Identity Management with Biometrics

Explore the latest innovative solutions to provide secure identification and authentication

Lisa Bock

BIRMINGHAM—MUMBAI

Identity Management with Biometrics

Commissioning Editor: Vijin Boricha
Acquisition Editor: Rahul Nair
Senior Editor: Arun Nadar
Content Development Editor: Pratik Andrade
Technical Editor: Sarvesh Jaywant
Copy Editor: Safis Editing
Project Coordinator: Neil Dmello
Proofreader: Safis Editing
Indexer: Pratik Shirodkar
Production Designer: Alishon Mendonca

First published: October 2020

Production reference: 1170920

Published by Packt Publishing Ltd.
Livery Place
35 Livery Street
Birmingham
B3 2PB, UK.

ISBN 978-1-83898-838-8

www.packt.com

I dedicate this book to the thousands of information technology students that I had the honor of instructing over 17 years at Pennsylvania College of Technology (Williamsport, Pennsylvania). Teaching you was the best part of my day. You made it fun! I enjoyed your curiosity, ambition, sense of humor, and willingness to learn. I look forward to hearing about all of your accomplishments, as I am so proud of you. Thank you for letting me be part of your life.

– Lisa Bock

`Packt.com`

Subscribe to our online digital library for full access to over 7,000 books and videos, as well as industry leading tools to help you plan your personal development and advance your career. For more information, please visit our website.

Why subscribe?

- Spend less time learning and more time coding with practical eBooks and Videos from over 4,000 industry professionals

- Improve your learning with Skill Plans built especially for you

- Get a free eBook or video every month

- Fully searchable for easy access to vital information

- Copy and paste, print, and bookmark content

Did you know that Packt offers eBook versions of every book published, with PDF and ePub files available? You can upgrade to the eBook version at packt.com and as a print book customer, you are entitled to a discount on the eBook copy. Get in touch with us at customercare@packtpub.com for more details.

At www.packt.com, you can also read a collection of free technical articles, sign up for a range of free newsletters, and receive exclusive discounts and offers on Packt books and eBooks.

Contributors

About the author

Lisa Bock is an experienced author with a demonstrated history of working in the e-learning industry. She is a Security Ambassador with a broad range of IT skills and knowledge, including networking, Cisco CyberOps, Wireshark, biometrics, and the IoT. Lisa is an author for LinkedIn Learning along with being an award-winning speaker who has presented at several national conferences. She holds a MS in computer information systems/information assurance from UMGC. Lisa was an associate professor in the IT department at Pennsylvania College of Technology (Williamsport, PA) from 2003 until her retirement in 2020. She is involved with various volunteer activities, and she and her husband Mike enjoy bike riding, watching movies, and traveling.

I would like to thank Dr. Paras Shah, Regenerative Interventional Orthopedic, North Kansas City Hospital, for introducing me to biometrics in the early 2000s. This knowledge prompted my passion for the subject and helped me while teaching and presenting biometric technology over the last several years.

About the reviewers

Roger Konecny is a Senior Director of Systems Implementation for a global biometrics corporation. He leads project management, systems engineering, and quality assurance teams in the implementation of multi-modal biometric identification systems. Roger has implemented biometric systems around the world for national, state, and local entities to provide safety and convenience to citizens. Among his accomplishments is the implementation of the United States' largest **Identity as a Service** (**IDaaS**) system, providing cross-jurisdictional biometric services to multiple state law enforcement agencies. A veteran of the United States Marine Corps, Roger previously served as a law enforcement officer in patrol, investigations, and forensic capacities.

Derek Northrope has over 20 years' experience in biometrics and identity management covering architecture, system integration, testing, evaluation, consulting, education, and International Standards development. This experience has been gained in a number of different countries and domains, including passports, visas, national ID, and defense systems. Derek has a Bachelor's of Information Technology degree, with a major in management, from the University of Canberra. Originally from Australia, Derek now lives and works in Canada with his wife and three children.

> *I would like to thank my wife, Charlotte, and my three children, Archer, Zahra, and Lailah. You are my guiding lights in this journey through life.*

Packt is searching for authors like you

If you're interested in becoming an author for Packt, please visit `authors.packtpub.com` and apply today. We have worked with thousands of developers and tech professionals, just like you, to help them share their insight with the global tech community. You can make a general application, apply for a specific hot topic that we are recruiting an author for, or submit your own idea.

Table of Contents

3

Recognizing Biometric Characteristics

4

Comparing Advantages and Modalities

Section 2 – Applying Biometric Technologies

5
Implementing Fingerprint Technology

6
Using Facial Recognition

7
Learning Iris Recognition

8

Using Voice Recognition

9

Considering Alternate Biometrics

Section 3 – Deploying a Large-Scale Biometric System

10
Selecting the Right Biometric

11
Integrating the Biometric System

12

Testing and System Deployment

13

Discovering Practical Biometric Applications

14
Addressing Privacy Concerns

Assessments

Other Books You May Enjoy

Index

Preface

Identity Management with Biometrics will teach you the broad strokes of biometric technology. You'll compare the different types of biometrics and learn why one may be a better fit than another according to your needs. With easy-to-follow details on the various types of biometric identification and authentication, examples, and self-assessment questions, this guide will outline the next generation of identity management.

By the end of this book, you will be well versed in a variety of recognition processes and be able to make the right decisions when implementing biometric technologies.

Who this book is for

This book is appropriate for IT managers, security professionals, students, teachers, and anyone involved in the selecting, purchasing, integrating, or securing of a biometric system.

What this book covers

Chapter 1, *Exploring Biometric Technology*, covers the concept of biometrics and the methods available to provide identification and authentication. We'll compare physiological versus behavioral biometrics, and examine common biometrics such as fingerprint, facial, iris, and voice recognition.

Chapter 2, *Biometrics and Mobile Devices*, teaches you the real-world applications of biometrics in mobile devices. This chapter covers the various biometric methods used in Fintech, such as voice and facial recognition, to enable authentication and payment processing.

Chapter 3, *Recognizing Biometric Characteristics*, outlines the desired qualities of a biometric, including uniqueness, performance, distinctiveness, and permanence, and reviews the general operation of biometric technology in various environments.

Chapter 4, Comparing Advantages and Modalities, explains the many types of biometric systems, along with their advantages/disadvantages. It describes the different types of biometrics systems, system errors, multimodal usage, and practical examples of different applications.

Chapter 5, Implementing Fingerprint Technology, provides a basic understanding of the evolution of fingerprint technology. We'll cover feature extraction and minutiae along with the different types of fingerprint systems in use today.

Chapter 6, Using Facial Recognition, provides an overview of the process of acquiring facial images using **two-dimensional** (**2D**) and **three-dimensional** (**3D**) sensors, and covers how systems extract the features along with how facial recognition is used today.

Chapter 7, Learning Iris Recognition, outlines the unique nature of the iris along with the structure of the eye. We'll step through capturing and sensing iris images, to matching templates and preventing spoofing, and will examine some of the applications for iris recognition.

Chapter 8, Using Voice Recognition, first reviews the evolution of two related technologies: voice recognition and speech recognition. We'll then step through the process of enrolling and matching and discuss the various ways we can use voice recognition.

Chapter 9, Considering Alternate Biometrics, outlines several lesser-known biometrics such as gait recognition and **deoxyribonucleic acid** (**DNA**). We'll cover an overview of keyboard dynamics and signature verification, along with using tattoos, scars, and ear biometrics.

Chapter 10, Selecting the Right Biometric, begins with an overview of the System Development Life Cycle and the requirements process for a biometric system. We'll also cover the factors that need to be considered when selecting a system, including usability, accuracy, speed, and efficiency.

Chapter 11, Integrating the Biometric System, moves through network and implementation considerations, compression methods, and securing biometric data, along with business continuity, disaster recovery, and integrating with the directory.

Chapter 12, Testing and System Deployment, stresses the importance of testing the system, and some of the tasks that the team will need to complete prior to deployment, such as providing education and awareness, enrolling the users, and tuning the decision process.

Chapter 13, Discovering Practical Biometric Applications, covers the use of biometrics in law enforcement and forensics. You'll see how we can use biometrics for large venues; to control access to assets, buildings, and systems; and some other novel uses of biometrics.

Chapter 14, Addressing Privacy Concerns, compares privacy laws in the US and Europe, and covers biometrics and the US' Fifth Amendment. We'll see the importance of biometric standards, and take a glimpse into the future of biometrics.

To get the most out of this book

This book is an introductory-level book. The reader should have a basic understanding of biometric authentication techniques, such as fingerprint and facial recognition, and the importance of providing a secure method of authenticating an individual.

Download the color images

We also provide a PDF file that has color images of the screenshots/diagrams used in this book. You can download it here: http://www.packtpub.com/sites/default/files/downloads/9781838988388_ColorImages.pdf.

Conventions used

There are a number of text conventions used throughout this book.

Bold: Indicates a new term, an important word, or words that you see onscreen. For example, words in menus or dialog boxes appear in the text like this. Here is an example: "Once in this dialog box, you can modify any settings, test the voice levels, or select **Record**."

> **Tips or important notes**
> Appear like this.

Get in touch

Feedback from our readers is always welcome.

General feedback: If you have questions about any aspect of this book, mention the book title in the subject of your message and email us at customercare@packtpub.com.

Errata: Although we have taken every care to ensure the accuracy of our content, mistakes do happen. If you have found a mistake in this book, we would be grateful if you would report this to us. Please visit www.packtpub.com/support/errata, selecting your book, clicking on the Errata Submission Form link, and entering the details.

Piracy: If you come across any illegal copies of our works in any form on the Internet, we would be grateful if you would provide us with the location address or website name. Please contact us at copyright@packt.com with a link to the material.

If you are interested in becoming an author: If there is a topic that you have expertise in and you are interested in either writing or contributing to a book, please visit authors.packtpub.com.

Reviews

Please leave a review. Once you have read and used this book, why not leave a review on the site that you purchased it from? Potential readers can then see and use your unbiased opinion to make purchase decisions, we at Packt can understand what you think about our products, and our authors can see your feedback on their book. Thank you!

For more information about Packt, please visit packt.com.

Section 1 – Understanding Biometric Authentication

In this section, we'll learn the various uses of and locations where biometrics are employed, and explore their use on mobile devices. We'll also review the characteristics of an optimal biometric, compare advantages and modalities, and learn about the different types of errors.

This part of the book comprises the following chapters:

- *Chapter 1, Exploring Biometric Technology*
- *Chapter 2, Biometric and Mobile Devices*
- *Chapter 3, Recognizing Biometric Characteristics*
- *Chapter 4, Comparing Advantages and Modalities*

1
Exploring Biometric Technology

Companies today are designing devices and computer systems to provide password-free authentication by using biometrics, which are the behavioral or physiological characteristics that are unique to an individual. Devices now include fingerprint technology, facial and voice recognition, and other methods such as haptics to provide authorized access to a device. Today, many organizations are adopting the use of biometrics to enable their employees to enter buildings, access cloud resources, and log in to phones and computers. As a result, IT managers may have to face the prospect of deploying a large-scale biometric system.

But just what is meant by biometrics, and why is the global market share of biometrics expected to double in the next five years? This chapter will answer these and other questions. It will cover the basics of biometric technology and terminology and compare various methods. We'll see how, in addition to providing authentication, we can also use biometrics to identify an individual.

We'll take a look at early biometric use in identifying prisoners and criminals. We'll then travel through the evolution of modern biometric history from 1924, through a discussion on digital signal processing to today's sophisticated systems. We'll compare physiological versus behavioral biometrics and some common biometrics in each category. You'll learn how physiological biometrics are attributes that can be measured, such as a face and fingerprint. You'll understand how behavioral biometrics are the way we do things now, such as signature or gait recognition. By the end of this chapter, you'll fully appreciate how biometrics provides a solid method of providing identification and authentication because of the unique characteristics we all possess.

In this chapter, we're going to cover the following main topics:

- Describing biometric technology
- Appreciating modern biometrics
- Comparing biometric categories

Describing biometric technology

Today, when you use your mobile device, you may need to use your fingerprint or face to gain access to the device. More and more companies are adopting biometric technology to provide password-free authentication for mobile devices, **Internet of Things (IoT)** devices, and computer systems. In addition, the use of biometrics in financial technology (fintech) has accelerated as a method for securing financial transactions.

For many of us, using biometrics has become commonplace, as biometric authentication is being used to sign in to websites along with applications on your mobile device. Today, many other biometric techniques are being explored and developed to automatically recognize and authenticate an individual.

Because of the widespread use of biometrics, in this section, we'll take a look at the definition of biometrics and compare how using biometrics can provide identification and authentication. Let's begin by exploring what defines biometrics.

Defining biometrics

Biometrics are the behavioral or physiological characteristics that are unique to an individual, and include fingerprints, iris patterns, and voice recognition.

A biometric system recognizes patterns and then determines whether the specific physiological or behavioral characteristic is unique to the individual. It's important to note that a biometric system must first have a database of enrolled individuals from which to compare. Enrollment can be either of the following options:

- Voluntary, where an individual willingly provides their biometric identifier to the system, along with some personal information.
- Completed by someone who populates the database with information, for example, enrolling with a database of police mug shots.

The use of the term *biometrics* can be broken down into two components, *bio*, or life, and *metrics*, or method to measure. The term biometrics has been in use for many years in a number of different scientific communities, for various statistical and mathematical analyses. Scientific communities and how they use biometrics include the following:

- Forestry to quantify vegetation
- Agriculture for predicting crops
- Medicine to measure the effectiveness of a treatment

The term biometrics has been in use for many years. However, the popularity of the term increased significantly from the 1950s to 2020, mainly because of the expanded use of biometrics for recognition and verification in modern-day applications.

Today, there are many technologies in use that we can use to validate and authenticate an individual. Each technology has a specific method of extracting the unique identifiable attributes of an individual. In the following section, let's see how we can use biometrics to identify an individual.

Providing identification

We can use biometrics to identify an individual, as it answers the question *who are you?* and are used in a number of different applications. To identify an individual, the system first takes a biometric in which to compare, and then searches a biometric template database to attempt to correctly identify the person. Biometric identification is a one-to-many comparison, as shown in the following diagram:

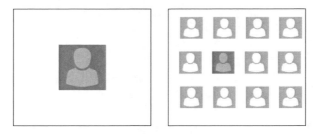

Figure 1.1 – Biometric identification, a one-to-many comparison

Applications for biometric identification have many uses that include identifying criminals involved in a crime or recognizing a friend while face tagging on social media. Let's start with how law enforcement uses biometrics to apprehend criminals.

Recognizing criminals

Law enforcement has long used biometrics, mainly fingerprints, to solve crimes. Other forms are used as well, as biometric techniques are used in forensic identification. Many individuals with a criminal past are in repositories such as the **Federal Bureau of Investigation's (FBI's) Integrated Automated Fingerprint Identification System (IAFIS)**. IAFIS is a powerful system that contains a vast number of records and includes fingerprints, faces, scars, and tattoos and helps law enforcement identify criminals. There are also other large biometric databases, including the **Unique Identification Authority of India (UIDAI)** system, that can be used to identify a person of interest.

Tagging faces

The social media giant Facebook has been using facial recognition for over a decade. Since 2010, Facebook has used the technology to suggest a tag on a face that looked similar and then used the data obtained to suggest more tags it perceived as a match. Facebook improved the technology over time, mainly because of the vast amount of data available from tagged faces in every possible setting, angle, and lighting variable. The science has evolved to become Deep Face, a nine-layer, **Deep Convolutional Neural Network (DCNN)** that provides approximately 97.35 percent accuracy in matching and identifying an individual.

There are many other uses for biometric identification. Uses include providing proof of citizenship, such as an image on a passport, a photo ID on a driver's license, or in forensics, where biometrics are used to identify someone who may have been a victim of a crime.

We can see how biometrics can be used to recognize an individual. Next, let's see how we can use biometrics to provide validation when a user claims an identity.

Verifying authentication

Authentication is showing something to be true or proving your identity, as it answers the question, *who do you claim to be?* Authentication can be achieved in one of three ways:

- What you know, such as a password, passphrase, or PIN
- What you have, such as a smart card or **Universal Serial Bus** (**USB**) token
- What you are, such as a fingerprint or iris pattern

We all want security. As a result, many solutions have been developed to provide a way to restrict access only to authorized individuals. Let's compare the three types, starting with passwords, the most common way to authenticate into a system.

Supplying a password

Using something you know such as a password or PIN is a simple and inexpensive way to prove our identity and has been widely used for several decades. Why is this important? When you go to a bank in person and you want to cash a check, you may have to present your driver's license to prove who you are. Today, If I go to a protected website, such as a banking site, the login page asks, who are you? I then enter my user ID to say *I'm Lisa Bock*. Then I am asked to prove it, and I put in my password.

After the internet became public in 1992, it seemed that by the late 90s, everyone was surfing the web, banking, and shopping at e-commerce sites. As a result, companies and governments early on sought ways to protect our data and our identities while online and we began to use passwords.

When passwords first came out in the 1990s, many of us were not familiar with the concept. To help us remember them, we wrote them down on sticky notes and we put them under our keyboards, and organizations said stop doing that. After that, we came up with passwords that were our pet's names or anniversaries, and that was also discouraged. The **National Institute of Science and Technology (NIST)** told us to make passwords complex, with upper and lowercase characters and special characters, so we came up with really good passwords. Then what did we do? We used them for every single one of our accounts, and many of us are still guilty of doing just that.

Current recommendations include using a passphrase, which is a sequence of characters that is longer and more secure than a password. There are many known attacks against passwords such as brute force and social engineering attacks. However, over the years, there have been many damaging data breaches involving the loss of billions of passwords, and other sensitive information.

To see how many companies have suffered from a data breach, go to the World's Biggest Data Breaches and Hacks, found at `https://www.informationisbeautiful.net/visualizations/worlds-biggest-data-breaches-hacks/`, where you will see the names of many well-known companies that have been breached in some way, possibly taking your password or credit card information.

If you aren't sure if you have been hacked, you can go to *haveibeenpwned* found at `https://haveibeenpwned.com/Passwords`. Once there, enter your password in the field to check and see whether your password has been compromised. The site also has many other tips and techniques on keeping your data secure.

The password is a sequence of characters and, of the three methods, it's the least expensive but is the least secure method to authenticate. In addition to the many attacks, many have found that the complexity requirements have led to frustration, as passwords can be difficult to remember. We all know that strong authentication is important. Using what you know in the form of a password is a common method, but what you have in the form of a smart card or token can provide a stronger method, as outlined in the following section.

Presenting a device

Another way to authenticate into a system is by using what you have, such as a smart card or USB token. Of the two, the smart card is the more commonly used and comes in a variety of forms, as discussed next.

Swiping a card

Smart cards and memory cards can house a user's credentials and process information. They are the size of a standard credit card and can be in one of two forms:

- **Smart card**: These can retain and process information.

- **Memory card**: These can house information but cannot process data.

The card can be either contact or contactless. With a contact card, you must physically interact with a device to exchange information. A contactless card has an antenna that, when in close proximity to a device, will garner enough energy to power the chip and transfer the data.

Memory cards hold information such as a user's credentials, medical information, or credit card numbers. The card can be used to provide information to a medical facility, make a credit card transaction, gain access to a building, or obtain currency at an **Automatic Teller Machine** (**ATM**). When using the card, the user will interact with the card reader, which will transfer information such as a password. In some cases, to provide a more robust authentication, the memory card can also provide two-factor authentication by requiring the user to enter a password or PIN in addition to presenting the card to the device.

Smart cards have been in use for many years in Europe and are now gaining traction in the United States (US). They are small and look like a credit card, as shown in the following graphic, yet they can do much more, as they generally house an embedded microprocessor. Today, many credit card companies are embedding a chip into the card and are called EMV (Europay, Mastercard, and Visa) cards, as shown in the following image:

Figure 1.2 – Smart card

The cards can process information and some have a tamper-proof feature where, if any unauthorized access is detected, the device can automatically wipe the data or lock users out so that the card has to be taken to the issuer to reset the PIN. Several card manufactures are incorporating fingerprint biometrics within the card. The user must present their fingerprint to make a purchase, which is a test for liveness that provides more robust security.

Although more expensive, the use of smart cards is expected to increase substantially over the next five years, as the banking and finance industry have turned to this type of method to provide an additional layer of security and deter theft.

Similar to a smart card, a token provides a physical method of interacting with a system to provide authentication, as discussed next.

Inserting a token

A **USB** token is a small durable device that resembles a flash drive. The token can house a user's credentials and is inserted into a USB port on a system, many times without the use of additional drivers. Because a token is a physical device, it provides a stronger and more reliable method to verify identity and secure data than using a password or PIN.

Some tokens are able to store private keys that can be used to encrypt files and emails or create a digital signature. In many cases, the token will require a password to gain access to the device. As a defensive measure, some tokens can self-destruct if someone tries to access the device following too many failed attempts.

Although smart cards and tokens provide an additional layer of security, they can be lost, stolen, or damaged. One of the most secure ways of authenticating an individual is by using something you are, in the form of a biometric such as a fingerprint, as we'll see next.

Comparing a biometric feature

Authentication uses a one-to-one comparison by matching the captured biometric with a pre-stored biometric template in the database. After the individual presents the biometric to the system, the features are extracted. The system will then determine whether or not there is a match, as shown in the following graphic:

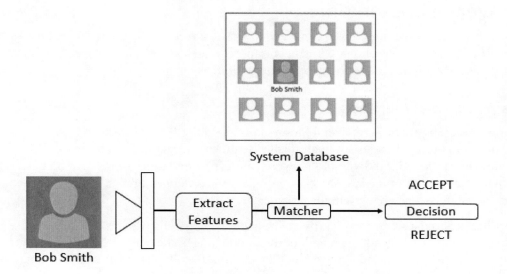

Figure 1.3 – Biometric authentication, a one-to-one comparison

Using a biometric to provide authentication can identify an attribute that is not only unique to the individual, but also defies duplication.

Most modern devices now include fingerprint technology and facial recognition, but can also include other methods such as voice recognition and haptics to provide authorized access. Today, many organizations are adopting the use of biometrics so their employees can enter buildings and access cloud resources. In addition, biometric authentication is used to log in to phones, devices, and computers.

We know that we can authenticate into a system in one of three ways. However, a password or token is not truly able to prove the identity of an individual and can be either attacked, stolen, forgotten, or obtained using social engineering techniques.

Everyone has several physical or behavioral characteristics that can be used to authenticate their identity. What you are, such as a face or fingerprint, provides a more robust method of authentication. In the next section, let's take a look at the evolution of biometrics.

Appreciating modern biometrics

When we discuss biometrics, and specifically using automated systems, you might ask, where did the concept originate? In this section, we'll travel through the evolution of biometrics, from the early use of body measurements to the FBI's identification division's use of fingerprints in 1924, to today's sophisticated systems. Let's have a look at some of the early uses of biometrics to identify an individual.

Traveling back in time

Historically, the use of biometrics can date back over several centuries, where the use of a fingerprint was used to validate a business transaction. Next, let's start by learning how the early manual methods paved the way to automation.

Using manual methods

In the late 1880s, there were several individuals, including *Henry Faulds* and Sir *Francis Galton*, who outlined the use of quantifiable identification methods such as face and fingerprints to identify individuals. However, a more formal utilization of physiological metrics came about in the late 1800s when *Alphonse Bertillon*, a French police officer, designed a measurement system for prisoners.

Bertillon devised a system to identify an individual's physical attributes that included measurements of the head, the length of the middle finger, the cubit, which is the length from the elbow to the middle finger, and the left foot. Bertillon supplemented his analysis with a photograph or mug shot of the prisoner, which has remained a staple of every criminal apprehension.

The Bertillon system began in the United States in 1887 at the *Illinois State Penitentiary*, and soon became a widely adopted standard in the prison system. However, the system had flaws. One of the challenges of a manual measurement was that not every guard would measure each attribute in the same manner or as accurately as the next guard, but it was the only method that they had at that time. During this period, cities began to populate, and therefore the prison population expanded as well.

The Bertillon system was used without issue until 1903, when two identical prisoners with the exact same name had the exact same measurements:

- In 1901, *William West* was detained at *Leavenworth Penitentiary*.
- in 1903, *Will West* was detained at *Leavenworth Penitentiary*.

At that point, it became evident that the system could no longer provide a reliable way to identify prisoners. Soon afterward, the use of fingerprint identification began to gain popularity. Then, in 1924, the FBI's identification division began using fingerprints.

Although a better method than the Bertillon system, using a fingerprint to identify an individual also experienced issues with quality control. In 1924, law enforcement used a card system to record the fingerprint. This worked in the following manner:

1. The guard had a card with the prisoner's name.
2. Ink was placed on a flat surface and rolled out.

3. The prisoner's fingerprints were placed on the ink.

4. The fingerprint was then transferred onto the card.

Similar to the Bertillon measurement method, it was important to have a guard who knew how to take a visible fingerprint, and not all of them were trained correctly. In addition, if a prisoner is detained in prison, they may try to smudge the print in some way so that it doesn't appear legible.

If the officer was able to get a good fingerprint that is visible on the card, the officer had to put those fingerprint cards somewhere and later retrieve them. As a result, by around the 1960's, the FBI had amassed millions and millions of these cards to identify potential persons of interest.

In the following section, we'll see how manual methods evolved into the use of automated systems.

Automating the process

Digital signal processing (**DSP**) began in the 1960s. The FBI, Royal Canadian Police, NIST, and other such organizations around the world began to see the value of using automation to search biometric identifiers, instead of using manual methods, and how automation would greatly improve overall efficiency.

In 1969, the FBI sent out a **Request for Proposal** (**RFP**) to come up with a technology to achieve an automated fingerprint identification system. Development of the system was slow. The main reason was we weren't quite ready yet, in that there was no scanning technology in existence during those early days of automation. All these things had to take time to develop. Eventually, the FBI began using the IAFIS on a large scale in 1999. The IAFIS system continued to evolve into **Next Generation Identification** (**NGI**), which has expanded capabilities from fingerprints to other biometric identifiers such as facial identification, iris, and palm prints.

Concurrently, there was more interest to study other forms of biometric identification. Scientists started to explore speaker recognition. The use of hand geometry systems started to gain interest as a method of restricting access to buildings in the early 1970s. Interest in biometrics expanded during the 1980s and 1990s, from signature verification to iris recognition systems. Government interest in automated personal identification increased and large-scale testing soon followed.

In the next section, let's take a look at how this expansion has led to the many places where we see the use of biometrics today.

Applying a unique attribute

Through advances in technology, automation, and a greater understanding of biometric identifiers, the science began to gain traction. Today, biometrics are used in a variety of ways. Uses include access control to get into cellphones, laptops, networks, buildings, and border control. Next, let's take a look at how law enforcement is stepping up the use of biometrics to apprehend criminals.

Enforcing the law

Law enforcement in agencies around the world have been using biometrics to aid in locating and identifying potential criminals. Organizations such as Interpol, the FBI, and CIA have many tools at their disposal. The tools include massive databases such as IAFIS, the **Automated Biometric Identification System (ABIS)**, and the **Unique Identification Authority of India (UIDAI)** system.

These systems provide law enforcement with the ability to not only search for possible persons of interest but assist in threat management during a massive sporting event, such as in a large stadium during a sports event.

Next, let's see how biometrics can aid in securing our borders.

Controlling the border

It is essential to provide security to all citizens, but it's also important to track and manage the flow of individuals entering a country. Using biometrics at the border provides a higher level of security and safety.

Currently in the US, the **Department of Homeland Security (DHS)** is amassing a biometric database that consists of fingerprints, faces, and iris scans of over 200 million individuals. The DHS also has access to the databases of other US agencies, along with foreign intelligence agencies of several countries. The Department of Homeland Security uses the database to scan individuals to identify potential persons of interest.

Biometrics also helps to simplify the airport experience when traveling. In many countries, automated biometric identification is replacing manual methods. You present your passport to the reader, and then are asked to look at the camera. The system then does a modified facial recognition scan to compare it to your passport and identify you. In addition to using biometrics for border control and while traveling through an airport, let's see the many ways we can use biometrics to recognize individuals.

Identifying individuals

The range of possibilities for biometric identification is extensive. Uses include the following:

- Recognizing customers in commercial locations such as stores, where an individual can pay for goods using facial recognition instead of using a cashier

- Verifying the identity of staff and volunteers upon entry and exit from a correction facility and managing prisoner identities

- Detecting military personnel from allies and enemies on a military base

- Identifying residents and citizens at the polls during an election

Over time, we will continue to see the growth of biometric technology worldwide to provide identification. Many countries such as the US, China, and many parts of Europe are using facial recognition to enhance security. But using biometrics for identification is only part of the wide range of applications. Next, let's take a look at how biometrics can replace the use of a password.

Replacing the password

Using a PIN or password is a traditional way to prove our identity and has been widely used for several decades. Many feel that authentication tactics such as passwords are insufficient for personal identification. As a result, biometrics are now being used around the world for a more secure method to gain access to our homes, vehicles, and mobile devices.

More and more mobile devices are offering the use of biometrics to sign in to your device. Under device security, you may have a choice of biometrics, where you can select from one of the biometrics methods, as shown in the following diagram:

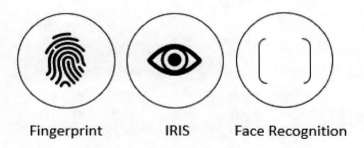

Fingerprint   IRIS   Face Recognition

Figure 1.4 – Mobile device biometrics

Today, using a biometric identifier can offer a unique advantage and replaces what you know or what you have with what you are to identify someone. Now that we have seen the evolution of modern biometrics, let's examine the two main types of biometrics.

Comparing biometric categories

Biometrics can verify an individual's identity by using a unique attribute or behavior. Although we may think of biometrics as one general topic, the science of biometrics is divided into two separate categories:

- **Physiological biometrics**: Represents attributes that can be measured

- **Behavioral biometrics**: Represents the way we do things

Although both categories provide a way to evaluate a unique attribute, each category is significantly different in the way they are assessed, as shown in the following diagram:

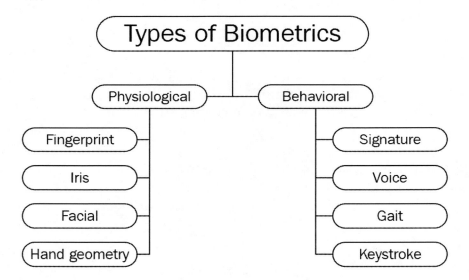

Figure 1.5 – Physiological versus behavioral biometrics

In this section, we will compare physiological and behavioral biometrics, so that you can get a better understanding of each type. We'll also cover some of the common biometrics in each category. First, let's outline physiological biometrics.

Measuring physiological attributes

Physiological biometrics are based on measurements or parts of the human body. Some of the common methods include the following:

- **Fingerprint recognition**: This was one of the very first biometrics used and is an optimal biometric. Each fingerprint is unique and is made up of ridge endings, bifurcations, and other detailed characteristics called minutiae.

- **Iris recognition**: This uses the iris or the colored part of the eye. Using iris recognition presents a unique, non-invasive biometric in that the image is captured with a camera and the participant does not have to touch a device.

- **Facial recognition**: This is done when a camera scans a person's face and takes measurements of the face, including the width of the nose, eye spacing, the forehead, and chin.

- **Hand geometry**: This is one of the oldest automated biometrics, as it was developed in the late 1960s–1970s. The hand is placed on a device, which then measures each finger and the hand as a whole.

The use of physiological biometrics has a wide range of applications. One of the newer techniques is using a token that can house biometric information, such as a fingerprint, and then using random numbers to encrypt data. The process is shown in the following diagram:

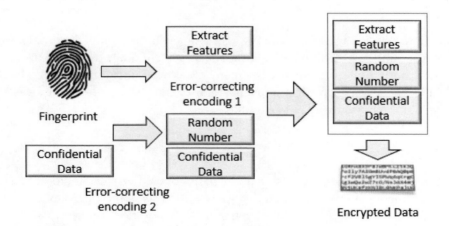

Figure 1.6 – Using a biometric to encrypt data

As you can see, this method can provide a higher level of security in that only the individual who encrypted the data can decrypt the data.

Now that we can see how physiological biometrics provide a measurable attribute, let's take a look at the other category of biometrics, and examine the behavioral aspects of an individual.

Observing behavioral biometrics

Behavioral biometrics are how we do things and are based on a person's actions, such as how you walk, talk, or sign your name. Behavioral biometrics include the following:

- **Signature verification**: This is the way someone signs their name. It takes into account the pressure of the stroke, the curves, and other unique characteristics of your signature.

- **Gait recognition**: This is a newer biometric, and is simply the way someone walks. It is a non-invasive biometric, and is used in large venues for threat management, such as in stadiums or during a large outdoor event.

- **Voice recognition**: This can recognize who is speaking by comparing the way they speak, including their inflection and their patterns.

- **Keystroke biometrics**: This gathers information regarding the way each individual hits the keyboard, along with the cadence and rhythm of each stroke in the way they press each key and how long it takes to release the key.

Although used less frequently, scientists are now finding that behavioral biometrics provide an enhanced ability to verify an individual and offer a more robust and secure alternative.

We are still in the early stages of developing all possible biometric applications. However, we are seeing a trend of using biometric authentication technology to replace the traditional methods. Using a biometric has many advantages, including the fact that they can't be lost like a key, smart card, or a token, and they can't be forgotten, like a password, and what you are can essentially last a lifetime.

Summary

By now, you have a better understanding of the basics of biometric technology. In addition to providing authentication, we learned that we can also use biometrics to identify an individual. You can now appreciate the rich history of biometrics, from early manual methods to today's advanced systems. In this chapter, we explored how biometrics can provide a straightforward simple authentication process. You then learned how biometric technologies are ideal in many different applications and environments.

You now understand that biometrics can be assessed in one of two ways. We can use physiological biometrics or attributes that can be measured, such as a face and fingerprints. We can also evaluate behavioral biometrics, which are the way we do things such as signature or gait recognition. Because each individual has both behavioral and physiological characteristics, we may find that using both can complement one another and provide a more robust method to secure a system.

We are now only just beginning to see the many possible applications of biometric systems. Unlike a password, which can be stolen or even forgotten, using a biometric such as a fingerprint can be used to provide proof, or reassurance that it is really you.

In the next chapter, we will examine how biometrics are used in mobile devices. You'll learn how using biometrics can simplify access control on devices without having to use a password that can be forgotten, or a device that can be lost. You'll understand how to use your voice or face in the fintech domain (financial technology) to make a payment, or activate a command, and why a PIN or password will soon be a thing of the past.

Questions

Now it's time to check your knowledge. Select the best response, and then check your answers, found in the *Assessment* section at the end of the book.

1. Which of the following would fall under *Something you know* authentication?

   a. Smart card

   b. Password or PIN

   c. Fingerprint

   d. Token

2. Which of the following would fall under *Something you have* authentication?

   a. Smart card

   b. Password or PIN

   c. Fingerprint

   d. Voice

3. _____ uses a one-to-one comparison.

    a. Smart face

    b. Identification

    c. Deep face

    d. Authentication

4. _____ represents biometric attributes that can be measured.

    a. Smart face

    b. Behavioral

    c. Physiological

    d. Authentication

5. Using voice recognition is an example of a _____ biometric.

    a. Smart face

    b. Behavioral

    c. Physiological

    d. Authentication

6. The FBI's identification division began using fingerprints in _____.

    a. 1924

    b. 1960

    c. 1999

    d. 2010

7. Keystroke biometrics are a _____ biometric that gathers the way each individual hits the keyboard, along with the cadence and rhythm of each stroke.

    a. Smart face

    b. Behavioral

    c. Physiological

    d. Authentication

Further reading

Please refer to the following links for more information:

- For a detailed look back at the end of the Bertillon system and the beginning of fingerprint identification, check out *A Fingerprint Fable: The Will and William West Case* found at `http://www.scafo.org/library/110105.html`.

- This site outlines the technology that converts a biometric such as a fingerprint into encrypted data: `https://phys.org/news/2015-10-technology-biometric-cryptographic-key.html`.

- This is a nice website with an overview of terms – *Glossary of Biometric Terms and Technique Classifications*: `https://www.biometricupdate.com/201205/biometric-terms-and-technique-classifications`.

2
Biometrics and Mobile Devices

Your mobile device is probably the most frequently used piece of technology you own. Mobile devices are convenient and are used for a number of different reasons. As a result, our devices hold a great deal of information about us, which includes photos we take, our contacts, location information, and our messages. No matter what we do on a mobile device, consumers continue to demand that the companies we interact with on a daily basis continue to provide the highest level of privacy and security.

In this chapter, you'll gain a better understanding of the many ways in which biometrics are used to secure mobile devices. Because more and more devices are using biometrics, such as fingerprint recognition, we'll compare various biometric methods. You'll gain a better understanding of how touch, gesture, voice, and facial recognition are used in fintech (financial technology) to enable payment processing, or by general applications to interact with the device. In addition, we'll outline the importance of having the option to provide continuous authentication while using a mobile device.

So that you can appreciate the technology that makes all this happen, we'll cover some of the optimal biometric application features for mobile devices that include the need to be intuitive, lightweight, and durable. Finally, you'll learn how a mobile device must have several key essential factors to support biometric technology, such as the ability to capture the image and be resistant to spoofing. At the end of this chapter, you'll learn how using biometrics may make using a PIN password a thing of the past.

In this chapter, we're going to cover the following main topics:

- Securing fintech and other applications
- Designing optimal biometrics for mobile
- Incorporating essential biometric technology

Securing fintech and other applications

Nearly 60 percent of Americans are using some type of mobile device, such as tablets and smart phones, on a daily basis, according to statistics listed on Pew Research: `https://www.pewresearch.org/internet/fact-sheet/mobile/`. Of those, over 80 percent use a smartphone, and that trend will continue to rise.

We use our devices to perform many common activities, such as shopping, chatting, browsing, banking, reading books, and making phone calls. Because of this, there can be a substantial amount of information that is housed on a mobile device. Using safeguards such as fingerprint and facial recognition helps secure our devices and protect data from unauthorized exposure.

In this section, we'll take a look at the importance of making sure the device limits access only to authorized individuals and processes, so as to prevent data loss and exposure. We'll then look at some of the laws that define how data is protected and how some device manufactures are moving toward using a token to pass credit card information as an extra layer of defense.

Let's start with outlining why we need to control access.

Ensuring access control

Access control prevents unauthorized individuals from accessing assets, either in an enterprise network, or on our own device, by using various methods. Biometric access control is an efficient method of accurately identifying and authenticating individuals and decreases the overall risk of an unwanted theft or data breach. As more and more companies and individuals adopt the use of mobile devices, the need to provide security for these devices will increase.

Let's start with a discussion on access control and why it is important.

Controlling access to assets

Access control is a basic concept in security that, when enforced, will decrease the risk of loss, misuse, or the misappropriation of assets. Assets can be either of the following:

- **Tangible**: Such as printers, laptops, or mobile devices
- **Intangible**: Such as intellectual property or sensitive information

Whether tangible or intangible, some assets are more valuable than others. Access controls help safeguard valuable assets and minimize exposure to loss. We apply access control methods to allow an individual to use a resource they have been granted permission to use by using physical or logical controls:

- **Physical access controls**: Limit the ability to access a structure, such as a building, a server room, or a device. Physical controls include card readers, door locks, or guards.
- **Logical access controls**: Limit access to intangible assets, such as files, networks, websites, or applications. Logical controls include **Access Control Lists** (**ACLs**), along with folder and file permissions.

Using both physical and logical controls improves an overall security posture. If access controls are misconfigured, broken, or missing, this could result in either loss of an asset or the exposure of sensitive data.

When a subject wants to access an object, access controls work in the following manner to identify, authenticate, and then authorize:

1. The system will first *identify* the individual or entity in some way, in other words, by providing a username, PIN, or supplying information from a smart card.

2. Once the subject has provided their identity, they then *authenticate* to the system, by means of either a password, token, or biometric identifier.

3. The system then grants appropriate *authorization* to the individual or entity.

The process is as shown in the following diagram:

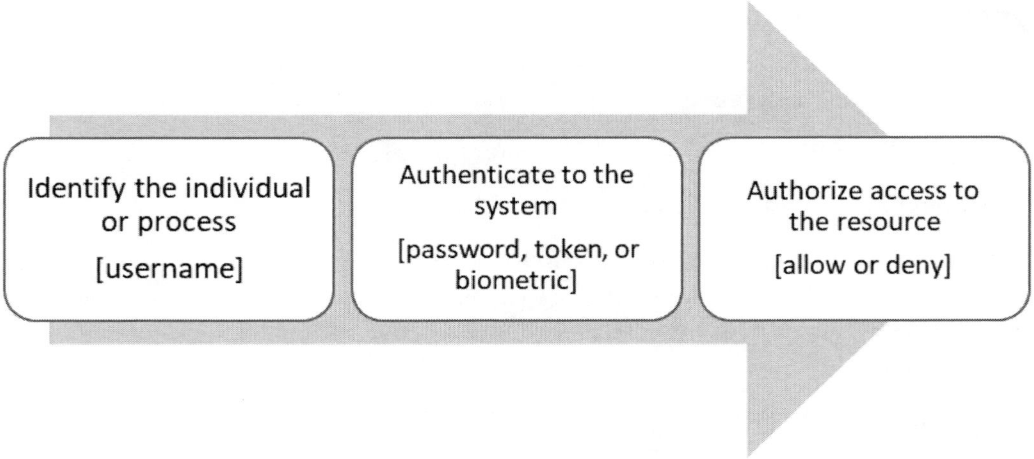

Figure 2.1 – Identification, authentication, and authorization

Access control policies can be extensive and include concepts such as the separation of duties, remote access, and least privilege. A list of references can be found at `https://nvd.nist.gov/800-53/Rev4/family/Access%20Control`.

We now understand why it is important to control access to assets such as equipment and sensitive data. Next, let's take a look at providing access control in an organization.

Deploying an enterprise solution

In an enterprise network, corporate data that is either on a mobile device or a secure website must be protected. Company-owned devices can be managed with different solutions that control every aspect of the device. However, many organizations do not provide company-owned devices. In an enterprise network, the concept of **Bring Your Own Device (BYOD)** adds to the complexity of managing an organization to secure corporate information while preserving employee privacy. While BYOD may not involve company-owned devices, they can be company-compliant to protect the resources.

Just as you would lock down a desktop or laptop, organizations enforce policies for access control methods for the mobile devices that interact with the organization's resources. Methods to prevent unauthorized users from gaining access to a mobile device include the following:

- Using biometric authentication and lock screen release
- Setting an idle timeout to lock the phone when not in use

However, while it's important to restrict access, the network administrator must enable individuals to conduct business while using their mobile device. The challenge is that corporate environments have diverse identities with varying levels of access. There are several things the administrator can do to lock down the device. Once the individual or process has been identified and authenticated, the system can authorize what services and directories they can access.

There are approaches to authenticate and authorize users and processes so they can connect to organizational resources and applications. Methods include **Security Assertion Markup Language (SAML)** and **Lightweight Directory Access Protocol (LDAP)**. In addition to restricting access, many services provide auditing and reporting to hold people accountable for actions taken on a system.

Now that we understand the importance of securing mobile devices used in an organization, let's examine some of the methods we can use to protect our own mobile device.

Protecting your own device

We rely on our mobile device to simplify our lives. To slow someone down from gaining access to your information, many of us use a passphrase or a password. If available, you can use a biometric, such as a fingerprint. In addition, many devices offer **Multifactor Authentication (MFA)**. MFA requires two or more authentication factors, such as a password and a biometric scan, and can improve the security of a device.

Several manufacturers are incorporating a single sign-in feature, where once you sign in to the device, you can then access all of your apps and websites without typing in a username and password. Because of an always-on connection and the amount of time we spend on mobile devices, there are some additional guidelines to keep your device safe. In addition to using access control, good practice guidelines include the following:

- Keep your mobile device updated. Patches and updates will ensure that the device has the latest software that will provide the best level of protection.

- Be cautious when using apps. Review the privacy policy. Make sure you understand what the app wants to access, such as your location, social media information, or any other data that is considered private before you download and install the app.

As we have seen, using access control is important to either an organization or on an individual device. Next, let's examine some of the reasons why it's imperative to employ methods to protect sensitive information, because of laws that dictate how a company must protect the data.

Staying in compliance

We know that it's important to manage risk and protect sensitive information in an organization. Using access controls helps keep data private, unchanged, and available. This concept is called the **Confidentiality, Integrity, and Availability (CIA)** triad, a well-known information assurance tenet, that is one of the basic principles of providing a secure system.

We prevent unauthorized access to ensure the following:

- **Confidentiality**: Keeping private information private
- **Integrity**: Protecting data from unauthorized changes
- **Availability**: Making sure that data is only available to authorized users

Either in an enterprise network, or on our own device, an organization must enforce access controls, not only to adhere to the CIA triad, but also to adhere to compliance requirements. When using a mobile device, individuals and the processes on the device may have to interact with corporate resources.

Next, let's take a look at a few of the standards, regulations, and guidelines to provide reasonable security and privacy, and help reduce the amount of data exposure. We'll start with the **Payment Card Industry Data Security Standard (PCI DSS)**.

Securing credit card transactions

PCI DSS is an industry standard that outlines requirements to secure credit card transactions. It's not a law or government regulation; it was developed by the payment card industry. The standard provides a set of widely accepted requirements to help financial institutions and merchants provide secure payment solutions.

PCI DSS applies to any sized organization that deals with credit card transactions, including transmitting or storing cardholder data. If you do deal with credit card transactions, you must comply, otherwise your company will face hefty fines, and you may lose the ability to handle credit card transactions. The extensive guidelines can be found at `https://www.pcisecuritystandards.org/pci_security/maintaining_payment_security`.

Next, let's look at the guidelines designed to protect our medical information.

Protecting patient information

The **Health Insurance Portability and Accountability Act** (**HIPAA**) is also known as the Privacy Rule. HIPAA governs data privacy for anyone working in U.S. medical facilities, along with any of their subcontractors and business associates. This legislation outlines security practices that safeguard **Protected Health Information** (**PHI**) from any past, present, or future information on a patient.

HIPAA outlines three areas of focus for best security practices that ensure that everyone works together to protect patient data. The three areas are as follows:

- **Physical controls**: As defined earlier, these limit the ability to access a structure such as a building, or a server room, and include door locks or video surveillance.

- **Technical controls**: These, or logical controls, as defined earlier, limit access to files, applications, or websites, and include encryption, ACLs, and file permissions.

- **Administrative controls**: These deal with the people in the organization who might interact with **Personally Identifiable Information** (**PII**). Administrative controls include **Security Education Training and Awareness** (**SETA**), record keeping, and disaster and recovery plans.

Using the controls in a layered approach will help ensure that patient data is protected. The law also includes mandatory requirements to report any breach. Anyone who is in violation of the policies and procedures will face penalties. HIPAA has extensive and granular guidelines. For a closer look, visit `https://www.hhs.gov/hipaa/index.html`.

As you can see, HIPAA outlines ways to protect patient data. Over the years, many laws have evolved and extended their reach. Let's now take a look at the **General Data Protection Regulation** (**GDPR**).

Giving consumers control of their data

Everyone has a reasonable expectation of privacy. Many of us willingly expose our personal information on social media, blogs, and other public forums. In many organizations, the need to protect data is not mandatory but a choice. However, some laws mandate the need to keep data private.

One such law is the General Data Protection Regulation or GDPR, a comprehensive data privacy law that affects companies located in and outside the European Union. Formalized in 2018, this replaced and significantly updated the Data Protection Directive, which had been in place since 1995, when many were still getting access to the internet.

GDPR outlines how personal data must be processed. You can find the regulations here in the language of your choice: `https://eur-lex.europa.eu/legal-content/EN/TXT/?qid=1532348683434&uri=CELEX:02016R0679-20160504`

Although the regulations are extensive, it's in a company's best interests to adhere to the regulations. If a company is found in violation of the rules, they can face hefty fines of up to four percent of total global turnover.

As you can see, compliance guidelines force us to stay within the boundaries of the law. Because of regulations, an organization must incorporate methods into their security compliance plan to reduce overall risk, and protect our health, financial, and personal information, whether it is at rest or in transit.

One way to secure credit card data is by using a token instead of the actual card number, as we'll learn next.

Tokenizing credit card information

Many of us use our mobile device to make purchases. To protect our devices from prying eyes, we secure them with biometrics such as facial recognition and fingerprint technology. Using a biometric along with a PIN or password provides a strong first layer of defense. Because of the popularity of making purchases with a mobile device, developers conceal your real credit card information with a digital token. The process is outlined in the following diagram:

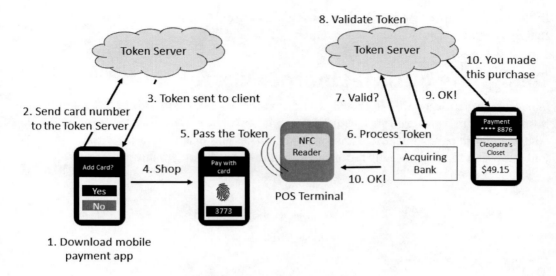

Figure 2.2 – Payment card tokenization

The process works in the following manner:

1.   The consumer must first download the appropriate mobile payment app, enter their information, and the card data is then sent to the **Token Server**.

2.   The server then returns a token to the client. At that point, the consumer can then shop, at a **Point of Sale (POS)** terminal, by passing the token.

3.   The token is then processed by sending it to the **Token Server**, which either validates or rejects the token.

4.   If all goes well, the token is validated. The vendor and the consumer are notified of the successful transaction.

The consumer's actual card information is stored off-site in a secure, PCI-compliant server. The token is used to make transactions without interrupting day-to-day operations. To further secure the card, many credit card vendors have worked to integrate biometric solutions to limit the damage if someone steals the device. If someone were able to access the phone, they would need to use the fingerprint sensor, making fraudulent purchases nearly impossible.

As we can see, because of the widespread use of mobile devices to shop, surf, and manage personal finances, we need to provide strong access control. Using a biometric identifier can improve security beyond using a password or PIN. As a result, more and more manufacturers will incorporate the use of biometric identifiers that will enhance the security level of the device.

In the next section, let's take a look at what makes a good biometric for a mobile device that improves security without inconveniencing the user.

Designing optimal biometrics for mobile

When we authenticate, we are proving to be genuine or true. Passwords have been used in some form to provide a form of authentication since the early 1960s. While we will continue to use passwords, there are some advantages and disadvantages to using what you know as a form of authentication, as shown in the following diagram:

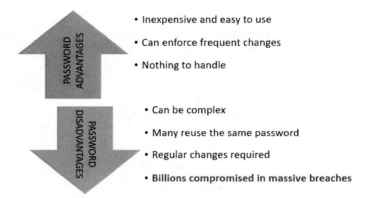

Figure 2.3 – Pros and cons of using passwords

The one thing we can't overlook in the disadvantages of using passwords is the fact that, over the last decade, billions of passwords have been stolen. As a result, the concept of password-free smartphones is becoming more attractive as an option to authenticate or interact with the device.

In the next section, we'll look at methods to provide optimal design, along with exploring the concept of using haptics as a compliment to biometric technology. Let's start with exploring ways we can improve the user experience while using biometrics on a mobile device.

Simplifying the user experience

Using biometrics in fintech is gaining ground. Manufacturers are incorporating the use of gesture, voice, touch, and facial recognition to enable the user to process payments or access general applications. However, there are a couple of core considerations app developers should include during the design phase. Consumers want basic functionality, while allowing the device to be enhanced, along with keeping everything reasonably priced. Let's start with the need to supply some basic features.

Providing the basics

Using biometrics on mobile phones is becoming more and more commonplace. As we transition to depending solely on biometrics on our mobile device, it's important to provide a core set of functionalities that works with minimal errors.

While developers are working hard to incorporate the latest biometric technology on a mobile device, it's imperative to make sure the user is comfortable with the approach. For example, if a fingerprint scanner that is designed for speed and accuracy performs slowly and in a clumsy manner, users will attempt to circumvent the technology, or discard it altogether.

In addition to optimal performance, users must accept the chosen biometric. Although there are many different types of biometrics, the most commonly used include fingerprint, face, iris, and voice. Fingerprints are gaining popularity when authenticating into someone's personal device. However, will everyone feel as comfortable using iris recognition? Cultural and diversity challenges may result in people accepting one form of biometric over another.

One other consideration is that the biometric reader must be easy to enroll and train the user on how to properly interact with the device. In most cases, it should be designed with intuitive instructions and self-guided prompts. Users will also need clear instructions on what to do if the biometric process doesn't work.

Next, let's take a look at how biometrics are evolving to transform and enhance a variety of services while using a mobile device.

Allowing for enhancements

In addition to using our mobile devices as a convenient method of making purchases, the technology is expanding to include biometrics that can enhance other services. For example, voice recognition is the only biometric that you can use over the phone. Using your voice to prove who you are is an added benefit as it lets you bypass the lengthy security questions to the agent. Businesses are finding voice recognition attractive, as instead of an agent, they only need an **Interactive Voice Response System (IVR)**. The customer must first register with the system. Then, when they call, the IVR gathers the required information, authenticates the user, and then connects the user to the appropriate department.

Although still an evolving technology, the use of biometric systems over the last several years has improved, along with the surrounding technology. Concurrent to the improved technology, biometrics have become more cost effective.

Security while using your mobile device is important. However, there is more to simply checking out at the convenience store; it's also about the psychology and user experience. In the next section, let's take a look at using haptics, or sensations the phone delivers when specific conditions are met.

Understanding haptics

Haptics are sensors that deliver a physical sensation in response to an action. Manufacturers are incorporating haptic technology into more mobile devices because of its responsive nature. In addition, because the technology is improving, developers are starting to investigate the use of haptics for other uses. That includes exploring ways in which haptics can provide continuous authentication, or how they can be used in place of a CAPTCHA to prove that you are not a robot. Let's start with how haptic technology is being used to signal a response.

Returning a response

The term is derived from the Greek word *haptesthai*, which means to contact or touch. Even though the term dates back in time, the modern connotation has taken off in a whole new context. We are only just beginning to see the potential of this technology.

Haptic technology is being used in a wide variety of applications, including the following:

- Haptic clothing
- Gaming joysticks
- Equipment controllers
- Barcode scanners
- Mobile devices

In a mobile device, using haptics provides a way for your mobile phone to communicate with you. The feedback can range from a slight buzz to heavy thud, depending on the application. This makes your mobile device seem almost lifelike in its response.

In your own device, you can control how loud or soft the haptics should respond by modifying the controls. The settings might look like the following graphic, where you can increase or decrease the intensity or sharpness of the response:

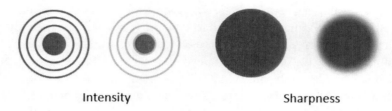

Intensity   Sharpness

Figure 2.4 – Haptic controls

Haptics relates to the **Human Computer Interface (HCI)** as the sense of touch. This technology is expanding as researchers are exploring the possibility of providing haptic-based biometric systems, as discussed next.

Actively authenticating

Traditional biometrics are based purely on behavioral or physiological characteristics. In a device, you provide a discrete one-time identifier, and then authenticate to the device. However, researchers are expanding the possibility of providing continuous authentication of an individual while using the device. While still in its infancy, the use of haptic-based authentication is showing promise. After acquiring and training the sensor by continuously monitoring an individual's movements over a period of time, the results are saved. The individual's identity is then periodically confirmed by comparing the haptic signature.

In addition to active authentication, the use of haptics is also being explored as a way to provide proof of life, as discussed next.

Identifying a human

When entering data in a web page, you may have to complete a **Completely Automated Public Turing test to tell a Computer and Humans Apart (CAPTCHA)**, as shown in the following diagram:

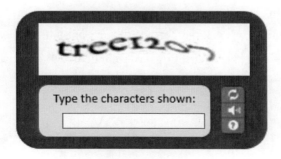

Figure 2.5 – CAPTCHA example

Captchas are used in web services such as account registration to prevent bot attacks. Users are presented with an image and asked to type the characters they see. In the graphic, the characters are **tree1207**. When looking at the characters in a CAPTCHA, it may be difficult to identify the characters. If needed, you can refresh the image to generate a new set of characters. Although some CAPTCHAS are difficult to read for many of us, studies have shown that these tests are especially difficult for elderly people. As a result, when using a mobile device, researchers are exploring the use of a haptic-based response as an alternative to this type of test.

Although haptics is not a biometric technology, we may find that using haptics in the future will complement biometrics, as scientists are discovering many different uses, as shown at: `https://www.cs.ubc.ca/labs/spin/projects`.

Optimal biometrics are important for enhancing the user experience and ensuring adaptability and cooperation. In the next segment, we'll examine some of the parameters required when designing essential technology, such as accuracy, throughput, cost, security, privacy, and usability.

Incorporating essential biometric technology

These emerging technologies allow for a more mobile workforce, while securing the enterprise network. Using checks and cash are becoming less commonplace as digital payment options are more convenient, secure, and flexible, which will reshape the retail and financial ecosystems. Vendors are discovering that biometrics are providing a realistic solution to authentication. Using a mobile phone for biometric authentication has multiple benefits that helps provide improve security. Benefits of mobile biometrics include the following:

- **Cost effective**: Mobile phones have become more powerful over time and most are easily able to process biometrics.

- **Built-in sensors**: Most devices have an onboard sensor such as a camera in order to capture the biometrics.

- **Widespread popularity**: A large percent of the population use a mobile device.

- **User acceptance**: Regularly handling a mobile device makes using biometrics on a mobile device almost natural.

- **Portable and convenient**: Mobile devices are used in a variety of applications and locations.

Along with the benefits come the challenges of using biometric authentication with a mobile device. Incorporating biometric technology in a mobile device must meet exceptional standards. The device must be able to not only capture the image, but go through the same steps related to enrollment, matching, and storage.

In this section, we'll discuss the necessary requirements when incorporating biometric technology. Requirements include methods to properly capture the biometric and seamlessly integrate within the device. In addition, the device needs to provide a quick and accurate response time, while ensuring security and privacy. Let's start with capturing the image.

Capturing the image

When using a biometric to identify and authenticate, the first step is to register with the software. The interface must focus on the user experience. Simplicity is key. In most cases, the user should be able to register on their own, because if the method becomes too frustrating, the user might abandon the process. The system itself must be capable of high-quality capture, be durable, and water resistant or waterproof.

When selecting a sensor, there are many considerations, as there are different biometrics, all of which have subtle differences as discussed next. Let's take a look at a few biometric techniques, starting with scanning a fingerprint.

Scanning a fingerprint

Using the fingerprint is a common biometric. Most of us are able to present their fingerprint without any issues. However, a small percentage of individuals face challenges, such as the finger surface being worn from excessive use of the hands while doing manual labor, or the prints being unintelligible because certain diseases and age can make the fingerprint difficult to capture. Newer photoelectric sensor scanners improve on the ability to capture fingerprints. Photoelectric sensors use light-emitting as opposed to optical sensors and are able to read a fingerprint through several layers beneath the surface.

Another common biometric we must consider when capturing the image is iris recognition, which we'll learn about next.

Imaging an iris

One of the qualities of a good biometric is persistence, which means unchanging over time. The iris is the colored part of the eye that is clearly visible and remains mostly the same throughout someone's lifetime. Iris recognition is a convenient, non-invasive biometric.

A few mobile device manufacturers are capable of capturing and processing an iris. Iris recognition uses near infrared optical technology to image the iris and is able to obtain the image with greater detail. To improve the precision of the iris scanner, manufacturers use a three - or greater megapixels lens. Other improvements include the ability to capture in varying lighting conditions, and whether or not they are wearing glasses.

Next, let's take a look at another common biometric – facial recognition.

Recognizing a face

Facial recognition is gaining support as a biometric, as nearly every mobile device has a built-in camera that is able to capture a facial image. This, in itself, is an advantage, as no additional hardware or software is needed. Using the face as a biometric is almost natural as the user experience of capturing a selfie is commonplace and convenient. Mobile device cameras are improving along with the quality, which leads to higher matching accuracy rates.

Researchers have found that authentication is not a cumbersome exercise, but rather a ritual that becomes part of our daily routine. In many ways, this process improves our sense of security. With time, there may be other biometrics developed to gain access to your device. Microsoft is now offering Windows Hello for Business, a method in Windows 10 that allows the user to authenticate by using their face or fingerprint on mobile devices, laptops, and desktop computers.

Once the biometric is captured, the device will need to have a way to process and then store the biometric, as we'll discuss next.

Handling the biometric

After a biometric is captured, the identifier must go through the same steps as any other biometric system. This includes preprocessing, extracting the features, and then storing the template for later comparison. However, there may be additional challenges associated with dealing with a mobile device, as it's small, may be moving, and must be able to capture in varying lighting.

A mobile biometric solution must provide the same or a better degree of errors and throughput that a standard system can provide. The device must be able to capture the biometric and remove any artifacts. This includes any non-biometric data, such as backgrounds, glasses, or jewelry.

The device must have adequate processing power, as well as exceptional image quality, in order to properly capture and process the biometric. In addition, the device will need the appropriate on-board memory to store the application and the biometric template. Manufacturers are seeking other improvements to mobile device authentication. Improvements include optimizing the algorithms to include ways to deal with new use cases and different scenarios, and the ability of the software to integrate well with existing systems.

In addition to capturing and processing the biometric, we also need to keep our biometric secure, as we'll see next.

Providing security and privacy

Although biometrics are widely used, and are more secure that a PIN or password, we need to be aware that there are security issues.

Users may be concerned that upon enrollment, they may be required to provide additional information such as an address, phone number, and email, along with a password or PIN. All of this information is considered private and must be protected. In addition, the biometric data itself is viewed as our identity, which should not be compromised.

In some cases, the biometric data will remain on the device, or it may be sent to a server for processing. Whether on the device or on a server, the stored biometric data must be protected using encryption. If the data is sent to a server, any communication must be sent using **Transport Layer Security** (**TLS**) or another **Virtual Private Network** (**VPN**), which will encrypt the data while in transit.

As we can see, there are many possibilities of using biometrics on fintech. As mobile device manufacturers gain a better understanding of the benefits of biometrics, the standards and interoperability will evolve, which will spur exponential growth of biometric authentication.

Summary

Every day, people are moving from their laptops to a mobile device to access information. With the amount and type of data that we are accessing every day, we need to protect our mobile devices from security hazards. Passwords and PINs are inherently weak authentication mechanisms and, as a result, more and more device manufacturers are using biometrics to ensure access control.

In this chapter, we examined the need to incorporate optimal attributes for mobile biometric applications. We also learned some of the optimal biometrics for mobile devices, with the importance of streamlining the user experience and how the use of haptics may play a more significant role in ensuring continuous authentication. Lastly, we now understand the need as to why it is important to incorporate key biometric technology when designing methods to capture the image, as well as integrate with the backend, while ensuring security and privacy.

In the next chapter, we'll take a look at what makes a great biometric and review the desired quality characteristics of biometrics. So that you have a better understanding of how a biometric system works, we'll step through the general operation of biometric authentication. Finally, because biometric technology can have different application variables, we'll examine how to implement the best system according to the environment and your purpose.

Questions

Now, it's time to check your knowledge. Select the best response, and then check your answers, found in the *Assessment* section at the end of the book.

1. _____ limits access to intangible assets, such as files, networks, websites, or applications, and includes ACLs along with folder and file permissions.

   a. Physical access controls

   b. Logical access controls

   c. Turing measurements

   d. GDPR clipping levels

2. When we protect data from unauthorized changes, we are ensuring _____.

   a. Integrity

   b. Confidentiality

   c. Availability

   d. Non-repudiation

3. When we use a _____ instead of a credit card during a transaction, this can prevent the payment database from being compromised.

   a. Token

   b. Haptic

   c. GDPR

   d. ACL

4. _____ requires two or more authentication factors, such as a password and a biometric scan, and can improve the security of a device.

   a. Tokens

   b. Haptic

   c. GDPR

   d. MFA

5. _____ is an industry standard that outlines requirements to secure credit card transactions.

   a. PCI DSS

   b. HIPAA

   c. GDPR

   d. ACL

6. _____ are sensors that deliver a physical sensation in response to an action.

   a. Tokens

   b. Haptics

   c. GDPR

   d. MFAs

7. _____ sensors use light-emitting as opposed to optical sensors and are able to read a fingerprint through several layers beneath the surface.

   a. Token

   b. Haptic

   c. Photoelectric

   d. GDPR

Further reading

Please refer to the following links for more information:

- You can learn more about how Windows Hello can provide multifactor authentication at: `https://docs.microsoft.com/en-us/windows/security/identity-protection/hello-for-business/hello-overview`.

- Learn about the many considerations when using biometrics and mobile devices in a paper entitled *Recent Advances in Biometric Technology for Mobile Devices*, available at `https://hal.inria.fr/hal-01894140/document`.

3
Recognizing Biometric Characteristics

Biometrics have been around in some form for many years, as they provide a solid method to identify and authenticate individuals. However, industry in general has been slow to adopt the technology. That is until now, where the expanded use of mobile devices has empowered the use of biometrics as a method to secure the device and restrict access to data. Businesses are recognizing that because biometrics can complement strong security policies in the fintech industry, organizations can now offer a wide range of features for their mobile workforce.

Because of this widespread adoption, industry leaders are seeking ways to ensure that the best biometric is employed for each use case. We know that there are several options in the type of biometric identifier we can select. To start us on our journey, this chapter begins with a review of just what makes a solid biometric choice. We'll compare the desired qualities of a biometric, such as uniqueness, performance, distinctiveness, and permanence. We'll then take a look at the general operation of biometric authentication, from initial registration to processing, to a one-to-one or one-to-many comparison within a database.

So that you have a better understanding of the ways industry is implementing biometric authentication, we'll compare how modern technology can adjust to varying conditions. You'll then understand how these modifications work to improve object detection in a wide range of application environments. We'll then take a look at open versus closed systems, and then compare whether the system can operate attended or non-attended and whether the biometric templates are privately managed or publicly accessible. Finally, we'll see the ways different biometrics are imaged, using either one-dimensional, two-dimensional, or the more recent three-dimensional imaging.

In this chapter, we'll cover the following main topics:

- Assessing the desired qualities of a biometric
- Summarizing the operation of biometrics technology
- Comparing application environments

Assessing the desired qualities of a biometric

When selecting a biometric identifier, we have many choices, such as our fingerprint, face, iris, or even our ears. Before deciding to implement a specific biometric type, device manufacturers run tests and consult studies that help us understand the most desired biometric qualities. Careful selection is important, as we don't want to change to another biometric once we have invested in a system.

Some of the key performance metrics for biometrics include the need to be unique, universal, permanent, collectable, acceptable, offer exceptional performance, and able to avoid circumvention. Let's take a look at each of these, starting with the need to be unique.

Having uniqueness

One key biometric characteristic is that of uniqueness, or something that is one of a kind. When selecting a biometric, the chosen biometric identifier cannot be the same for any two individuals, even between two identical twins.

Using a unique attribute as a method to identify someone has been in use in some form for centuries. In the late 1800s, *Alphonse Bertillon* devised a system to identify an individual based on measurements of various physical attributes of a person's body. Measurements included the head, the cubit, and the left foot.

The Bertillon system was widely accepted and used as a method to identify prisoners. In theory, it seemed everyone would have sufficient differences in those physical attributes. However, in 1903, it was revealed that the system had a major flaw. The discovery occurred when two prisoners, both named *Will West*, had the exact same measurements. It was then determined that the Bertillon method was not an accurate way to identify individuals, as the chosen bodily measurements were not sufficiently unique.

Uniqueness is an important attribute when selecting a biometric. Another desired characteristic is universality, in that everyone must possess the biometric, as discussed next.

Being universal

Because a biometric identifier measures a physiological attribute or observes a specific behavior, it's important to select a characteristic that everyone in the cohort will have.

If a biometric authentication system is to be installed in a facility, careful consideration should be made prior to implementation. For example, while nearly everyone has fingers, not everyone can successfully use fingerprint identification. If you need to implement biometric technology where there are individuals that have engaged in manual labor for many years, a fingerprint reader may not be the best choice. The fact is that many manual workers may not have sufficient detail in their prints for the device to even enroll the individuals, let alone be consistently accurate for the device to work properly.

Another attribute that is essential when selecting a biometric is that it does not change much over time, as we'll learn next.

Staying permanent

Permanence is the stability of a biometric that does not change or changes only minimally over time. Consider your voice. Many of us will experience subtle changes that occur over time. Think of the way you spoke as a child, and then think about how your voice may change as you grow into adulthood.

While some biometrics experience changes over time, others are more stable. For example, if you need a more permanent biometric, a fingerprint or iris will change only minimally over time.

The characteristic of permanence is essential, but as important is the need to accurately capture the biometric.

Performing accurately

When considering a biometric system, performance is a key indicator. An optimal system will provide reliable and consistently correct results with every measurement of a given biometric sample. For example, if we use the right index finger to enroll, the same finger must be identified correctly each time it is measured.

The system must be tuned to adjust for variables such as environmental factors that may affect the accuracy of the identification. For example, when using a mobile device, capturing the details of a fingerprint using a camera may produce a lower quality image that an image captured using a touch-based sensor. If the system is not able to properly capture an image, there may be errors. The outliers that can occur are:

- The **False Match Rate** (**FMR**), also called a Type II error, measures the rate by which the results are accepted as valid, however, they are not from an authorized individual.

- The **False Non-Match Rate** (**FNMR**), also called a Type I error, measures the rate by which the results are from an authorized individual, however, they are not accepted as valid.

- The crossover or **Equal Error Rate** (**EER**) is where both the FMR and FNMR are equal and therefore are at a crossover point.

When assessing performance, these values are monitored, as the ideal system will measure the biometric identifier accurately, reject impostors, and accept only authorized individuals.

Along with wanting the biometric system to be fast and accurate, it's also important to make sure the system provides a reasonably simple way to capture an image using an automated system. Next, let's take a look at the concept of collectability.

Ensuring collectability

A system may have exceptionally high accuracy, universality, permanence, and uniqueness. However, the system must also have collectability, or a method by which a biometric sample can easily be obtained from an individual.

Collectability takes into account the various parameters that are taken into consideration when obtaining a sample. Parameters may include checking to see if the system has the following properties:

- Simple to use and readily available

- Mobile and can be used in a wide range of settings

- Equipped with affordable hardware and software
- Able to quickly obtain the given feature set

In general, collectability measures how effortless it is to obtain the given biometric data. If the system is too complex or requires expensive devices, the collectability of the chosen biometric will be less than optimal. For example, retinal scans and **deoxyribonucleic acid (DNA)** are two of the most precise and reliable biometric identifiers. However, because the data collection process can be either complex, time-consuming, or expensive, this makes using retinal scans or DNA less than optimal identifiers.

Another optimal characteristic is acceptability, or how willing we might be to use the selected biometric identifier, as discussed next.

Providing an acceptable biometric

When we think of having someone present a biometric identifier, it's important to implement a user-friendly system. An acceptable biometric is one that the population is willing to use.

The user interface should not only be able to capture a high-quality image that can be sent to the backend for processing, but also physically comfortable so that the user does not have to manipulate any devices to obtain a capture.

While it's important to obtain a high-quality capture, developers must keep in mind the perception of intimate and personal space. As shown in the following graphic, the intimate space is considered to be less than 0.5 meters (or 1.6 feet):

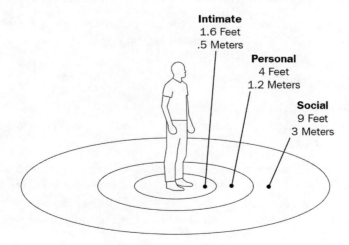

Figure 3.1 – Intimate and personal space

When attempting to obtain a biometric identifier, as you get closer to the protected intimate space, the user may become anxious, or hesitant to use the reader.

For example, when dealing with the eye, there is a significant difference between the iris and the retina, as shown in the following graphic. The iris is the colored portion in the front of the eye, the pupil is in the center of the iris, and the retina is in the back of the eye:

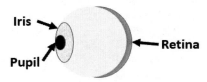

Figure 3.2 – The eye showing the iris, pupil and the retina

While users may feel comfortable using iris recognition, they may not agree to a retinal scan. The reason is the two work completely differently when collecting a biometric identifier.

- An iris recognition system can capture the iris and produce a high-resolution, sharp iris image at a reasonable distance.

- A retinal scan uses an infrared light that passes through the pupil in order to gain access to the retina, and requires the system to be very close to the user.

As you can see, the retinal scan is perceived by many to be invasive and is not an optimal biometric for that reason. When selecting a biometric identifier, users need to feel comfortable and protected, and the identifier should be acceptable to everyone.

While acceptability is an important characteristic, we also want a system that prevents spoofing. Let's take a look at this concept in the next section.

Avoiding circumvention

Another important consideration when selecting a biometric identifier is the need to prevent impersonation attacks. Circumvention deals with the ability to spoof the system in order to gain access to it.

Current biometric technology actively incorporates a variety of tools and techniques to prevent someone from tricking or spoofing the system. There are a few methods that developers can use to detect spoofing. The predominant technique is the use of liveness detection, which prevents someone from using an image or video as a biometric identifier.

Liveness detection methods can be as simple as requiring the user to complete an action such as nodding, smiling, or blinking. However, with advances in technology, malicious actors are finding creative ways to spoof systems using techniques such as high-quality images, videos, and masks. Vendors are incorporating advanced liveness or realness detection into systems.

Advanced liveness methods do not require any participation from the user and can include the following:

- Software that can detect anomalies, such as the pupillary reaction when presented with a light source

- 3D imaging that can distinguish between a high-quality 2D image, and a real face

- Multispectral imaging, which can assess sub-surface information such as the vascular system of a finger, which makes spoofing difficult, if not impossible

Liveness detection is a strong anti-spoofing method, and according to the **National Institute of Standards and Technology (NIST)**, this method has a high accuracy rate at preventing fraud.

All key characteristics are important, but ultimately the use case will decide what indicators are most important to the organization. One way to help you decide is to create a matrix, as shown in the following figure, which can help you review all of the key characteristics before making a decision:

Biometric	Uniqueness	Universal	Performance	Acceptable	Circumvention	Concerns
Face	High	High	Medium	High	High	Lighting, artifacts
Fingerprint	High	Medium	High	Medium	Medium	Age, wear, dryness
Iris	High	High	High	Low	Medium	Lighting
Voice	Low	High	Low	Medium	Medium	Health, stress level

Figure 3.3 – Comparison of different biometrics and their characteristics

As you can see, there are many considerations when selecting an appropriate biometric. Next, let's look at the basic operation of using a standard biometric system.

Summarizing the operation of a biometric system

A biometric system validates the identity or authenticity of an individual, by comparing the physiological or behavioral characteristics against a stored template. The process can be performed by either of the following:

- **A person**: Comparing the characteristics using a manual method
- **A machine**: Comparing the characteristics using an automated method

Today, much of the work in biometric identification and authentication is done using automation. Most systems have a common sequence of events. The process begins at the user interface, then the system acquires the image, prepares the image for comparison, determines if there is a match, and then presents the results.

The basic process is outlined in the following diagram:

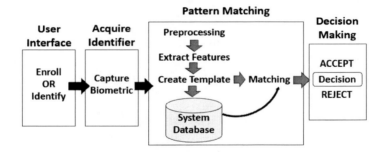

Figure 3.4 – Basic operation of a biometric system

Let's take a look at each step, starting with the user interface.

Initiating contact with the user interface

The user interface is where the subject initiates contact with the biometric system, which can either enroll, identify, or authenticate, according to the design:

- **Enrollment** is the process of processing a biometric identifier for the first time so that it can be stored in the system database for later comparison. During enrollment, the user may need to provide additional information such as their name or a user ID.
- **Identification** occurs after enrollment, when there is a template in the database that can be used to compare the sample to the template. Identification is a one-to-many comparison, as the database is not indexed.

- **Authentication** occurs after enrollment and is a one-to-one comparison that matches the captured biometric sample with a pre-stored template in the database. Because the process is indexed, the user must enter a name or other form of identification into the system.

The interface must have many of the collectability qualities, such as being user friendly, simple to use, readily available, and able to quickly obtain the feature set. After the user initiates contact with the system, the biometric is then captured, as discussed next.

Obtaining the biometric identifier

At this point, the system acquires the biometric traits for further processing. A biometric system must be able to accept a variety of settings and possibly be used on different devices. The capture devices on modern systems have more robust acquisition modules that are able to provide speed and accuracy.

Many are able to remove noise such as non-biometric information, which improves the overall process. Once the biometric identifier is presented to a sensor, the output is prepared to be sent to pattern matching. In some cases, the image is compressed to reduce storage requirements. Standards for compression include the following:

- **Wavelet Scalar Quantization (WSQ)**, used for fingerprints
- **Joint Photographic Experts Group (JPEG)**, used for facial images

Although compression reduces the size of the image, in some cases it is not used, as compression and the resultant expansion can cause a loss in image quality.

Once captured, the image moves to the next phase in the system, pattern matching, as discussed in the next section.

Matching the pattern

Once a biometric identifier is obtained, the image moves through the system to the pattern matching phase, which is a key part of the system. The measurement of the given behavioral or physiological characteristic must be prepared so a template can be placed in the database.

This component has the following modules: preprocessing, feature extraction, template creation, matching, and the system database:

- **Preprocessing** obtains the biometric pattern within the transmitted signal. For example, if we are using facial recognition, the system must find the boundaries of the face in the transmitted image.

- **Feature extraction** pulls the true biometric pattern from any noise and signal degradation, preserves the critical information, and discards any unnecessary or redundant data.

- **Template creation** converts the features into a compact digital template for storage in the system database that is available for matching purposes. In most cases, the template is stored in the form of a non-reversible format so the biometric cannot be reconstructed from the template.

- A **database** is available so the system can update the templates that are stored in it for later comparison.

In most cases, the system will check the quality to ensure the sample can be used for comparison. If the sample is not acceptable, the system will signal a failed attempt, and the subject must present another sample for consideration. In addition, any biometric system can have errors during acquisition or capture, so there should be policies in place for exception handling.

At the heart of this module is pattern matching, discussed next.

Comparing the sample

Pattern matching involves comparing the subject's sample with a pre-stored biometric template in the database. This process evaluates the interval of the sample to the template on file. If two patterns are compared and are apart by an acceptable distance, then the sample would be considered a match.

For example, in the following graphic, we see a biometric sample with an acceptable distance, which would be considered a match:

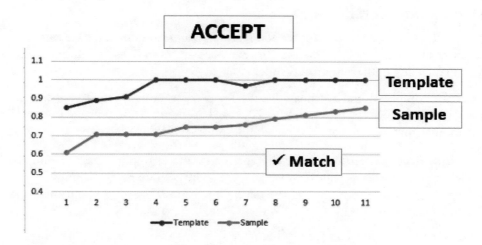

Figure 3.5 – A biometric sample with an acceptable distance

In the following graphic, the sample is too far from the template and this would not be considered a match:

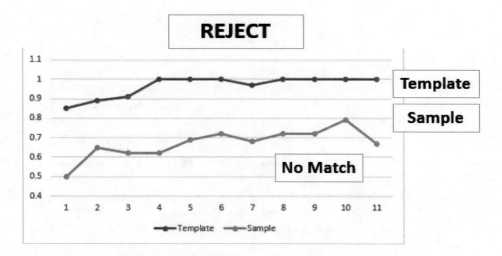

Figure 3.6 – A biometric sample without an acceptable distance

Keep in mind that, unlike a password, which will always return a 100 percent match, a biometric will rarely if ever be a 100 percent match.

In a large-scale system, there can be thousands of templates. In the next segment, we'll discuss ways to improve the searching process.

Narrowing the search

Comparing the sample against all of the templates in a large system database can be process intensive, which only worsens as the database grows in size. At that point, the speed and efficiency of the system can suffer.

To reduce the computational overhead during this process, biometric patterns are classified, which involves partitioning the database based on certain types of information. Two techniques that are used are binning and filtering, which optimize the search process:

- **Binning** groups together similar characteristics. For example, a fingerprint has various Level One features such as loops, whirls, and arches. Taking advantage of binning can group the Level One features together to optimize the searching process.

- **Filtering** narrows in on specific characteristics, such as which finger was used during capture, or the sex of the individual. Removing unnecessary information can speed up the searching process.

Although helpful in narrowing a search, binning and filtering can result in errors, so the algorithm must be carefully written and thoroughly tested before widespread deployment.

The last phase in a biometric system is to make a decision, as we'll see next.

Making a decision

Once the sample passes through the pattern matching component, the last step is to make a decision based on received inputs. The results will show either a positive or negative identification and will either accept or reject the individual. At that point, the individual can begin the process again. In some cases, the threshold may need to be readjusted.

Important note

One common misconception is that the system can recognize anyone at any time, as there is a super database of pre-stored templates available. You may have seen a television show or a movie where law enforcement is able to instantly recognize someone when trying to track down a criminal. However, as we have seen, the first step in the process is the creation of the template, which is used to compare the sample. If the template is not in the database, the sample will be rejected.

As we can see, the standard operation of a biometric system has a number of complex components to provide methods to enroll, identify, or authenticate an individual. In the next section, let's take a look at the various application environments you may encounter.

Comparing application environments

When dealing with obtaining biometric samples, there are various configuration profiles. The selected method will depend on how we need to collect the biometric, where this will take place, and what type of inputs are required.

Next, let's take a look at the various methods of obtaining a biometric sample.

Classifying different methods

When evaluating various ways to obtain a biometric sample, we have a number of different choices. Before deciding on a method, it's important to gather the requirements so that you select the best method for the organization.

Let's take a look at the different types of biometric systems as shown in the following table:

Type of system	Explanation
Habituated or Non-Habituated	• Habituated systems are used on a daily basis and become a habit. • Non-habituated systems are not used regularly, and the user must refamiliarize themselves before using the system.
Overt or Covert	• An overt system is used when the user is aware that a biometric identifier is being measured, and include access control and any non-forensic applications. • In a covert system the user is unaware that a biometric identifier is being measured, for example during a forensic evaluation.
Attended or Non-Attended	• Attended requires someone to monitor the user. • Non-attended systems allow users to interact independently with the system.
Public or Private	• A public system is designed to be used by customers. • A private system will be used internally by the employees.
Open or Closed	• An open system uses standards for data collection, compression, and format, so that the original signal can be reconstructed. • A closed system will use internally developed proprietary formats.

Figure 3.7 – A comparison of different types of biometric systems

In addition to the various environments, biometric system design can include the ability to accepts different types of input, as we'll see next.

Accepting various forms of input

When designing a biometric system, it's important to understand the type of input that will need to be accepted. The system must be able to accept the appropriate image. Depending upon how the biometric is collected, the images can be either **one-dimensional** (or **1D**), **two-dimensional** (or **2D**), or **three-dimensional** (or **3D**).

Let's compare the differences, starting with how we measure a 1D biometric image.

Representing a 1D image

A 1D image only needs one measurement to describe the sample, for example, a span of time such as 5 hours is one-dimensional.

1D images include voice samples and handwritten signatures. A voice sample is a single 1D image. A handwriting sample is considered to be multiple simultaneous single 1D signals.

When a person speaks, their voice can be represented by a waveform. In the following graphic, you can see my voiceprint:

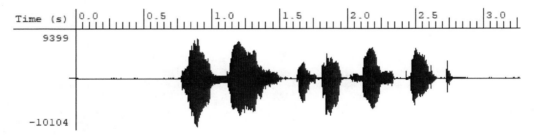

Figure 3.8 – "My voice is my passport" voiceprint

More complex identifiers have multiple dimensions. Next, let's evaluate what's involved in obtaining a 2D image.

Viewing a 2D image

When you need more than a single dimension to describe the biometric identifier, the next option is 2D, which is represented as the height and width. However, a 2D object does not possess depth. If you think of plotting points on a graph, here, it would be plotted on an *x* axis and a *y* axis.

2D images use measurements that include length and width. Images that have more than one dimension can include irises, faces, fingerprints, and hand geometry.

When you need more than two measurements to describe the identifier, you'll need to use a 3D image, as we'll learn next.

Capturing a 3D image

A 3D object has length, height, and depth, such as this cube:

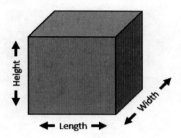

Figure 3.9 – A three-dimensional object

If you think of a mathematical representation, this would require x, y, and z axes.

3D images are a newer trend as they improve on the measurements obtained by 1D and 2D methods. In any given situation, there will be issues with obtaining a biometric identifier. Here are some examples of less than optimal scenarios:

- When taking a fingerprint, if the finger has residue such as dirt or grease on it, or there is movement during capture, the quality will suffer.

- During iris recognition, individuals that have diabetes may not be able to provide a readable iris image.

- Issues with voice recognition can occur as when a person ages, their voice can change. In addition, having a cold or allergies can affect the quality of voice input.

The challenge in biometrics is to improve the quality of the identifier for feature extraction. Using 3D imaging provides a more robust illumination and pose variations than using 2D imaging. Using 3D imaging is capable of providing a richer source of information during feature extraction. In addition, because a 3D image is more complex, it is more difficult for it to be spoofed or duplicated, and is thus more resistant to attacks.

The bottom line is that in a biometric system, quality is multi-dimensional. To obtain an acceptable image, there are three key factors that will influence the quality:

- The capture *process* will govern the quality of the biometric sample.

- The capture *device* will govern the quality of the image.

- The *algorithm* will govern the quality of the feature extracted.

In general, over time, the use of biometrics will improve and evolve. As shown in the following image, we'll see an expansion of technology from our mobile apps, to desktops and websites, and then to ATMs and kiosks, along with IoT devices and more:

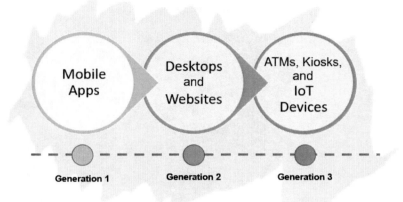

Figure 3.10 – Evolution of biometrics

It's an exciting time for biometric authentication. In the near future, we will see the use of biometrics for access control in a variety of settings, from factories to nuclear power plants, college dorms, and even our homes.

Summary

With the rapid advances in the ability to capture and process biometric identifiers, along with overall improvements in technology, we now see that the business world has embraced biometrics as a people-centric solution to authentication. In this chapter, we took a look at what makes a good biometric identifier as we examined some of the desired qualities, such as robustness, its unchanging nature over time, its collectability, and the need to prevent circumvention. We examined the general operation of biometric technology, from initiating contact with the system, to acquiring the image and preparing it for comparison, and then determining whether there is a match and presenting the results.

We evaluated how you may encounter different environments when dealing with biometric authentication, including whether the system is attended or non-attended, public or private, and whether or not the system will use standards for data collection, compression, and format, or internally developed proprietary formats. Finally, we learned how the different systems are capable of obtaining a 1D, 2D, or 3D image, and how 3D is a more desired imaging technique for a variety of reasons.

In the next chapter, we'll compare some of the pros and cons of various biometric identifiers. We'll take a closer look at the different types of errors that can occur, such as Type I, Type II, and crossover points. You'll get a better understanding of the value of using multi-factor authentication in today's complex digital environment. Finally, we'll see how many industry leaders are working on more universal biometric standards to help promote interoperability among systems.

Questions

Now it's time to check your knowledge. Select the best response, then check your answers, found in the *Assessment* section at the end of the book:

1. When selecting a biometric identifier, the characteristic of _____ means that everyone must possess the biometric.

    a. Uniqueness

    b. Universality

    c. Collectability

    d. Circumvention

2. A biometric system must have _____, or a method to easily obtain a biometric sample from an individual.

    a. Uniqueness

    b. Universality

    c. Collectability

    d. Circumvention

3. A(n) _____ biometric is one that the population is willing to use.

    a. Unique

    b. Universal

    c. Acceptable

    d. Collectable

4. _____ is the process of processing a biometric identifier for the first time so that it can be stored in the system database for later comparison.

    a. Identification

    b. Authentication

    c. Filtering

    d. Enrollment

5. _____ is a one-to-one comparison by matching the captured biometric with a pre-stored biometric template in the database. Because the process is indexed, the user must enter a name or other form of identification into the system.

    a. Identification

    b. Authentication

    c. Filtering

    d. Enrollment

6. _____ narrows in on specific characteristics, such as what finger was used during capture, or the sex of the individual.

    a. Binning

    b. Authentication

    c. Filtering

    d. Enrollment

7. When you need more than two measurements to describe the identifier, you'll need to use a(n) _____ image.

    a. Binning space

    b. Authentication

    c. Three-dimensional

    d. Enrollment

Further reading

- You can learn more about protection biometric templates by using a non-reversible method to create the template, with more information available at `http://www.bromba.com/knowhow/temppriv.htm`.

- To obtain your own voice sample, go to `https://www.phon.ucl.ac.uk/resource/sfs/wasp.php` and download the free Windows Tool for Speech Analysis.

4
Comparing Advantages and Modalities

Today, many of us are able to unlock our phone or tablet by using our face or fingerprint. Making use of a biometric identifier not only provides a stronger method to authenticate, but also provides an easier login experience for the user. In addition to our mobile devices, biometric technology is being used in a number of other applications to make everyday life safer and more convenient. Using fingerprint, face, and voice recognition can help make secure transactions, but these techniques are also used in many other areas. Biometrics are used in border control, airports, commercial applications, and law enforcement.

With the evolution of technology over the years, we now find that we have many choices in terms of how we implement biometric identification and authentication. In this chapter, we'll examine whether or not the biometric system must be a standalone solution, or whether it can be networked and integrated with the organization's directory. In addition, we'll discuss what happens when a system has to integrate with another system, and why you might need a middleware solution.

We know that one of the desired qualities of a biometric is the need to perform accurately. So that you have a better understanding of performance metrics, we'll compare some of the advantages and disadvantages of common biometrics. We'll then go into detail on Type I and Type II errors, and discuss some of the reasons as to why system errors can occur. In addition, we'll look at how biometrics can strengthen a standard login by using multi-factor and, in some cases, multi-modal authentication. Finally, because of limitations in system interoperability, you'll learn why many industry leaders and scientists are promoting biometric standards.

In this chapter, we're going to cover the following main topics:

- Reviewing system approaches
- Understanding system errors
- Using multi-factor authentication
- Recognizing the push for standards

Reviewing system approaches

Today, many companies are choosing biometrics, which are the behavioral or physiological characteristics that are unique to an individual, to provide password-free authentication into devices, facilities, and computer systems. When faced with a decision to implement a biometric solution to provide identification and authentication to an organization, there are a couple of questions:

- What is our approach on how to implement the system; will it be standalone or networked?
- Of the many choices we have, what are some of the advantages and disadvantages of some common biometric identifiers?

In this section, we'll review these questions. Let's start with evaluating how a networked system works.

Networking the biometric system

A complex corporate environment will most likely need a networked solution that is capable of centralized administration. Most systems will have the ability to manage the system remotely using a web interface. This will allow for easier configuration modifications. In addition, this can give you the control needed to manage all devices, so that you can verify the same person in different locations. In addition, a networked system will allow users' templates to be housed within a central database. This will allow users to enroll and sign in at multiple remote locations, as their template will always be available for comparison.

Prior to implementation of a networked biometric system, the administrator must do a complete requirements analysis to ensure that there is appropriate support for the system. Several assessments should be made in terms of bandwidth across the **Local Area Network (LAN)** and/or **Wide Area Network (WAN)** for reliable data transfer. In addition, it's important to make sure that the end devices are able to quickly, reliably, and securely obtain the sample.

While providing a networked solution has many benefits, an organization may not be able to implement a networked biometric system. An alternative is to use a standalone system, as we'll see next.

Operating in standalone mode

Standalone systems have been in place for decades. In some cases, it's simply easier and faster to use than a networked solution to provide biometric identification and authentication. There can be a few reasons why this type of system might be a better and easier alternative to networking the device. Some of these reasons are mentioned here:

- The organization doesn't have a central directory, so there is no need to network the device.
- The system is in a remote office with a limited network, so a standalone system is the only alternative.
- Because of the nature of access control needed, there is no need for integration into the directory.

A standalone system can provide a plug and play form of access control, where the administrator can enter the users and then monitor the output. One example is a company that might choose to implement a biometric reader as a time clock for more accurate time and attendance. Using the biometric system can avoid the threat of 'buddy punching', where someone punches in the time clock for someone who is running late. While most employees are honest, there are a few that might try to circumvent the system.

Using a biometric identifier can add value to the company by preventing theft of service. Once in use, the administrator can run reports, similar to the one shown in the following diagram, where the report can identify activity such as early or late punches, which can be highlighted in red:

	A	B	C	D	E	F	G	H	I	J	K	L
1						**Time Card Report**						
2						*02/09/2020 - 02/15/2020*						
3												
4												
5	**Employee ID**: 78321		**Employee name**: Roxy Blake				**DEPT**: Sales		**SHIFT**: 8:00 - 5:00		Totals	Notes
6	Date	Week	(IN)	(OUT)	(IN)	(OUT)	(IN)	(OUT)	(IN)	(OUT)		
7	9-Feb	SUN										Not assigned
8	10-Feb	MON	7:59	12:00	12:59	17:01						
9	11-Feb	TUE	8:03	11:55	12:55	17:04						
10	12-Feb	WED	7:59	12:10	13:00	17:01						
11	13-Feb	THU	8:01	11:52	13:06	17:02						
12	14-Feb	FRI	7:58	12:00	12:55	17:01						
13	15-Feb	SAT										Not assigned
14												
15	Work Total (hrs):				Overtime (hrs):				Flags: 3			

Figure 4.1 – Time card report on a biometric time card system

Standalone time clock systems have a wide range of offerings, such as fingerprint, facial recognition, and hand geometry. The systems are easily customized with employee start and stop times and holidays, and the administrator can pull the reports for analysis.

In addition to determining whether or not the biometric system will be a standalone or networked solution, there may be a need to incorporate the biometric device with an existing system, such as the company directory, as we'll see next.

Integrating with other systems

Interoperability is when two or more systems are able to work together to exchange information. In a biometric system, this could be the biometrics themselves or the results of a comparison.

A biometric system can have several components. One of the key components is the **identity management system (IDMS)**, that provides the backend tasks that include enrollment, identification, and authentication.

When considering a biometric system, one of the concerns is making the system capable of integrating with a backend, which includes the system directory or other database.

In some cases, there may be a need to use a middleware wrapper to maintain the biometric workflow. As shown in the following diagram, we see a logical representation of middleware being used. This is in place so that the proprietary system can communicate with the backend:

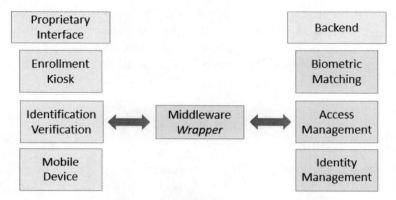

Figure 4.2 – Using middleware to bridge systems

Middleware essentially bridges separate systems together by enabling communication between the proprietary biometric interface and the backend systems. The chosen solution can be either a dedicated appliance or a software solution.

In addition to recognizing the different approaches for implementing a biometric system, it's important to understand the various different modalities, as discussed in the next section.

Reviewing common modalities

Some of the common attributes that ensure an optimal biometric include the need for uniqueness, staying permanent, and ensuring collectability. In this section, let's compare several biometric identifiers, along with some pros and cons for each one. Let's start with using the face as a biometric identifier.

Recognizing the face

Facial recognition is being used in a wide variety of applications. The algorithms have improved over the years, along with the cameras that capture the face, so we are seeing an increase in the use of facial recognition.

Using facial recognition has a couple of key benefits. One is that it's fairly non-invasive, in that the subject does not have to touch anything when authenticating into the system. In addition, facial recognition can work without the subject having any knowledge they are being observed, so this type of identification can be used for threat management.

On the downside, there are cases where systems are unable to discern identical twins, and may return a false match on a non-authorized individual. Facial recognition can also be affected by non-facial artifacts, such as glasses, moustaches, makeup, and hats, which can result in a high face non-match. Facial recognition can also have the potential for privacy abuse because it's so easy to use.

Another common option is to use fingerprints, as we'll see next.

Verifying a fingerprint

One of the oldest methods continues to be one of the more common biometric identifiers. Fingerprint technology is a mature biometric that is in use in commercial and government applications.

Some of the benefits include the fact that fingerprints stay about the same throughout someone's lifetime. Most people find using a finger as a method to identify and authenticate into a system to be non-intrusive, and easy to use. In addition to being fairly accurate, multiple fingers can be enrolled and many of these systems have low costs.

Disadvantages include the fact that fingers can be affected by skin conditions, such as dry or cracked skin, and less expensive systems may not be able to identify older workers, individuals wearing gloves, or fingers that are dirty, dry, or wet. In addition, fingerprint sensors will get dirty and this mandates frequent cleaning for more accurate scanning. In addition, in rare cases, some individuals cannot be enrolled into the system because the system is unable to obtain an accurate fingerprint.

Using a fingerprint is also associated with law enforcement and forensics. Because of this, some individuals may be hesitant to use a system, as they may fear their fingerprint can be recognized in some manner.

Another common biometric is voice recognition, as we'll evaluate next.

Comparing the voice

While there are many different biometrics, using our voice for identification and authentication is becoming more commonplace. Voice recognition is gaining popularity because of the built-in tools required for voice recognition, such as the telephony infrastructure, along with components such as speakers and microphones that are built into mobile devices.

Using our voice as a biometric identifier seems almost natural, and there are no negative connotations associated with voice recognition. Some of the industry leaders using voice recognition to identify and authenticate individuals include financial services, healthcare providers, and governments.

Although voice recognition is becoming a popular biometric, there are some concerns such as the potential for a pre-recorded attack, difficulty in filtering out background noise, along with issues with variations in someone's voice if they are ill.

Iris recognition is another common biometric with both advantages and disadvantages. Let's take a look at this now.

Scanning the iris

An iris scan is one of the most secure biometric identifiers. Iris recognition uses the iris or the colored part of the eye, which is captured using a camera, without the need for the participant to have to touch a device.

Using iris recognition has many advantages. Some of the reasons are as follows:

- The iris is extremely stable throughout someone's life.
- Obtaining an iris image is considered to be non-invasive.
- Most systems are easy to use and can scan the iris from a comfortable distance.

Although the iris is a popular biometric, there are certain disadvantages. One negative aspect is the fact that the eye can be obscured by heavy lashes or even eyelid hooding. Another concern is that the eye or the individual may move during the capture and may have to repeat the sequence.

In general, we see there are many approaches to implementing a biometric system. In addition, along with the advantages, you'll want to review the disadvantages before making a decision.

Along with understanding some of the high-level features and benefits, the network administrator should have a basic understanding of the application or system errors that can occur, as we'll see in the next section.

Understanding system errors

In most cases, an organization will choose to implement a biometric system to control access to a facility, room, or system. Careful consideration prior to implementation includes weighing the pros and cons of the different types of systems. We also want to make sure the selected biometric has most of the desired qualities, such as having uniqueness, ensuring collectability, and avoiding circumvention. In addition, we'll want to make sure the system is capable of performing accurately.

Next, let's take a look at what errors can occur while making a decision.

Making a correct decision

You may see a figure from a vendor that lists the error rate. For example, you might see the following listed in the specifications:

FNMR: = 1%

FMR: <0.1%

Figure 4.3 – Error rate specifications

A biometric system will commonly have the following errors:

- Type I error: **False Non-Match Rate (FNMR)**: This represents the number of authorized individuals who are rejected for one reason or another.

- Type II error: **False Match Rate (FMR)**: This represents the number of unauthorized individuals (or imposters) who are accepted into the system.

- **Failure to acquire (FTA)**: This represents the number of times the system was unable to distill or extract the features. Reasons include the fact that the system was unable to obtain enough features, such as fingerprint minutia, or the sample was too small.

- **Failure to enroll (FTE)**: This represents the number or percentage of individuals who cannot enroll for one reason or another. Reasons are similar to FTA, in that the system could not obtain a decent sample or enough features to create a template.

When graphing errors, the **Equal Error Rate (EER)** is the point at which the FNMR equals the FMR, as shown in the following diagram:

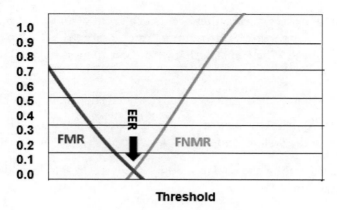

Figure 4.4 – Graph showing the EER

The EER, also known as the **Crossover Error Rate** (**CER**), is a method to assess the accuracy of a given biometric system. In general, a lower EER will provide an optimal biometric.

As shown in the following graph, we see a comparison of various biometric identifiers and their respective EER. Iris recognition, the third value, is shown to have a low EER. That makes iris recognition an optimal biometric:

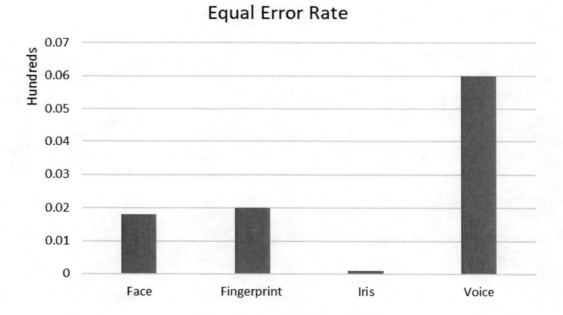

Figure 4.5 – Comparison of various biometric identifiers and their EER

During the matching process, verification occurs as a result of an acceptable threshold, instead of a *yes* or *no* comparison. System tuning can modify the FNMR and FMR and therefore change the EER. When considering what value to modify, you'll want to take this into consideration:

- A higher False Non-Match Rate leads to frustrated clients but is more secure.
- A higher False Match Rate is more dangerous as it can allow unauthorized individuals into the system, and should be avoided.

Therefore, when faced with what value to modify, it's always best to lean toward increasing the FNMR instead of the FMR.

But how do we get the values that represent system errors or anomalies? In the next section, let's take a look at some considerations to factor in when testing a biometric system.

Testing a biometric system

When assessing the quality and performance of a biometric system, there are a couple of key considerations that come into play. Testing will assess several aspects, including the environment, the technology, and the operational aspects of the device.

Let's start with the testing environment.

Evaluating the environment

When evaluating a biometric system, it's important to assess the system response in a variety of settings. A key consideration is that the environment must be in line with a potential real-life application.

For example, if the device is a fingerprint reader and it will be used to control access to a building where the temperature will range from -10 degrees to 95 degrees Fahrenheit, testing needs to be done in the same environment.

Another consideration is the actual technology in use, as we'll see next.

Gauging the technology

In any situation where multiple participants will use the biometric system, the technology must be evaluated. Testing will determine whether the sensor/capture device and algorithm will perform with the appropriate speed and accuracy, in various constraints and time limits.

In addition to the algorithm, you'll also want to consider the following guidelines when selecting a database:

- The database must be large enough with a variety of samples to provide a rigorous test.

- The same database must be used throughout all the testing. Switching the database will lead to skewed data.

- The database should include various demographic groups that will use the system.

- The database should contain a small number of irregular biometric samples.

Just as important as the technology and database is the ability of the system to easily collect the biometric sample from the individual. This is essential, and is discussed next.

Determining operational effectiveness

In general, collectability measures how effortless it is to obtain the biometric data. If the system is too complex or requires expensive devices, the collectability of the chosen biometric will be less than optimal.

Measuring the operational effectiveness will determine the efficiency and effectiveness of the **Human Computer Interface (HCI)** across a wide population. Because of the multiple variables that exist in capturing a biometric identifier, careful design should include a good quality sensor that is able to accept a wide range of inputs.

Prior to testing, make sure the system instructions should be almost intuitive, with immediate verification of success or failure. In addition, the test volunteers must range in age, gender, and educational level, and be adequately trained on the system so they can use the device properly.

When testing the system, consistency is the key. For example, if conducting fingerprint verification testing, the same finger(s) must be used in all cases, so a fair comparison can be made.

In the next section, let's take a look at the value of using multi-factor authentication in today's complex digital environment.

Using multi-factor authentication

When you need to gain access to a computer system, building, or mobile device, we generally enter our username, and then we must provide a form of authentication, in one of several ways:

- What you know, such as a password or PIN
- What you have, such as a smart card or token
- What you are, such as a fingerprint or iris pattern
- Where you are, using geolocation and geofencing

While many of us have only ever used one form of authentication, it's becoming more apparent that more than one identifier should be used to validate a user's identity.

In the next section, let's take a look at combining two or more types of authentication to improve the security of a system.

Strengthening a standard login

Multi-factor authentication (**MFA**) is becoming popular, as companies aim to improve the security of their systems. Multi-factor authentication requires two or more ways to authenticate, such as a smart card and PIN, or a PIN and fingerprint. There are different types of authenticators. What you are required to use as a second authenticator will be determined by the organization.

Let's start with using a security question as a second authenticator.

Employing security questions

A security question is an example of something you know. Generally, the user will pre-answer the questions on enrollment, which can include questions such as the ones shown here:

- What is your youngest sibling's birthday, month, and year?
- What is your paternal grandmother's maiden name?
- What is the name of the city or town where you were born?

Although this is a common method to provide validation, the type of questions asked can be confusing, as your answers may change or you might forget. For example, what color was your first car? You might answer teal, as it was a cross between green and blue. Time will pass and when you think about it again, you might answer blue, and that would be wrong.

Another option can be to use a push notification via a mobile device.

Pushing a notification

In addition to security questions, the network administrator may choose to implement the use of either a mobile push notification, or a one-time token that is sent via email or text message. This is often called an out-of-band notification, and will appear on a mobile device, as shown in the following diagram:

Figure 4.6 – One-time token

Although a handy option, this may not be possible if the user is in a location that does not have cell service, or they don't have their cell phone with them.

Another form of multi-factor authentication includes the use of blockchain technology. Let's take a look.

Leveraging a blockchain

A blockchain is a distributed ledger, comprised of a chain of immutable blocks. Originally developed in 2009, blockchain technology was primarily used for bitcoin mining. As time has passed, industry leaders have found value in using blockchain technology for a host of other applications.

One such application is using blockchain-based multi-factor authentication. Using blockchain technology provides a secure form of verification. The process uses a token, which is validated only with the user's private key, and prevents unauthorized individuals from gaining access to protected sites.

> **Important note**
> You can find an example of using blockchain-based authentication here:
> `https://saaspass.com/mfa/blockchain-authenticator-multi-two-factor-authentication-2fa-mfa/`

In addition to all of the other options for providing an additional authenticator, companies are examining the use of biometrics as a second authenticator, as discussed next.

Using a biometric identifier

Biometric technology has evolved in the last few years, and using a biometric identifier as a second authenticator will improve the security of the system. Using what you are provides a more robust way to supply proof of identity, as this is the only factor that can't be shared or modified.

Industry leaders and government organizations are seeing the value in tapping into the biometric market because of the many benefits of using something you are, such as a fingerprint or facial recognition. Biometric technology is evolving to improve and secure the login experience, as part of a multi-factor authentication process.

In addition to using multi-factor authentication to strengthen a standard login, some companies are using multimodal authentication as a more robust authentication method, as discussed next.

Adding a biometric identifier

In addition to a second authenticator, such as a token or security question, another trend is using multimodal biometric authentication, which uses a second biometric as the authenticator.

A multimodal system can be used in one of two ways, either as a second authenticator, or as an alternative biometric.

Let's see how multimodal authentication is used as a second authenticator.

Requiring a second authenticator

Using multimodal authentication requires a second biometric authenticator. For example, a user will need to provide their fingerprint and iris scan prior to gaining access to a system. Using a second identifier improves overall security, as it is more accurate, reliable, and resistant to spoofing attacks. While someone may be able to spoof a single biometric identifier, such as a fingerprint, there is a significantly less chance someone would be able to spoof a fingerprint and a second biometric, such as facial recognition.

In addition to being a second identifier in a multimodal system, this can be an alternative to another biometric, as discussed next.

Providing an alternative

Another way to use a multimodal system is by offering a choice for the individual to use one or another biometric, depending on the situation. In that case, a user can provide either their fingerprint or iris scan prior to gaining access to a system.

For example, if the system is to be used for individuals working in a factory, there is a good possibility that the fingerprints may be damaged, dry, or cracked, and not an appropriate identifier. In that case, having a second identifier, such as facial recognition, will provide an alternate option for gaining access to the system.

With the increased use of biometrics in all types of organizations, industry leaders are seeking standards for biometric transmission, quality, capture, and interfaces. Let's examine this concept in the following section.

Recognizing the push for standards

Technical standards provide guidelines as to how a method, process, protocol, or device must work. On many occasions, standards are developed by a governing body to ensure consistency and interoperability. For example, the governing body IEEE defines 802.11, a family of specifications that outlines best practices for wireless networks.

We know that using biometrics provides a simpler sign-in experience with added security. Providing standards when dealing with biometrics will help the industry expand the use of biometrics across all vertical markets.

Just like the early days of IEEE 802.11, biometrics did not have any formalized standards until the 2000s, when the United States (US) and foreign governments began to take a closer look at providing a strong identity management infrastructure. Let's examine this in the following section.

Taking a closer look at biometrics

One of the most significant events that pushed the US government to evaluate the use of biometrics as a way to prove identity occurred shortly after September 11, 2001 (9/11). On that date, the US fell victim to a terrorist attack. Soon afterward, the US began several initiatives to combat terrorism, which included a group of individuals called the 9/11 Commission. The group listed a *biometric entry-exit screening system* as one of the key findings required to improve national security. The complete report can be found: z .

During that time, using biometric identification and authentication was still an emerging technology. No defined standards existed, and very few entities had conducted rigorous testing. In addition, the mainstream media had very little knowledge or experience in working with biometric technology, and did not report all efforts.

Early efforts saw the beginnings of testing, collaboration, and experimentation on biometric technology. In the course of cooperation across several agencies, it soon became apparent that there were several challenges that had to be addressed in order to meet the proposed counter-terrorism needs. The challenges included the following:

- The need to ensure privacy
- More advanced technology to implement a large-scale solution
- Improved intra-agency trust and cooperation
- More education on biometric technologies for the public and media
- Transparency on what the proposed solution was capable of achieving, along with the limitations

The years following 9/11 began a wide range of activities that gave biometric technology the momentum needed to come of age. Many significant events took place that helped shape today's current biometric environment.

Next, let's take a look at how leaders in biometric technology began to take a good hard look at developing standards.

Developing biometric standards

Biometric technology was quietly evolving, from the 1960s through to the early 2000s. After the attacks on the United States, several key government agencies began working cooperatively together to strengthen border control by using biometric technology.

Many agencies were involved, from intelligence and counterterrorism, to border management and immigration. In addition, numerous scientists were influential in advancing biometric technology and techniques to provide enhanced security.

The following lists some of the milestones after 9/11:

- 2002 saw the establishment of the ISO/IEC SC 37 standards subcommittee on biometrics. This organization actively works to define and refine standards for file frameworks and profiles to promote system interoperability.

- 2002 also saw the **Face Recognition Vendor Test (FRVT)**. This ongoing effort is driven by NIST to assess the quality of facial recognition algorithms for commercial systems.

- 2004 started the **Face Recognition Grand Challenge (FRGC)**. In the true spirit of competition, the challenge sought to inspire developers to improve their systems and reduce error rates. In addition, the competition helped expand public awareness of facial recognition technology.

- 2004 was when the fingerprint **Minutiae Interoperability Exchange (MINEX)** was launched. MINEX provides continuous testing of fingerprint templates in an effort to improve overall quality.

- In 2006, the US government launched www.biometrics.gov. This now falls under the **Department of Homeland Security (DHS)**, which is home to the **Office of Biometric Identity Management (OBIM)**. The OBIM provides the resources to match share and store biometric information.

- In 2006, the US government announced the National Biometrics Challenge, which sought to improve the performance of identity management systems. A newer version, completed in 2011, can be found at: https://www.fbi.gov/file-repository/about-us-cjis-fingerprints_biometrics-biometric-center-of-excellences-biometricschallenge2011.pdf/view.

- 2007 saw the release of *ANSI/NIST-ITL 1-2007 – Data Format for the Interchange of Fingerprint, Facial, and Other Biometric Information – Part 1*. This provided best practice specifications on methods to exchange various biometric identifiers, such as fingerprint, iris, and even tattoos.

- 2018 saw the release of Biometric Air Exit, which uses facial recognition to verify the identity of travelers as they move through airports. The process takes a photo of the traveler and compares this to the one on their passport to confirm their identity. Read more at https://www.bidnet.com/bneattachments?/571360129.pdf.

As you can see in this short list, many significant advances took place following the events of 9/11. There were many other activities besides in the years that followed that helped expand and improve biometric technology. You can find the entire list at: `https://fas.org/irp/eprint/biometrics.pdf`.

In addition to government standards, other efforts to improve biometric technology exist. For example, the **Fast IDentity Online (FIDO)** Alliance is an organization designed to provide guidance and standardization of specifications that allow scalable and interoperable biometric systems. The organization offers guidelines on best practice techniques regarding methods such as capture settings, scanning parameters, and how best to digitize images.

Today, the influence of biometrics is being felt in many aspects of our lives. The work in this realm continues, so that biometrics can help secure our mobile devices, organizations, homes, and borders.

Summary

As you can see, there are many choices and considerations to take into account before deploying a biometric system. In this chapter, we examined some of the approaches we might take, along with questions we need to ask before implementation. The questions include the following: *How should we approach the installation? Will we need a middleware solution? What are the advantages and disadvantages of some common biometric identifiers?*

So that you appreciate what makes a biometric system exhibit exceptional performance, we reviewed some of the system errors. We then looked at what's involved in testing a biometric system, and what's necessary to provide a true picture of system performance.

We then took a look at the use of requiring more than one identifier, such as a security question or a token, and in some cases, more than one biometric modality. Finally, we examined why it is important to have standards, to ensure interoperability, and improved performance.

In the next chapter, we'll examine one of the most common biometrics available today – fingerprint technology. You'll gain an appreciation of how fingerprint systems work, from scanning, digitizing, storage, and matching. We'll cover what's involved when examining a fingerprint for use in identification and what it means to extract the features along with a discussion on minutiae. Finally, you'll get a better view of the many applications for using fingerprints, such as government, forensics, and commercial use in today's world.

Questions

Now it's time to check your knowledge. Select the best response, and then check your answers, found in the *Assessment* section at the end of the book:

1. _____ recognition can work without the subject having any knowledge they are being observed, so this type of identification can be used for threat management.

    a. Voice

    b. Retinal

    c. Facial

    d. Cloud

2. If you need to implement a system in a remote office with a limited network, you'll need to use a _____ system.

    a. standalone

    b. cloud

    c. networked

    d. scanning

3. When installing a biometric system, in order to maintain the biometric workflow, there may be a need to use a _____ product so that the proprietary system can talk to the backend.

    a. malware

    b. cloudware

    c. scan-box

    d. middleware

4. A(n) ___ is a Type 1 error.

    a. FMR

    b. FNMR

    c. FTE

    d. CER

5. Adding a second biometric identifier, either as a required second authenticator, or as an alternative to another biometric, is called _____ biometric authentication.

   a. far reaching

   b. blockchain

   c. standalone

   d. multimodal

6. _____ is an ongoing effort driven by NIST to assess the quality of facial recognition algorithms for commercial systems.

   a. MINEX

   b. FRVT

   c. FTE

   d. CER

7. _____ provides continuous testing of fingerprint templates in an effort to improve overall quality.

   a. MINEX

   b. FRVT

   c. FTE

   d. CER

Further reading

- Learn how US-VISIT has enhanced security at `https://www.dhs.gov/ xlibrary/assets/usvisit/usvisit_edu_biometrics_brochure_ english.pdf`.

- To understand some of the various biometric systems in use today, go to `https:// www.researchgate.net/publication/322680611_A_Survey_on_ Biometrics_and_Cancelable_Biometrics_Systems`.

- Read more on ISO/IEC JTC 1/SC 37 at `https://www.iso.org/ committee/313770.html`.

- To learn more about how facial artifacts can affect facial recognition, visit `https://pdfs.semanticscholar.org/dabf/269f516adc6bf87a7ceb455cceda4466917a.pdf`

- Biometrics in government after 9/11: `https://fas.org/irp/eprint/biometrics.pdf`.

Section 2 – Applying Biometric Technologies

In this section, we'll cover commonly used biometrics, such as fingerprint, face, iris, and voice recognition. You'll learn how each of our unique features is extracted for comparison for each biometric. We'll then review the advantages and disadvantages of the various technologies, and then outline some of the lesser-known biometrics, such as gait, signature dynamics, and tattoos.

This part of the book comprises the following chapters:

- *Chapter 5, Implementing Fingerprint Technology*
- *Chapter 6, Using Facial Recognition*
- *Chapter 7, Learning Iris Recognition*
- *Chapter 8, Using Voice Recognition*
- *Chapter 9, Considering Alternate Biometrics*

5
Implementing Fingerprint Technology

Take a moment and look at your right index finger. You may have to use a magnifying glass, to view the tiny details we are interested in investigating. Upon close examination, you will see ridges, along with the other tiny details that make your fingerprint distinct. Today, many of us are familiar with using fingerprints to uniquely identify someone. However, using friction ridges, or the raised areas on our fingers and palms, were used for identification long ago by the ancient Chinese. The fact is that everyone's fingerprint is unique, even for identical twins, which makes using our fingerprints as a biometric identifier ideal.

In this chapter, we'll learn about one of the most common biometrics available today. We'll first explore early systems and learn how the Henry Classification System and Vucetich's Comparative Dactyloscopy helped overcome the challenges of examining fingerprints. We'll then review the early role of the **Federal Bureau of Investigation (FBI)** in fingerprint verification. We'll also take a look at today's **Automatic Fingerprint Identification System (AFIS)** and **Next Generation Identification (NGI)**. You'll gain an appreciation of how fingerprint systems work, from scanning, to digitizing, storing, and matching. We'll then cover what's involved when examining a fingerprint for use in identification and what it means to extract the features, along with a discussion on minutiae. Finally, we will see the many uses for fingerprint technology in use today.

In this chapter, we're going to cover the following main topics:

- Exploring the evolution of fingerprint technology
- Understanding fingerprint systems
- Discovering feature extraction and minutiae
- Realizing the many uses of fingerprint technology

Exploring the evolution of fingerprint technology

Scientists as early as the 1600s were taking a closer look at the finger itself as a method to identify someone. In 1686, a biologist named *Marcello Malpighi* identified the loops, ridges, and spirals consistently found in most fingertips. Then, from the mid 1800s to the late 1880s, there were several groups who began using fingerprints to identify individuals, mainly while conducting forensic exercises.

Although most agreed the friction ridge patterns were a practical method to use for identification, the main problem was that there was no formal method to classify the patterns found in fingerprints.

That was until classification systems were developed, as we'll discover in the next section.

Classifying fingers

During the late 1800s, anyone who was involved in using fingerprints for identification saw the value in this promising method. The use of fingerprints was being accepted as evidence in several cases, as this era began the use of forensic fingerprinting.

However, if more than one fingerprint was obtained, there was no organized method to reference what was being matched. It was obvious that a formal method was necessary to improve the process. In the late 1800s, a group of several respected scientists developed systems to categorize fingerprint characteristics. Two methods were developed at the time, the *Henry Classification System* and *Vucetich's Comparative Dactyloscopy*.

> **Important note**
> The methods described are used to classify, not identify, fingerprints.

In this section, we'll take a look at each of the two methods to classify fingerprints. In addition, so that you have an idea of what's involved when we examine a fingerprint, we'll simulate fingerprints using an application called SFinGe.

Let's start by generating some samples.

Generating prints

When assessing the effectiveness of a fingerprint algorithm, most studies require a generous database of samples. To create a database from live candidates can be complex and expensive. You would need to gather volunteers and obtain the prints. In addition, because of privacy concerns, the volunteer pool may be hesitant to offer their biometric identifier, even if it is for testing purposes.

So that you can generate your own set of prints to study, the Biometric System Laboratory has developed a synthetic fingerprint generator. The application is called SFinGe, which will provide us with a set of prints to study, as we'll see next.

Using SFinGe

In addition to generating a database of prints, SFinGe can generate individual samples so that you and other students can learn how to recognize the different patterns and, more specifically, the tiny details called minutiae.

> **Important note**
> To generate your own set of prints, go to `http://biolab.csr.unibo.it/research.asp?organize=Activities&select=&selObj=12&pathSubj=111%7C%7C12&` and download SFinGe, found in the middle of the page.

The installation process is fairly standard. Once installed, you can launch the application and begin generating prints. The process goes through various steps where you can make a selection on different variables to make a realistic fingerprint.

Steps include the ability to modify the following:

- Selecting a finger, adding scratches, or creating areas that appear dry or worn

- Rotating the image, and adding noise such as variations in color, brightness, or contrast.

Although there are ten steps in SFinGe, we'll only go through the first three so you can get an idea of the types of fingerprints the software can generate.

Complete the steps as follows:

1. Once you launch SFinGe, you will see the splash screen. From the menu choice, select **Generate**, and you will see the window as shown in the following screenshot:

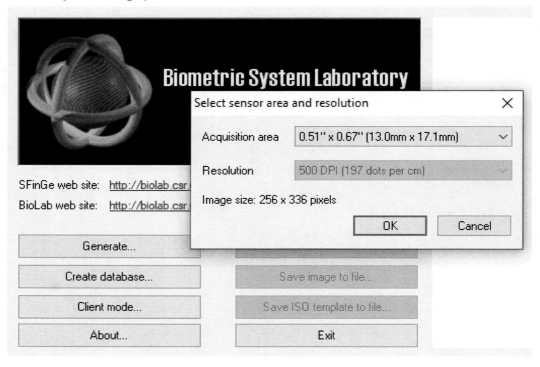

Figure 5.1 – SFinGe Generate option

Accept the defaults, and the program will present **Step 1 - Fingerprint mask generation**. Once you are there, you can select a finger type from the drop-down menu, as shown in the following screenshot. Select **Index** finger, and then select **Generate** without modifying the settings:

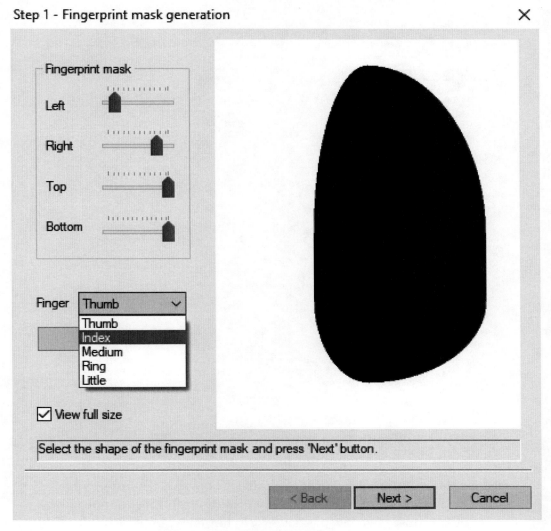

Figure 5.2 – Fingerprint mask generation

2. Select **Next** and that will bring up the **Step 2 - Directional map generation** section. This is where you can generate the first-level detail, such as **Arch**, **Left loop**, **Right loop**, **Whorl**, or **Tented arch**, as shown in the following screenshot:

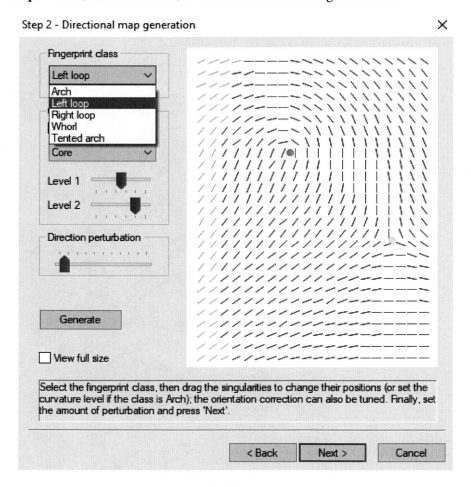

Figure 5.3 – Directional map generation

Once you are on **Step 2**, select **Left loop** and do not modify the settings. Then select **Generate**. You will see the singularities (the colored dots) change position. If you want, you can move them into position by selecting one of the singularities, hold down the left mouse button, and then drag them into another position.

When you are happy with the position, click **Next**.

3. This will bring up **Step 3 - Density map and ridge pattern generation**. Check the box to **View Minutiae**.

> **Important note**
>
> For now, we will focus on the first-level details. We'll get into a discussion of minutiae later on in the chapter.

Select **Start ridge generation**. You will then see your fingerprint as shown in the following screenshot. Your print will look different than my image, as the software renders each print slightly different. At that point, you can do a screenshot and save your print for later analysis:

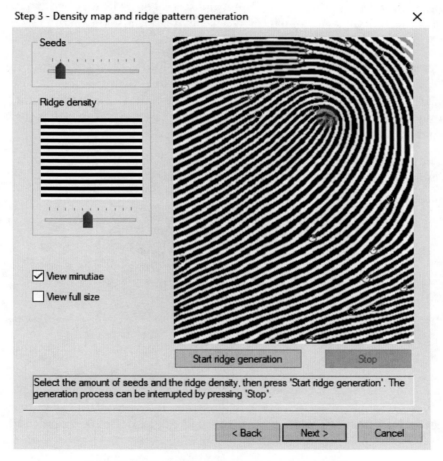

Figure 5.4 – Density map and ridge pattern generation

SFinGe has several more steps. As you move through the steps, you'll see the ability to modify different variables, which includes scratches, dryness, and fingerprint distortion. I encourage you to experiment with SFinGe and generate various prints, so that you can see what an investigator might see when evaluating a fingerprint.

As demonstrated, there are many variables that make analyzing a fingerprint challenging. To have a sense of order when dealing with a large number of fingerprints, two classification systems were developed in the late 19th century, the Henry Classification System and Comparative Dactyloscopy.

Let's take a look at each of these, starting with the Henry Classification System.

Using the Henry Classification System

Sir Edward Richard Henry, *Sir Francis Galton*, and several other learned individuals collaborated together to devise a method to classify fingerprints. The method developed was the Henry Classification System, a ten-finger system.

When referencing the first-level details, we are looking for the presence of one or more deltas. A delta point is the convergence of two or more lines that resemble the Greek letter delta (Δ). The position and presence of the delta point(s) will determine the type of fingerprint pattern. In addition to the delta, we will also see the core, which is the center area of a fingerprint.

When examining the fingers, each finger has a first-level detail that is in the form of a whorl, loop, or arch, as shown in the following diagram:

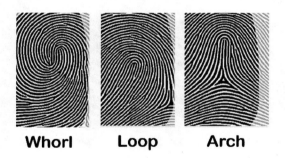

Whorl   Loop   Arch

Figure 5.5 – First-level details

When evaluating the types of characteristics across the population, loops are the most prominent, appearing in 60 to 70% of the fingerprints. Whorls contain two or more deltas and are the second most prevalent, as they are seen in 25 to 35% of the population. Arches are rare and appear in only about 5% of the population.

The method developed by *Sir Henry* was widely adopted. However, while the Henry Classification System provided a great starting point in identifying prints, the FBI later further defined the basic first-level details: whorl, loop, and arch (as shown in the *First-level details* diagram).

The result was eight distinct categories as outlined here.

The three subgroups of whorls are as follows:

- **Plain whorl**: The simplest and most common.

- **Central pocket loop whorl**: These make one complete circle.

- **Accidental whorl**: These contain at least two deltas and occur when two different pattern types are present.

The three subgroups of loops are as follows:

- **Radial loops** relate to the position of the radial bone in the arm as they present as a loop running from the little finger to the thumb. Radial loops are rarely seen.

- **Ulnar loops** relate to the position of the ulnar bone in the arm as they present as a loop running from the thumb to the little finger. Ulnar loops are rarely seen.

- **Double loops** have two separate loop patterns, each having their own shoulder and creating their own circuit.

The two subgroups of arches are as follows:

- **Plain arches** will start on one side of the finger, arch upward, and then end on the other side of the finger. This pattern resembles an ocean wave.

- **Tented arches** are similar to plain arches. However, they have a more abrupt arch that looks similar to a tent.

> **Important note**
>
> To see a more detailed description of the eight most common fingerprint patterns, visit `https://www.touchngoid.com/8-common-fingerprint-patterns/`.

Classifying the fingerprints

Once the fingerprints are obtained, and the examiner is able to identify the details of the prints, then fingerprints can be classified. Each component assigns a value according to a specific formula.

The components of the Henry Classification System are as follows:

- **Primary classification** is determined by calculating the value of the fingers that have a whorl pattern.

- **Secondary classification** is determined by calculating the value of the patterns; that is, tented arch, double loop, or whorl, of the right and left index fingers.

- **Subsecondary classification** further defines the secondary classification, and is determined by examining specific fingers and assigning a value. This examines the following:

  a. Ridge counts of the fingers that have *loops*

  b. Ridge tracings of the fingers that have *whorls*

- **Final classification** is evaluated only if the right little finger has a loop pattern. The value is determined by calculating the ridge count and assigning a value. If the right little finger does not have a loop pattern, no final classification is assigned.

- **Key classification** examines every finger (except the little fingers) starting with the right thumb. If the finger has a loop pattern, the ridge counts are calculated. If none of the fingers have a loop pattern, no key classification is assigned.

- **Major classification** examines the ridge counts of the right and left thumb.

Classification is important as it helps to provide order when searching a massive number of fingerprints and can result in easier data retrieval.

> **Important note**
>
> The Henry Classification System method is still in use today by the FBI's **National Crime Information Center** (**NCIC**). A more detailed explanation can be found here: `http://www.pbso.org/qualtrax/ QTDocuments/3304.PDF`

Another method for classifying fingerprints was developed by *Juan Vucetich*, called Comparative Dactyloscopy, as we'll see next.

Applying Dactyloscopy

In 1892, two boys were found brutally murdered in a small village near Buenos Aires, Argentina. The boy's mother, Francisca Rojas, had a suitor named Velasquez. Law enforcement originally suspected the suitor as the culprit. However, after interviewing and torturing Velasquez, they were unable to obtain a confession.

After examining the crime scene, investigators found evidence in the form of a bloody fingerprint. At the time there was no formal method to deal with fingerprints. Authorities contacted Juan Vucetich, an anthropologist and police official, to assist with the investigation. Vucetich examined the blood print and found it was a match to Rojas' fingerprint. Investigators confronted Rojas, who eventually confessed to the crime.

The murder investigation and successful use of fingerprints during the investigation, prompted Vucetich to develop a formal fingerprint system called Comparative Dactyloscopy. Soon afterward, the technique was adopted by many countries worldwide, and the Spanish-speaking community in particular.

Although Vucetich's method was widely used, he did not translate his method to English. As a result, it did not gain as much recognition as the Henry Classification System. However, the method is still employed by many Spanish-speaking countries today.

The use of fingerprints continued to evolve and improve in the early 1900s. As a result, various governing bodies sought to organize and house the large number of fingerprints acquired over time. One organization was the FBI, as we'll learn next.

Managing US fingerprints

Soon after fingerprinting became part of a standard investigation, filing systems for fingerprints soon followed. Here are some of the early efforts:

- In 1891, Juan Vucetich formalized a system in Argentina.
- In 1901, Sir Edward Henry established a system for Scotland Yard.
- In 1904, the US Federal Penitentiary in Kansas established a fingerprint bureau, with the help of Scotland Yard.

The years from 1905 to the early 1920s saw law enforcement, military, and government agencies adopting the use of fingerprint technology.

In 1924, the FBI began work in the newly formed identification division. This then positioned the FBI as a national repository for fingerprints along with related criminal records. During those early years, over 800,000 fingerprints were classified using Henry Classification System method. The FBI soon became the keystone of fingerprint identification records. Over the years, the fingerprint files grew along with the demand for identification services.

During the period from the early 1900s to the mid-1970s, it took anywhere from weeks to months to process fingerprints for law enforcement agencies. The main reason it took so long was because the method used at the time was a manual, labor-intensive process. In addition, the prints for the most part were transmitted using the **United States Postal System** (**USPS**), and could take several days to deliver.

Along with the time it took to process the prints, a manual method had several other shortcomings. One was the high possibility of errors; in fact, the accuracy rate was only 75%. Also, someone had to properly classify and then file the prints. However, sometimes the prints were not properly filed. As a result, in addition to the initial process to classify and then store the prints, the next significant challenge was to search and match the prints.

With the expanded need for fingerprint identification, it soon became apparent that a manual system would not be able to keep up with continued demand.

Interest in early automation efforts began in the 1960s with the expansion of **Digital Signal Processing** (**DSP**). This led to efforts to create an automated system, as we'll see in the next section.

Developing an automatic system

During the mid-1960s, agencies around the world saw the value of creating a computerized system to improve efficiency. After many years, the hope of an automated system began to become a reality. On July 28, 1999, the FBI began the wide-scale use of the **Integrated Automated Fingerprint Identification System** (**IAFIS**), a totally automated system.

The FBI's IAFIS compares, sorts, stores, and exchanges digitized fingerprints. IAFIS contains billions of prints, most of which are identified; however, some are unknown. Using IAFIS significantly reduced search time and improved accuracy. The IAFIS system continued to evolve into **Next Generation Identification** (**NGI**), which has expanded capabilities from fingerprints to other biometric identifiers, such as facial identification, iris, and palm prints.

Early fingerprint technology was primarily done by law enforcement in the course of investigating a crime. From the early 1980s, when the use of personal computers began to evolve, fingerprint technology started to see a value in non-criminal applications such as a means to provide identification. Current fingerprint technology uses minutiae and singular points as the recognized features.

In the next section, we'll take a look at how fingerprint systems work, from scanning, digitizing, and storage, to matching.

Understanding fingerprint systems

Today, fingerprint technology is not only used in identifying criminals; its use has expanded to provide identification and authentication. But just how does a standard system work?

Let's take a look at the first step in the process – scanning the fingerprints.

Scanning the fingers

When scanning fingerprints, the user will press (gently) and hold on the scanner to obtain the image. Today, there are several methods that may be used, depending on the device. You might use an optical or capacitive technology, or the newest technology, ultrasonic sound waves, to capture an image.

Let's take a look at each of these in turn, starting with the oldest method – optical scanners.

Optically capturing an image

Optical scanners have been in use for many years, and work by capturing an image using light. Once captured, an algorithm detects the fingerprint details, such as ridges and minutiae, by sensing the dark and light areas on the image. Unlike a regular camera, the optical scanner has a higher resolution and higher contrast and can identify minutiae with more granular detail.

Once you place your finger on the sensor, **Light Emitting Diodes** (**LEDs**) illuminate your finger and pass through a prism and then capture the ridges and valleys of the finger. The details are then passed to the lens and to the image sensor, as shown in the following graphic:

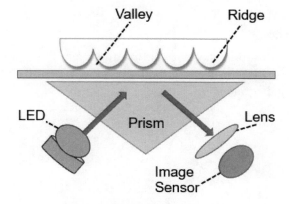

Figure 5.6 – Optical scanner

While the optical scanner is commonly used, it has a couple of drawbacks. One disadvantage is that the image is only **two-dimensional** (**2D**), while another disadvantage is that this type of technology is easily spoofed.

Because of the limitations, this technology is slowly being replaced by higher quality sensors. However, some manufacturers are developing smaller optical modules that are able to capture an image under 1 mm of glass, with an improved ability to capture an image.

Next, let's take a look at another type of fingerprint scanner, the capacitive scanner.

Measuring currents

Another choice in scanning fingerprints is the capacitive scanner, which is one of the most common scanners in use today. Like the optical scanner, capacitive scanners only create a 2D image. However, instead of using light, a capacitive scanner uses electrical currents to capture the image.

When you place your finger on the scanner, hundreds (and sometimes thousands) of capacitor circuits gather data about your fingerprint. Once the scanner gathers the details, a digital image of your print is assembled. Using more capacitors improves the quality of the image.

Capacitive scanners are more compact than optical scanners and are used in most smartphones today. They are more expensive than optical scanners, but provide a more secure capture as they are harder to spoof.

Over the years, the technology has improved. The latest technology is an ultrasonic sensor, which creates a 3D image of your print, as we'll see next.

Using sound waves

An ultrasonic sensor uses sound waves to capture an image. To use an ultrasonic sensor, you place your finger on the scanner, and then the sensor transmits ultrasonic pulses, as shown in the following diagram:

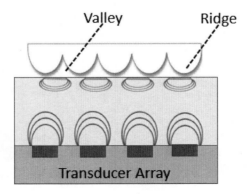

Figure 5.7 – Ultrasonic sensor

Depending upon what the pulse encounters, some of the pulse is absorbed and some of it bounces back to obtain details of the ridges, valleys, pores, and other details. As a result, an ultrasonic sensor creates a 3D image and is faster and more accurate in its readings. In addition, a longer scan will result in a more detailed print, which improves security.

Not all smartphones are equipped with ultrasonic technology. In addition, thicker glass and screen protectors will limit the ability to effectively capture a fingerprint. However, the technology is being used by a few smartphone manufacturers, which may vary in speed and accuracy.

As you can see, there are a few techniques to obtain a fingerprint image. Once obtained, the next step is to convert the image into a digital form, as we'll see next.

Digitizing the image

Once a fingerprint is captured, the image must be converted to a digital representation of fingerprints. Over the last 30-40 years, algorithms have been developed and improved to automatically process digital fingerprint images.

A fingerprint algorithm will prepare the image in a way that the features can easily be identified. This process goes through preprocessing, extracting the features, and then creating the template. Let's start with preprocessing.

Preprocessing the image

When capturing fingerprints, it's important to acquire a high-quality image, as this will affect the ability to extract the minutiae. While it's not always possible to have a high-quality image, the next step is to preprocess and enhance the image, in order to provide better feature extraction. This step is a key component of this process. The algorithm seeks to obtain the biometric pattern within the transmitted signal and improves the visualization of the ridges.

> **Important note**
>
> The **National Institute of Standards and Technology** (**NIST**) provides open source **Fingerprint Image Quality libraries** (**NFIQ**). The libraries are used to gauge the quality of a fingerprint, to ensure the best sample is provided during the matching process. The libraries can give real-time feedback or be used to evaluate previously captured fingerprints.

The process enhances the image by diminishing the noise that is present in the image, which is the variation of intensity or hue. During the process, a normalization phase corrects image distortion and smooths the intensity of each pixel. After that, there is a transformation of the image obtained into a more acceptable output. At that point, thinning may be necessary to reduce the ridges to one pixel.

Image enhancement is important when using biometrics. Because we are capturing a biometric identifier, the image will be slightly different every time we present our biometric to the scanner. As shown in the following image, the left fingerprint might be an example of what is captured. The following image shows enhancements, and the print is now ready so the minutiae can be more readily identified:

Figure 5.8 – Image enhancement

After preprocessing, the image moves to feature extraction and then template creation, as discussed next.

Pulling the true biometric

Once the image is enhanced, normalized, and thinned appropriately, the next step is to pull the true biometric pattern and then mark and extract the minutiae.

The features are ready to move to template creation. During this step, the features are converted into a compact digital template for storage in the system database. In most cases, the template is stored in the form of a non-reversible format so the biometric cannot be reconstructed from the template.

Once complete, the template moves to the database so that it is available for matching purposes, as discussed next.

Storing the templates

When using fingerprints for identification and authentication, the system will create a master template during enrollment. In most cases, the system will store the template, and not the fingerprint image. Each template will contain the details of the minutiae.

Enrollment is the process of processing a biometric identifier for the first time so that it can be stored in the system database for later comparison. During enrollment, the user may need to provide additional information such as their name or a user ID.

After the template is stored in the system database, the user will then access the system to either be identified, using a one-to-many comparison, or to be authenticated, using a one-to-one comparison. In either case, the template is stored somewhere until the time it is retrieved during comparison.

Depending on the system, templates can be stored in one of the following options:

- **Central database**: When biometric identification and authentication is used in an enterprise network, you will most likely use a central database that is a networked solution, capable of centralized administration. In this scenario, it's important to encrypt data in transport to ensure privacy, and prevent someone from obtaining the template, which can be used in a replay attack.

- **Smart card or token**: This can be an option when a networked solution isn't an option, as this option stores the template locally instead of a central database. By using a smart card or token, the user may feel more in control of their biometric information. However, portable devices can be lost or stolen. In addition, there may be more costs involved because specialized devices are required to interface with the device to read the biometric data.

- **Computer, laptop, or workstation**: These can be another option where you can store biometric templates, if a networked solution isn't available. This option can work if there is proprietary software that requires increased security and restricts login to only authorized individuals. For example, this might be a solution for a **Point of Sale** (**POS**) system in a restaurant to restrict access to only authorized individuals.

- **Sensing devices**: They are small devices that capture biometric information. The devices might be wall mounted, such as access control for a warehouse. This non-networked solution provides an option to ensure security. However, it will be limited if someone needs to log in at multiple locations.

Regardless of where the templates are stored, ensuring security and privacy is extremely important. Users need to know that you are taking steps to protect their templates from a breach.

The last step is pattern matching, as we'll see in this next section.

Matching the patterns

Once a fingerprint is scanned, digitized, and processed into a template, the pattern matching phase is when the user accesses the system to be identified and or authenticated. The user's print is processed and then compared to the master template. If the two are within an acceptable distance, then it is considered to be a match.

While this process sounds fairly simple, there are quite a few variables that can make pattern matching more complex. The one thing we must keep in mind is that a biometric identifier originates from a person, and each time they offer their biometric, they can change the manner in how they interact with the system.

During enrollment and training, the user should be given guidelines on the best way to interact with the system. Some suggestions include the following:

- Use the same finger you used during enrollment.
- Place your finger parallel to the sensor surface.
- Do not apply too much pressure, or move your finger, until the process is complete.
- If your fingers have food, oil, or dirt on them, clean them prior to using the system.
- Once done scanning your finger, clean the sensor with the approved method.
- If the biometric reader is in a public facility, the sensors must be cleaned in order to give accurate results.

Even with instructions and training, the fingerprint may be rejected because of problems during capture. As shown in the following diagram, we see three examples of potential issues:

Overlap   Dry Skin   Distortion

Figure 5.9 – Errors when matching prints

The first image shows an overlap, where the user's middle phalange was captured instead of only the distal phalange. The second image shows the result of dry and chapped skin. The third image shows distortion, which may have been the result of the user pulling, moving, or pressing too hard during capture.

While there may be errors during capture, the algorithms will attempt to adjust in order to match the sample to the template. If there is too much variation, the user may be rejected. In that case, they will need to go through the process again.

Now that we understand how a fingerprint system works, we'll take a look at the heart of fingerprint matching – identifying the minutiae.

Discovering feature extraction and minutiae

The core of a fingerprint system is extracting the features and identifying the minutiae, which are the tiny details of the fingerprint. As we have seen, there are many variables that can alter the fingerprint. Therefore, once a high-quality image is obtained, the system preprocesses and enhances the image in order to provide better feature extraction.

In the next section, we'll see just what's evaluated during feature extraction.

Extracting the features

During feature extraction, the algorithm enhances and pulls the features, so the system can better identify the minutiae. When matching fingerprints, the system can either use pattern matching or minutiae-based comparison:

- Pattern matching is a technique used to detect duplicates by comparing two images.
- Minutiae-based matching is the most common method, and matches the minutiae obtained when extracting the features.

When comparing fingerprints, minutiae-based matching has many advantages. Instead of comparing the entire print, only identified minutiae are compared, which reduces the computational power, and minimizes storage requirements.

So that you have a better understanding of what defines the details of a fingerprint, let's next take a look at the different types of minutiae.

Identifying minutiae

When examining a fingerprint, we are identifying the minutiae, which are also referred to as second-level details. In the following diagram, you can see several types of minutiae identified:

Figure 5.10 – Minutiae and a delta identified on a fingerprint

When describing minutiae, there are seven common types of minutiae that can be identified:

- Islands (or points) appear as a single dot.

- Bifurcations are where you see the ridges splitting off in a Y pattern.

- Ridge endings are where the ridge appears to stop and is not connected to any other ridge.

- Crossover will appear as an X as two ridges cross over one another.

- A spur is a small branch off the side of a ridge.

- A lake is when a ridge splits and forms a donut shape.

- An independent ridge is a ridge that sits in the center of two ridges.

In some cases, the system may also identify third-level details, which are the sweat pores, and any creases, breaks, or scars that may be present on a fingerprint.

During the matching phase, the user's print is processed, and the minutiae are identified. The sample is then compared with the master template. As shown in the following diagram, the sample is aligned over the template, and then the minutiae are compared to see how many correspond with one another:

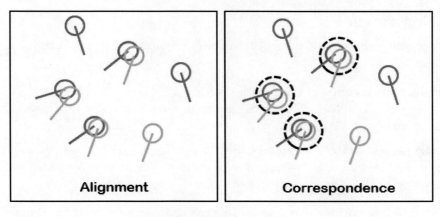

Figure 5.11 – Matching minutiae

If the sample and the template minutiae are within an acceptable distance, then it is considered to be a match.

In the next section, let's take a look at a few examples of where we might use fingerprint technology.

Realizing the many uses of fingerprint technology

Fingerprint recognition is one of the original biometric technologies developed. Using fingerprints first gained significant recognition from its uses in forensic science. As time passed, however, many saw the value of using the fingerprint to identify and authenticate an individual. In this section, we'll see the many applications and locations where fingerprint technology is used. In addition, we'll also see the pros and cons of using fingerprints as a biometric identifier.

Let's start with a few examples of where fingerprint technology might be used today.

Finding fingerprints everywhere

While the use of fingerprints was used mainly by law enforcement to identify individuals, commercial entities soon realized the value of using the fingerprint to prove identity. As a result, there are a number of different organizations and entities that employ fingerprint technology.

Let's start with using a fingerprint for access control in an organization.

Controlling access

Using fingerprint technology can help control both physical and logical access in an organization.

- **Physical access control**: A fingerprint reader can be used to identify and authenticate an individual for access to a facility, such as a hospital, private club, or a financial organization.

- **Logical access control**: Using fingerprint technology can be used to gain entry into a restricted computer system; for example, having an employee log in using a keyboard or USB fingerprint reader.

We also see how fingerprint technology can aid in border control, as outlined next.

Monitoring the border

Several countries, including South Korea, the United States, Italy, and Brazil incorporate the use of fingerprint technology to identify its citizens. This information is then used when verifying your identity at the border or when traveling through an airport.

Because of the sheer volume of people entering and exiting a country, it's important to track and manage the flow of individuals entering a country. Using biometrics at the border provides a higher level of security and safety.

In addition to using biometrics for border control and while traveling through an airport, let's see the many ways in which we can use biometrics to identify individuals.

Identifying an individual

One of the original uses of fingerprint technology was used by law enforcement. The technology continues to be essential in identifying an individual during a forensic exercise. For example, we use fingerprints to uncover the truth as to whether or not the suspect was at a crime scene.

In addition to other identifiers such as dental records, height, and weight, medical examiners also rely on the use of fingerprints to positively identify a deceased individual.

Using fingerprints can also provide proof that someone completed a task or logged in to a system or building, as we'll see next.

Ensuring accountability

A fingerprint reader can also be used to ensure accountability, for example, using a fingerprint reader on a **Point of Sale (PoS)** system in a restaurant that controls who is covering each table and accounts for how much each waiter sells.

In addition, if a fingerprint reader is used to gain access to a facility, the data obtained during login can be integrated within a time and attendance system to monitor an employee's true login patterns.

While we can see that using the fingerprint as a biometric is in use in many different applications, there are also a few limitations, as discussed next.

Comparing benefits with drawbacks

Using a fingerprint has been gaining popularity over the years as a biometric, as it is very unique, and it stays the same throughout most of your life. Let's compare the benefits and the limitations, starting with the benefits.

Embracing the benefits

Using a fingerprint as a biometric identifier has gained acceptance around the world. Fingerprint technology is a mature technology that has a comparatively low cost to implement.

Capturing a fingerprint has high accuracy and is considered minimally invasive. It is used in many different ways, from border control, to controlling access to a building, computer system, or a mobile device. In addition, unlike a password or PIN, you can't lose your fingerprint. And in most cases, they will stay the same thought your lifetime.

There are many benefits to using fingerprint technology. However, there are also some drawbacks, as discussed next.

Understanding the limitations

Using a fingerprint is also associated with law enforcement and forensics. Because of this, some individuals may be hesitant to use a system, as they may fear their fingerprint can be recognized in some manner.

Correct capture depends on the individual's fingers. Some individual's fingerprints cannot be read for the following reasons:

- Certain skin conditions, such as a skin disease or dry and chapped skin can affect quality.

- Manual workers may not have sufficient detail in their prints for the device to be consistently accurate.

- An individual may have missing or damaged fingers.

In these cases, using fingerprint technology cannot be an option, and they will need to be identified in another way.

Fingerprint technology continues to gain popularity as a method to identify and authenticate on a system. Everyone's fingerprints are unique, and they stay the same throughout most of your life. In the future, we'll most likely see continued improvements and enhancements.

Summary

Now, when you look at your fingers, you'll have a better understanding of what's involved when we obtain a fingerprint. In this chapter, we examined the evolution of fingerprint technology. We travelled back to the humble beginnings of law enforcement and the first official use of fingerprints as part of a forensic exercise. We then saw the development of the Henry Classification System and Comparative Dactyloscopy to help provide more structure in recognizing prints. We then traveled through the early days of manual fingerprint examination, to the use of automated systems, such as the FBI's IAFIS and NGI systems.

By now, you have a better understanding of modern-day fingerprint systems, from scanning, to digitizing, storing the templates, and matching the samples. We then covered what defines minutiae, and how examining the tiny details helps determine whether or not a fingerprint is a match to the template. Finally, we took a look at how fingerprint technology is used in the world today, along with some of the benefits and drawbacks of using fingerprint technology.

In the next chapter, we'll take a look at another popular biometric, facial recognition. You'll learn how we use the face as a biometric identifier and what facial features are measured during facial recognition. You'll gain a better understanding of how systems acquire the facial image using 2D and 3D sensors. Finally, you'll appreciate the ways in which we use facial recognition today for identification, social media, and surveillance, along with a discussion on deep fakes and spoofing.

Questions

Now it's time to check your knowledge. Select the best response, and then check your answers, found in the *Assessment* section at the end of the book:

1. The _____ system is a ten-finger method used by the FBI to classify fingerprints.

    a. Henry

    b. Marcello

    c. Rojas

    d. Vucetich

2. When referencing the first-level details, we are looking for the presence of one or more _____, which is the convergence of two or more lines.

    a. alphas

    b. betas

    c. gammas

    d. deltas

3. Instead of using light, a(n) _____ scanner uses electrical currents to capture the image.

    a. optical

    b. ultrasonic

    c. capacitive

    d. digital

4. When evaluating the types of characteristics across the population, _____ are the most prominent, appearing in 60 to 70% of fingerprints.

    a. whorls

    b. arch

    c. tented arch

    d. loops

5. Preprocessing enhances the image by diminishing the _____ that is present in the image, which is the variation of intensity or hue.

   a. noise

   b. delta

   c. beta change

   d. shimming

6. When identifying minutiae, a(n) _____ is a small branch off of the side of a ridge.

   a. island

   b. ridge ending

   c. spur

   d. lake

7. In some cases, the system may also identify _____ level details, which are the sweat pores, and any creases, breaks, or scars that may be present in a fingerprint.

   a. first

   b. second

   c. third

   d. fourth

8. A fingerprint reader can be used to identify and authenticate an individual for access to a facility, such as a hospital, private club, or a financial organization to provide _____ access control.

   a. logical

   b. physical

   c. merit

   d. delta

Further reading

- A booklet from the FBI on the science of fingerprints: `https://www.crime-scene-investigator.net/fbiscienceoffingerprints.html`.

- For a deep dive into fingerprints, visit `https://www.ncjrs.gov/pdffiles1/nij/225320.pdf`, where you will find *The Fingerprint Sourcebook*.

- There are many image enhancement techniques. To learn more about this important concept, visit `https://www.mathworks.com/discovery/image-enhancement.html`.

6
Using Facial Recognition

When we look at someone's face, we quickly scan their features, and see the circles, lines, and shadows that make up a person's unique attributes. In addition, many of us tune into microexpressions, which are the subtle movements that help indicate the mood someone is currently experiencing. Because of this rich source of information, **facial recognition technology (FRT)** has proven to be an optimal biometric identifier. Each face has many areas that can be measured, such as the width of the face, the space from pupil to pupil, and the distance between the forehead and the chin.

So that you have a better understanding of the many variables involved, this chapter will outline what features are measured during facial recognition. We'll take a look at how systems can acquire a facial image using **two-dimensional (2D)** and **three-dimensional (3D)** sensors, and see how modern systems can now detect emotion. You'll recognize how measuring the face can be challenging, as a face has shadows and color variation. In addition, you'll understand how a facial recognition system handles artifacts, such as eye glasses and jewelry. We'll also learn how the system extracts the features, through methods such as template- or feature-based. We'll cover the potential for deepfake videos and image spoofing. Finally, you'll appreciate the ways in which we use facial recognition today for identification, social media, and surveillance.

In this chapter, we're going to cover the following main topics:

- Understanding facial features
- Acquiring the facial image
- Extracting the features
- Using facial recognition today

Understanding facial features

Have you ever looked at someone and thought, *I can't remember that person's name, but I know that face*? Not remembering someone's name is not uncommon. Researchers explain that one of the reasons you remember someone's face and not their name is because the face is comprised of multiple details, many of which you commit to memory. However, someone's name doesn't have any real connection to the individual, which makes it difficult to remember. Why you might remember their face is because the brain has a remarkable ability to remember faces.

Let's step through what happens when you see someone's face.

Seeing someone's face

When you look at a face, as opposed to looking at an inanimate object, a number of different processes occur in the brain. We immediately begin scanning the face to examine the eyes, mouth, and nose. In addition to examining the features, we are processing what possible emotion they may be experiencing, which helps us determine how to react to the situation.

In studies that monitor eye tracking, they show how, when looking at someone for the first time, we quickly examine the entire face, in order to make visual assessments. In addition to observing the facial features, your brain continues to process emotions, such as whether the person is happy, sad, or angry, and also helps us determine what is being said.

A very small percentage (approximately 2%) of individuals can't recognize faces at all. These individuals suffer from a condition called prosopagnosia, or face blindness. The condition makes them unable to recognize someone's face, even their relatives. However, for the rest of us, we all have an ability to recognize faces.

On the other side of the spectrum are *super-recognizers*. These individuals have an exceptional ability to retain details of someone's face. They can recognize someone even after years have passed, if the person has changed their hair color, or is now wearing glasses.

However, in most cases, many of us fall within an average range of face recognition. In fact, studies have found that the average adult can recall approximately 5,000 faces. Some individuals can recognize up to 10,000 faces.

Understanding how humans can recognize faces led scientists to consider automating that process. In the next section, let's take a look at the concept of facial recognition over time, along with some of the significant advances in FRT.

Studying faces over time

Experiments in facial recognition began over 60 years ago. Since that time, significant advances in both technology and algorithms have led to today's widespread use of facial recognition.

Let's study the evolution of this technology, starting with manual methods that began in the 1960s.

Manually measuring attributes

In the early 1960s, a scientist named *Woodrow Wilson Bledsoe* developed a manual classification system to recognize faces using an individual's unique facial attributes. *Bledsoe* would manually mark the horizontal and vertical coordinates of features such as the eyes, nose, mouth, and hairline of a photograph.

The metrics were entered and stored on a RAND tablet, an early computer that provided the ability to input data using a stylus, and then digitize the information. Once the database was created, *Bledsoe* could input the facial metrics of a photograph of an individual, and the system would provide the nearest closest match. Although the system had limitations in computing power and speed, *Bledsoe's* work was a significant first step in recognizing that the face could be used as a biometric identifier.

In the 1970s, scientists *Goldstein, Harmon*, and *Lesk* improved the accuracy by adding an additional 21 variables, such as lip thickness and hair color. Even with the improvements, this process was slow, as it also involved manual calculations.

> **Important note**
> Read more on the advances in FRT over time in the article by the FBI, found here: `https://www.fbi.gov/file-repository/about-us-cjis-fingerprints_biometrics-biometric-center-of-excellences-face-recognition.pdf`.

Studies on facial recognition evolved in the late 1980s, as scientists worked to improve accuracy, as we'll see next.

Improving accuracy

The study of facial recognition expanded in the late 1980s to the early 1990s when two scientists, *Sirovich* and *Kirby*, applied techniques to pull the basic features of an image by analyzing the image, while preserving as much of the original dataset as possible.

During the studies of faces, the scientists recognized that coordinates on a face would best be obtained if the lighting was optimal, and each face had a consistent expression. An optimal image rarely is possible, because most of the time someone's face has variations in light and shade. This is mainly because a face is not smooth, like a table surface, but has several areas of shadowing.

As a result, the goal was to develop an algorithm that adjusted to the variation of light and expression.

Developing Eigenfaces

In the late 1980s, the two aforementioned scientists developed what is known as an *eigenface*, which is a set of eigenvectors derived during facial recognition. The eigenface approach uses facial images with lower dimensions, which results in a blurry representation of a face, as shown in the following figure:

Figure 6.1 – Eigenface

While the eigenface image is blurry, you can still see that several features, such as the eyes, nose, and the outline of the face, are still recognizable. Using a collection of eigenfaces, scientists were able to demonstrate that each face has similar features. In 1991, two other scientists, *Turk* and *Pentland*, were able to find the face within the face, by matching distances and ratios, meaning, instead of a collection of objects, that they were able to isolate the true facial features, such as the nose, eyes, ears, and mouth. Although some constraints existed in terms of computer processing and environmental artifacts, this heralded the dawn of automated facial recognition.

The eigenface approach showed promise in terms of being fast and effective, especially in a constrained environment. However, scientists experimented using *Fisher's* **linear discriminant analysis (LDA)**, and extended the eigenface method. This approach, known as a *Fisherface*, proved even more promising in terms of low error rates in dynamic facial recognition environments.

The advances and interest in facial recognition began to expand. By the early 1990s through the mid-2000s, we saw an increase in applications, as discussed next.

Encouraging improved algorithms

In the early 1990s, two major United States scientific agencies, the **National Institute of Science and Technology (NIST)** and the **Defense Advanced Research Projects Agency (DARPA)**, began to encourage innovation in the facial recognition arena and, more specifically, in commercial markets. Both agencies provided test sets with hundreds of high-resolution facial images to be used for testing and developing advanced algorithms for facial recognition.

In the early 2000s, NIST began providing government evaluations of existing algorithms, with the goal of encouraging additional development and improvements. The **Face Recognition Vendor Tests (FRVTs)** are designed to promote the widespread use of facial recognition, and are still offered today.

> **Important note**
> You can visit the site at `https://www.nist.gov/programs-projects/face-recognition-vendor-test-frvt`.

With the advances in technology and improved algorithms, we started to the increasing use of facial recognition systems in the private sector, along with government agencies.

Not all were successful implementations. For example, in the 2001 Super Bowl, law enforcement tested a facial recognition system to identify criminals. The system was unable to render the massive number of faces, threw numerous false positives, and was only able to identify a small number of petty criminals. While facial recognition wasn't quite ready for prime time, its use showed promise.

Later in that decade, in 2009, the *Pinellas County Florida Sheriff's Office* began successfully using FRT to aid in apprehending criminals. Then, in 2010, social media giant Facebook started using facial recognition to suggest a tag on a face that looked similar, and then used the data obtained to suggest more tags it perceived as a match.

As we can see, over the past six decades, there have been significant advances in FRT. Lastly, let's take a look at a general approach to facial recognition.

Moving through facial recognition

A standard facial recognition process begins with acquiring the image. The algorithm must then have a method to isolate the face, and then crop and normalize the image. Once the image is prepared, it then goes through the process of extracting the features before the final stage of determining whether or not there is a match:

Figure 6.2 – Stages of facial recognition

In the next section, let's examine just what is involved when a system acquires a facial image.

Acquiring the facial image

More and more applications are turning to facial recognition to identify and authenticate an individual. Recent years have seen dramatic improvements in the technology, both in image capture and processing. As a result, facial recognition is slowly replacing other biometrics, such as fingerprint technology.

Facial recognition is used in a wide range of applications, from enforcing the law and providing access control to securing our borders. In order to be the most effective, it's important to capture a high-quality image. During this process, there are several challenges to overcome, such as being able to handle non-face artifacts such as eye glasses and jewelry.

In the next section, we'll focus on what steps are involved in capturing the facial image. Let's start the discussion with evaluating 2D and 3D image capture.

Capturing images using 2D or 3D

In the past, there was mainly 2D, with limited 3D image capture available. However, there have been several advances in technology in the past two decades. As a result, there are more choices for capturing facial images, and we are seeing more and more options for enhanced 3D technology.

Let's compare the differences between the two, starting with 2D image capture.

Obtaining a 2D image

2D images use measurements that include length and width. A face has more than one dimension. As a result, it's common for devices that use facial recognition to use 2D capture, as it's convenient and widely available. In fact, almost all imaging used on social media is 2D. This type of imaging is fairly accurate and assumes the subject will look straight at the camera to obtain an image.

Although convenient and fast, 2D has several limitations. Obtaining a 2D image relies on the visible light spectrum, or the light a human can see. Because of this, it's difficult, if not impossible, to capture an acceptable image if there is dim light, or excessive shadowing on the face.

During capture on a mobile device, it's common to obtain a 2D image using the front-facing camera. If the subject isn't looking directly at the camera, or if the lighting isn't consistent, it may incorrectly identify someone. In addition, some 2D cameras can even be spoofed using a high-quality photograph.

2D is a flat representation of an individual. Although fairly accurate, a 2D object does not possess depth. 2D images cannot assess the finer details, such as the depth of your eye sockets, or the length of your nose.

In the next section, we'll see why 3D images have more advantages when used for facial recognition.

Procuring a 3D image

A 3D object has length, height, and depth. 3D imaging uses advanced techniques and cameras employing an **infrared** (**IR**) light to obtain a textured, realistic image. Additionally, built within most IR cameras is a flood illuminator, which helps brighten the face when in a dark room.

Let's take a look at some methods that are employed to obtain a 3D image.

Using dots to build a face map

Some mobile device manufacturers are using IR cameras that can project from 15,000–30,000 invisible dots onto your face to build your unique face map. Once obtained, the camera transfers the results to be processed into a template for comparison. In this type of system, more dots mean more detail, and results in improved recognition.

During capture, targets that are closer to the sensor (such as your nose) will reflect faster that the area under your eye. As expected, this type of imaging improves the accuracy of the facial recognition process, as complex sensors essentially construct a depth map of the face.

> **Important note**
>
> Read more and see just how many dots are used by visiting `https://www.imore.com/how-see-iphone-xs-dot-map`.

Some device manufacturers are also utilizing a **Time of Flight** (**ToF**) camera, as outlined in the following section.

Measuring the speed of light

Another technique used in capturing 3D images is by using **Light Detection and Ranging** (**LIDAR**). LIDAR illuminates the target surface with a **ToF** camera, and measures the differences in reflected light, which is used to construct a 3D model of the target.

Using ToF provides a fast, precise measurement of the target. There are, however, some issues that can interfere with an exact measurement. The issues are mainly due to very bright objects near the target. Interference such as sunlight or other bright lights can cause unwanted reflections, thereby preventing an accurate measurement of the response time.

> **Important note**
>
> To see an illustration of how ToF systems work, visit `https://` `d3eys52k95jjdh.cloudfront.net/wp-content/` `uploads/2019/03/FaceSafe-3D-Face-Recognition-How-` `3D-Systems-Work-1024x576.jpg`.

Another 3D technology is the use of thermal imaging, as outlined in the next section.

Imaging warm objects

Another 3D technology uses thermal imaging, which detects the IR light discarded from objects. A warm object emits IR light; cold objects are nearly non-responsive.

Thermal imaging is the preferred method if you need to detect and recognize faces at night, or in poor lighting conditions. The method is commonly used by the military and law enforcement. In addition to being able to recognize faces in dim light, images captured using thermal imaging conceal an individual's true image, thus adhering to privacy concerns.

As you can see, when using 3D capture, most will agree that images have exceptional quality and life-like properties. Additionally, when appropriate lighting is used, the results are quite satisfactory.

Even with the latest technology, while capturing images during facial recognition, any alterations in lighting, pose, and other variables can present a challenge in providing an acceptable capture, as discussed next.

Overcoming challenges

Properly capturing a facial image presents several challenges. The issues can alter the ability to obtain a quality capture, and/or alter the appearance of an individual. Some of the common issues include the following:

- Improper illumination that can cause excessive shadowing.
- Facial expressions, such as smiling, closing the eyes, or frowning.
- Artifacts such as glasses, hats, scarves, and jewelry can impact the capture if it partially obstructs a key measurement.
- The presence of noise such as visual distortion or splotchy discoloration.
- The face can be blurred by either someone moving the camera, or as a result of the subject moving during capture.
- Scaling factors that occur when the subject is closer or farther away.

Over time, there can be subtle changes in someone's appearance due to the aging process, which may influence the match rate. If this occurs, the subject may need to periodically re-enroll.

In addition, the system may have difficulty rendering a change in pose or head orientation. Some systems (such as passport control) require a face-forward approach to obtain the best image. However, when dealing in an uncontrolled environment, such as threat management in large venues, the system must adjust to slight face rotations. Furthermore, the algorithm should be tuned to adjust to the appropriate scale.

As you can see, there are many things that can prevent appropriate biometric template rendering.

Once the face image is obtained, the next process is to localize the face, and extract key features from the image and create a template. Let's take a look.

Extracting the features

Once an appropriate image is captured, the algorithm must complete the following steps:

1. Detect the face, and then crop and normalize the image.
2. Discover the facial landmarks.
3. Convert the metrics of the facial landmarks into a template to be either stored or compared to an existing database.

The first step in the process is to localize the face, as discussed next.

Localizing the face

After acquiring an image, the next step is to detect a human face in an image or video. Once the face is located, the image is prepared by cropping and normalizing. As shown in the following image, this phase seeks to prepare the image.

At a high level, you might see the following steps:

1. Remove any non-face artifacts.
2. Detect the eyes.
3. Rotate and scale the image appropriately.

The following diagram shows the high-level steps taken to prepare an image:

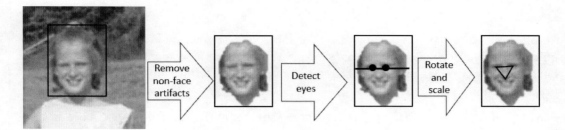

Figure 6.3 – Preparing the image

As shown in the far-right graphic, the points between the eyes and the mouth make up an isosceles triangle, as the distance from the center of each eye to the mouth is equal. This marker is used to verify facial orientation.

Once the face is isolated and optimized, the next step is to extract the features, as outlined next.

Identifying the features

Facial feature extraction detects the facial landmarks. This step pulls the most significant elements of a face, such as the eyes, nose, mouth, eyebrows, and cheeks. Before classifying a face, the system must pass the image through preprocessing. This stage readies the image by bringing out the details and texture.

In some cases, it's appropriate to apply white balance. Balancing the white will control the color distribution in an image, and help eliminate unnatural color tints, so as to provide an improved image. It's also advantageous to utilize skin segmentation, which isolates various skin tones that can occur in sub-optimal lighting conditions, or naturally occurring variations within different ethnic groups.

Once the key features are isolated, filters extract and sharpen the features. Filtering can include the following:

- Median filtering that normalizes color and removes noise
- Gaussian filters to give more weight to the center of the filter and less to the edges, which helps pull the features under different illumination conditions
- Gabor filters to detect and enhance the edges, and improve the visual textures

In some cases, a hybrid filtering approach may be used before moving to detect the facial features.

Over the years, scientists have developed several face detection algorithms. Next, let's review the four main categories.

Detecting the face

Think about what happens when you look at someone's face. Most of the time, you'll quickly scan the entire face and locate the key areas that uniquely identify an individual. Because of the complex process that occurs in our brains when we look at a face, the process is natural, and fairly quick.

For a computer to achieve the same task, there can be challenges, such as scale, pose, and lighting that degrade the performance of the process. To adjust to the various challenges, several methods have been developed over the years.

Face detection method categories include the following:

- **Knowledge-based**: This approach is similar to the way we recognize faces. The method uses what we know about the various landmarks and geometry of the face, such as the eyes, nose, and mouth. However, knowledge-based methods can have difficulty adjusting to extreme variations in pose or head orientation.

- **Appearance-based**: This method is achieved by training the system using **artificial neural networks** (**ANNs**) and Eigenfaces to distinguish a face. The algorithm discounts any non-face areas such as the background region or other irrelevant data. Appearance-based methods optimize **machine learning** (**ML**) and statistical analysis to make a decision, and can exhibit improved performance as compared to other methods.

- **Feature-based**: This method utilizes facial geometry such as the various points and curves to identify the facial features. This method works well with 2D images that easily display the distinctive facial features, such as the eyes, nose, mouth, and chin. However, this method might not perform well when dealing with a complex background.

- **Template-based**: This method uses a predefined template or model that defines either the face as a whole, or the individual features. When using template-based detection, the head is detected using a filter or mask. The features are pulled by using knowledge geometry of facial features.

In the next section, let's take a look at how systems optimize input to learn and improve their results.

Learning to learn

Most advanced systems utilize some form of **Artificial Intelligence** (**AI**) during face detection, tracking, and matching. AI is similar to the way we think, using tools such as problem solving, perception, and planning in order to make a decision. An application of AI is **Machine Learning** (**ML**), which uses data and deep learning to help a system learn how to learn.

A key component of AI and ML is an **ANN**. An ANN is similar to the way our brains work, as it is made up of interconnected neurons that provide input to one another. This feedback is essential in decision making, and helps facial recognition algorithms to collect, filter, and analyze data to provide more accurate decisions.

Deep learning is a subset of ML, which uses an ANN to make decisions. Most facial recognition systems use a **feed forward neural network** (**FFNN**) for pattern recognition and decision making. In an FFNN, we see three layers as shown in the following diagram:

- The input layer receives data.
- The hidden layer(s) perform analysis of the data.
- The output layer provides the results.

The following diagram shows the graphic representation of a FFNN:

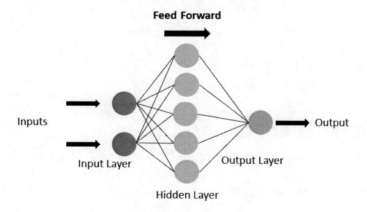

Figure 6.4 – Feed forward neural network

Prior to becoming useful, an ANN must be trained in order to help the system to understand the expected outputs. In order to learn the facial features, the system must have input, such as the database found here: `http://bosphorus.ee.boun.edu.tr/default.aspx`.

The final step is to compare the results to determine whether there is a match, as outlined in the following section.

Matching the template

Once the template is complete, the next step is to compare the newly created template against the stored template to see whether there is a match. Facial recognition can be used in one of two ways; to identify or authenticate an individual.

The system can identify an individual by searching a non-indexed database using a one-to-many comparison for a match. For example, identification might be used during threat management, to determine whether the system can identify the individual. If there is no matching template in the database, the search will fail.

The system can authenticate an individual by searching an indexed database using a one-to-one comparison for a match. For example, if you use facial recognition to authenticate and unlock your phone, if the template matches, you will gain access to your phone. If someone else tries to gain access to your phone, their facial template will not match, and they won't be able to unlock your device.

> **Important note**
>
> It's important to note that with any biometric system, you will never get a 100% match rate. Verification occurs as a result of an acceptable *threshold*, instead of a *yes* or *no* comparison.

In the next section, we'll examine the many applications and uses for facial recognition, along with a brief look at the pros and cons of using FRT.

Using facial recognition today

Over the last decade, we have seen advances in the use of FRT. FRT assists industries and government agencies in many ways. Uses include preventing crime, taking attendance in school, identifying hotel guests, and optimizing the shopping experience.

Let's start with a look at the ways FRT can help law enforcement improve public safety.

Enhancing public safety

FRT has found a home in providing surveillance in many locations. For example, in Panama's Tocumen airport, law enforcement uses facial recognition to monitor individuals as they travel through the airport. The system has successfully identified known Interpol suspects since its launch in 2010.

In the US, the **Automated Regional Justice Information System (ARJIS)** provides cooperating law enforcement agencies with information on known suspects. Agencies that benefit from the system include U.S. Marshals, the FBI, and numerous local police departments.

Law enforcement can also use a photo ID (for example, a driver's license or real ID) to run a search to identify and remand possible criminals. In addition to searching for known criminals, facial recognition helps during a forensic exercise in identifying known criminals.

FRT is also being used to secure our borders. Travelers present their passport to the reader, and then are asked to look at the camera. The system then does a modified facial recognition scan to compare it to their passport in order to verify their identify.

Law enforcement is optimizing the use of FRT. However, we see that FRT is improving user experiences across a wide range of applications.

Improving experiences

The benefits of being able to recognize an individual is being optimized by retail establishments, social media, and the gaming community.

First, we'll examine how FRT improves our experience at retail establishments.

Monitoring retail environments

Stores are using facial recognition to detect theft, as a thief's face is shared among other retailers, which may ban you from entering the store. A company called *Face First* (`https://www.facefirst.com/`) helps provide real-time threat management by monitoring traffic in large venues such as shopping malls.

Some retail establishments are experimenting with FRT to provide payment in order to streamline the process. In addition, FRT coupled with AI will monitor your shopping habits each time you visit, and then provide tailored suggestions delivered to your phone as you enter the building.

Next, let's examine how FRT optimizes social media.

Getting social online

Social media has been using facial recognition for over a decade. Since 2010, Facebook used the technology to suggest a tag on a face that looked similar and then used the data obtained to suggest more tags it perceived as a match. Facebook improved the technology over time, mainly because of the vast amount of data available from tagged faces in every possible setting, angle, and lighting variable.

In addition to identifying a face in the crowd, FRT is expanding to capture the emotion of an individual, as we'll learn next.

Detecting emotion

Today, several facial recognition apps are capable of performing basic mood analysis. Researchers are beginning to see the benefits of sensing what emotion a user is experiencing.

The ability to detect emotion is beneficial in retail settings in order to determine a customer's mood while they are looking at a product.

Monitoring emotion is also important while we are behind the wheel. Most cars today aren't quite ready to be self-driving; they need the operator to stay alert. By monitoring the driver's face, the car can send an alert if the driver's eyes are closed or if the driver appears drowsy.

Emotion detection can also aid health care providers. By observing facial expressions, providers can detect changes in health, such as lethargy or an increase in pain. By monitoring the emotions, health care professionals can be proactive in treating an individual.

Researchers are also investigating the use of emotion detection in gaming. The system monitors the player's mood, and then provides an appropriate response that reflects on the player's avatar. This technology will make games even more life-like and interactive.

Along with improving our day to day experiences, FRT is instrumental in controlling access in several areas, as we'll see next.

Providing access control

Controlling access is one of the cornerstones of biometrics technology. FRT is right in the mix, as it provides robust access control across a wide range of platforms.

In addition to controlling access for buildings and computer systems, facial recognition is gaining a foothold in the mobile market. Since its release in 2017, the Apple iPhone X has been using facial recognition for device security. Consumers have embraced this option, and other vendors have begun to implement the technology.

Airports are using the technology for threat management and to ensure consistent identity. Travelers are checked in using their ID, and then they are verified before boarding the plane, so as to prevent ticket swapping. In addition, concert venues are investigating the possibility of adopting similar practices with a view to prevent ticket scalping.

While the use of FRT has expanded in many different areas, it's important to understand the pros and cons, so we can better understand a system's capabilities. Next, let's compare the benefits and drawbacks.

Recognizing the pros and cons

Facial recognition is gaining attention in a variety of applications. As with any system, there are benefits and drawbacks.

Let's start with listing the benefits of FRT.

Acknowledging the benefits

Facial recognition is an optimal biometric, as it's unobtrusive and can track individuals at a distance. Using FRT can be used in a variety of situations and can operate covertly, without the cooperation of the individual. As a result, FRT is great for surveillance and law enforcement.

As the technology improves, FRT can provide an economical solution for identification and authentication. The technology can assist in locating missing and/or exploited children along with disoriented elderly patients.

In addition, many facial recognition systems are including the ability to detect whether a person is wearing some type of protective mask on the lower part of their face. The check is incorporated into employee access control systems to ensure that mask requirements are complied with during a medical crisis, such as an epidemic.

When compared against other biometric systems such as fingerprint or iris recognition, facial recognition is inexpensive and non-intrusive. Humans recognize one another by looking at their face.

As a result, most consider facial recognition as one of the most natural biometrics available.

While there are many advantages to using FRT, there are also some drawbacks, as discussed next.

Understanding the limitations

While we can accept the many benefits of FRT, there are some drawbacks. FRT can be affected by appearance and environment. There are systems that, unless tuned and trained properly, have a high false non-match.

FRT can suffer from an identical twin attack, where the system is unable to differentiate between twin siblings. In addition, some systems have difficulty recognizing certain demographics.

Although facial recognition is non-invasive, inexpensive, and convenient, it may not be as accepted as using a fingerprint. Privacy advocates claim concerns over unwanted surveillance along with a potential for privacy abuse.

Another drawback of FRT is its inability to distinguish a live face from a photo, and can be spoofed, as we'll learn next.

Spoofing a system

With advances in technology comes the ability to generate photo-realistic images and deepfake videos. Spoofing a system presents many challenges and can be dangerous, especially when authentication methods are attacked.

If a system is running unsupervised, such as access control on a mobile phone, someone could attempt a spoof or presentation attack. Spoof attacks can use a high-quality image or a mask.

One way to prevent a spoof attack is by employing liveness detection. There are several techniques that can test a subject's liveness, including the following:

- Use a challenge-response approach where the system prompts the user to turn their head or blink prior to capturing the image.
- Use algorithms that detect subtle facial movements of the lips or eyes.
- Use 3D capture to ensure that the face has height, width, and depth.

It's important to note that spoof detection is not recognizing an individual; it's a method for determining whether the subject is alive, and not a spoofed image.

Some individuals actively attempt to spoof systems by using special makeup, wigs, and other artifacts that include dots and synthetic hair to confuse FRT. This technique is used by average individuals and criminals to escape the eyes of facial recognition monitoring systems that are always active. One such site is CV Dazzle, `https://cvdazzle.com/`, which offers items designed to spoof facial detection systems, and provides privacy filters to those who do not want to be recognized.

In general, there are many ways in which we use facial recognition today. In the future, we will most likely see more creative applications of this fascinating biometric.

Summary

Facial recognition is one of the most natural biometrics available. When we see a face, our brains perform complex processing to take the image and make sense of what we are seeing.

In this chapter, we learned about the evolution of FRT, from the early beginnings in the 1960s, to advances in technology and algorithms in the 1980s, to the present day. By now, you can understand that, although the face is an optimal biometric, obtaining an image of the face to use in a facial recognition process can be challenging. We covered the differences in capturing a 2D image versus a 3D image, and how a 3D image can provide depth and provide a more life-like image. Even still, shadows, alterations in pose, and variations in color can negatively affect the recognition rate.

We then examined the process of facial recognition, from extracting the features, to localizing the face, and then identifying the features. We then saw the importance of using AI to make a correct decision. Finally, we examined the many applications of facial recognition that are in use today, along with comparing the pros and cons of this popular biometric.

In the next chapter, we'll take a look at another popular biometric: iris recognition. You'll learn how the iris is the colored part of the eye that provides a unique biometric. We'll cover the structure of the eye and what is captured when using iris recognition. We'll step through methods to sense and capture iris images, imaging techniques, and learn how the eye is normalized. You'll gain a better understanding of how template matching works and also a discussion on spoofing. Finally, you'll recognize the many uses for iris recognition for a variety of applications around the world.

Questions

Now it's time to check your knowledge. Select the best response, and then check your answers, found in the *Assessment* section at the end of the book:

1. A very small percentage (approximately 2%) of individuals can't recognize faces at all. These individuals suffer from a condition called _____, or face blindness.

    a. hyperopia

    b. near-infrared

    c. prosopagnosia

    d. myopia

2. The _____ approach uses facial images with lower dimensions, which results in a blurry representation of a face.

    a. eigenface

    b. hyperopia

    c. prosopagnosia

    d. myopic

3. 3D imaging uses advanced techniques and cameras employing a(n) _____ light to obtain a textured, realistic image.

    a. eigenface

    b. infrared

    c. myopic

    d. thermal

4. _____ illuminates the target surface with a ToF camera, and measures the differences in reflected light, which is used to construct a 3D model of the target.

    a. LIDAR

    b. Infrared

    c. Myopic

    d. Thermal

5. The points between the eyes and the mouth make up an isosceles_____, as the distance from the center of each eye to the mouth is equal. This marker is used to verify facial orientation.

   a. square

   b. ellipse

   c. rectangle

   d. triangle

6. A(n) _____ -based face detection method is similar to the way we recognize faces and uses what we know about the various landmarks and geometry of the face, such as the eyes, nose, and mouth.

   a. feature

   b. knowledge

   c. template

   d. appearance

7. One way to prevent a(n) _____ attack is by employing liveness detection.

   a. feature

   b. triangle

   c. spoof

   d. identical twin

Further reading

- To read about the secret history of facial recognition, go to `https://www.wired.com/story/secret-history-facial-recognition/`.

- See how Fujitsu is experimenting with ways to detect emotion using FRT: `https://www.fujitsu.com/global/about/resources/news/press-releases/2019/1015-01.html`.

- Visit `https://www.kairos.com/blog/60-facial-recognition-databases` to see a list of 60 facial recognition databases.

- Go to `https://nvlpubs.nist.gov/nistpubs/ir/2018/NIST.IR.8238.pdf` to view a report of the ongoing FRVT.

- To watch a video on using a RAND tablet, visit `https://youtu.be/LLRy4Ao62ls`.

7
Learning Iris Recognition

When we gaze into someone's eyes, we can sense a lot about how they may be feeling. The eyes can reflect if someone is worried or if they are truly happy. But there is more to the human eye. Within the eye is the iris, or the colored part of the eye, which is responsible for allowing light to reach the retina. And each of our irises is unique, which makes the iris an optimal biometric.

In this chapter, we'll start by taking a closer look at the structure of the iris, and outline some of the main functions. We'll discover the many markings in an iris, such as ridges, crypts, stripes, and freckles, which provide its uniqueness. We'll then cover the structure of the eye and what is captured when using iris recognition. We'll step through methods to sense and capture iris images, looking at imaging techniques and learning how the eye is normalized. You'll gain a better understanding of how template matching works, along with a discussion on spoofing. Finally, you'll recognize the many uses of iris recognition in a variety of applications around the world.

In this chapter, we're going to cover the following main topics:

- Understanding the unique nature of the iris
- Learning the structure of the eye
- Capturing and sensing iris images
- Matching templates and preventing spoofing
- Reviewing iris recognition applications

Understanding the unique nature of the iris

"The eyes are the windows to the soul" is a common phrase, as interpreted from the Bible verse, *Matthew 6:22-24*. The saying is appropriate when describing the iris, as it is responsible for allowing light into the eye by expanding and shrinking the pupil. In this section, we'll study how scientists began to evaluate the eye as an identifier as early as 1885. We'll then take a look at why the iris is an optimal biometric, and following this, examine the structure of the iris.

Let's begin with the evolution of iris recognition.

Recognizing uniqueness

Interest in using the iris to identify someone began as early as 1885. A French police officer, *Alphonse Bertillon*, designed a system to identify prisoners using bodily measurements, called the *Bertillon system*.

Concurrent to this development, Bertillon began investigating the use of the iris as an identifier. In the following screenshot, we see iris classification details, which outline a code to indicate the color of the eye:

```
3. Eye. (j) yellow, (or) orange, (ch) chestnut, (mar) dark chest-
          nut, (as) azure, (i) intermediate violet tinge, (ard)
          slaty, (v) greenish.
```

Figure 7.1 – The Bertillon iris classification details

Many years later, ophthalmologist *Frank Burch* recognized the unique nature of the iris. In 1936, Burch proposed its use in identifying individuals.

Half a century later, in the 1980s, ophthalmologists *Leonard Flom* and *Aran Safir*, along with *John Daugman* of Cambridge University in England, made significant strides in developing an iris recognition system. Flom and Safir ascertained that the patterns within each individual's iris are unique. The two ophthalmologists approached *John Daugman* to collaborate and develop an algorithm to provide automated iris recognition.

Flom, Safir, and Daugman continued their work together. In the 1990s, they developed a successful prototype. Then, in 1995, we saw the release of the first commercial iris recognition system. *Daugman* held the patent for the system from 1991 until the patent expired in 2005. The release of the patent paved the way for companies to develop their own iris recognition systems.

Concurrent to Daugman's work, another group of scientists, *Richard Wildes*, *W.W. Boles*, and *Raul Sanchez-Reillo*, developed methods to extract iris features to be used for pattern-matching algorithms.

After the diligence of the early pioneers and the development of a working iris recognition system, we saw a great deal of interest in this biometric. Next, let's outline some of the reasons the iris is an optimal biometric.

Providing an optimal biometric

When dealing with a biometric system, there are several key performance metrics that measure the quality of an optimal biometric. The metrics are the need to be unique, universal, permanent, performant, collectable, acceptable, and able to avoid circumvention.

When comparing biometric modalities, we know that fingerprint technology is an optimal biometric used in a wide range of applications. However, as far as acceptability is concerned, fingerprint technology has a lower acceptance rate for a couple of reasons, as follows:

- Many individuals feel that fingerprint technology is associated with law enforcement. As a result, some users are hesitant to offer their fingerprint for fear their fingerprints might be shared with the police.

- In most cases, when someone is using fingerprint technology, the subject must physically touch a device to be recognized by the system. The fact that you have to touch a sensor may result in a user's hesitancy to interact with the sensor, especially if it is used in a public place such as a bank.

Because of these reasons, iris recognition has an improved acceptance rate.

In addition to this, the iris has many other desired qualities, as follows:

- **Uniqueness**: Each iris has multiple characteristics such as ridges, crypts, stripes, and freckles, which makes everyone's iris unique.

- **Universal**: Nearly everyone has an eye that can be used to obtain an iris image.

- **Permanent**: The iris is developed in the womb, and once it is formed, it remains essentially the same throughout an individual's life.

- **Performance**: In a healthy eye, iris recognition is capable of consistently correct results and is shown to have more accurate rates than fingerprint technology.

- **Collectability**: Iris recognition provides an effortless way to obtain biometric data, as cameras can obtain a high-quality image at a comfortable distance.

- **Avoid circumvention**: As with other biometric systems, an iris scan can be spoofed by using methods such as high-quality images and specialty contact lenses. To avoid spoofing, systems should use iris liveness detection.

Next, let's take a closer look at the iris, and at what makes it an optimal biometric.

Using the iris as an identifier

When looking at someone, many times we notice the color of their eyes. Collectively, this colored portion of the eye area is called the uvea. The uvea is comprised of three structures: the iris, the ciliary body, and the choroid.

Let's take a closer look at the components that make up this notable structure.

Dissecting the uvea

The pigmented part of the eye is called the uvea. Within the uvea reside the following structures:

- The **iris**, or the most obvious structure, is the colored part of the eye.

- The **ciliary** body is a ring of muscle fibers that surrounds the iris, secures the lens of the eye, and helps keep intraocular pressure stable.

- The back of the uvea is the **choroid**, which has tiny blood vessels that provide nourishment to the retina.

Behind the iris is melanin pigment, which prevents too much light from entering the eye. The amount of melanin pigment in the iris will determine the color of the eye. For example, if an individual has a great deal of melanin pigment, their eyes will most likely have brown or chestnut coloring.

In the human eye, brown is the most common color. Lighter colors such as amber or silver are less prevalent. In rare cases, someone will have eyes that have two different colors. This condition is called heterochromia iridum and affects less than 1% of the population.

Next, let's get a better understanding of the role of the pupil.

Understanding the pupil

The iris is made up of smooth muscle fibers and connective tissue. In the center of the iris is the pupil, as shown in the following image:

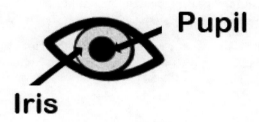

Figure 7.2 – The iris and pupil of the eye

In response to light, the iris reacts by doing the following:

- Widening the pupil in dim lighting
- Constricting the pupil in bright lighting

This involuntary response is referred to as pupillomotor function, which is controlled by the brain.

> **Important note**
>
> Doctors use the pupil to determine if the brain is working properly. If a patient has suffered a brain trauma, the doctor will test pupillary response by shining a light onto the eye. If the brain is healthy, the response will be noted as **Pupils Equal, Round, and Reactive to Light and Accommodation (PERRLA)**.

The pupils work with the autonomic nervous system to respond not only to light but also to emotion, meaning that your pupils will dilate if you sense danger or if you meet an attractive person.

Next, let's take a look at the eye itself so that you can get a better perspective of the various structures. In addition, we'll also examine possible diseases that can influence the ability to properly use iris recognition.

Learning the structure of the eye

Concurrent to understanding the concept of iris recognition, we'll want to take a minute to study the eye itself. We'll also want to take a look at some diseases and aging factors that can alter the effectiveness of obtaining an acceptable iris image.

Let's start with an overview of the most common eye elements.

Viewing the major elements of the eye

The human eye is in a family called *Camera Eyes*. It is referenced as such because a camera has a lens that opens during image capture to allow light to pass through and enter the camera. Similar to a camera, the pupil regulates the amount of light that enters the eye.

As shown in the following screenshot, we see the major structures of the eye. The iris is the colored portion in the front of the eye, the pupil is in the center of the iris, and the retina is at the back of the eye:

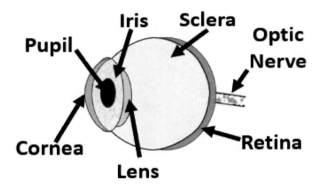

Figure 7.3 – Anatomy of the human eye

The human eye has a protective layer of white fibrous tissue called the sclera, also called the *white* of the eye. The cornea is a clear structure that sits over the uvea area and directs light through the pupil to the retina.

Between the iris and the cornea lies the aqueous humor. The clear transparent object behind the pupil is the lens. The retina resides at the back of the eye and has millions of photoreceptor cells. This highly vascular area accepts light and communicates directly with the brain to interpret visual stimuli.

The cornea and the eyelid provide protection for the uvea. However, the uvea can suffer from genetic- and age-related changes, along with diseases. Let's take a look at some of the issues that can occur in the eye.

Dealing with eye disorders

In most cases, there are minimal concerns when using iris recognition. However, there are some ailments that might influence the quality of the iris capture.

Let's first examine ways the pupil can be affected.

Altering the pupil shape or position

A pupil's position or appearance can be affected by two conditions, as follows:

- **Dyscoria**: This is a condition where the shape of the pupil is altered from a normal round appearance. The pupil does not dilate properly in response to light, and the patient may experience vision problems.

- **Corectopia**: This is a condition where the pupil is not in the center of the eye. With corectopia, the patient may experience eye pain, and surgery may be required.

It is common that a patient suffering from corectopia will suffer from dyscoria as well. The two conditions are shown in the following screenshot:

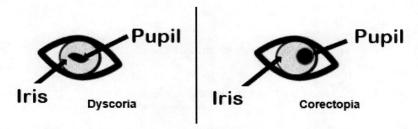

Figure 7.4 – Pupil distorted by shape (dyscoria) versus position (corectopia)

In addition to pupil shape or appearance, the iris can also have disorders that can be either hereditary or caused by an injury, as we'll see next.

Affecting the iris

The iris assists in helping you see better by adjusting to varying levels of light. The following list details a few conditions that can affect the iris:

- **Aniridia** is the absence of a pupil. The condition is either hereditary, where the individual is born without an iris, or occurs as a result of a penetrating injury. In either case, the affected eye is unable to constrict the iris, which can result in too much light entering the eye.

- A **coloboma** is a hereditary disorder where part of the iris tissue is missing. A coloboma presents as a hole in the iris.

- **Synechiae** are adhesions that are caused by trauma or disease. The affected iris will appear irregular and/or cloudy and this may lead to glaucoma.
- **Choroidal or iris nevus** is a benign pigmented freckle in either the choroid or the iris.

As you can see, some conditions can be serious and lead to diminished sight. Others, such as a nevus (or freckle), are not as serious, but should be observed for changes over time.

The uvea is also an area of concern when dealing with the eye, as outlined in the following section.

Impacting the uvea

Within the uvea are the iris, ciliary body, and choroid. Any of these three structures can be affected by disease or trauma, and can include the following:

- **Uveitis** is inflammation of the uvea. Uveitis can affect the iris and/or the ciliary body, and can cause the eye to be red, painful, and sensitive to light.
- **Uveal melanoma** is a rare cancerous growth that can affect any part of the uvea, iris, ciliary body, or choroid.

As you can see, there are several eye diseases and disorders that may negatively influence the ability to properly capture the iris.

In the next section, let's take a look at the process of obtaining an image of the iris.

Capturing and sensing iris images

Take a moment to look at your own iris. When examining your iris up close, you will see lines, waves, and dots, along with light and dark areas. All of these make a unique pattern that is used during iris recognition.

Obtaining an iris image goes through several phases, as shown in the following screenshot:

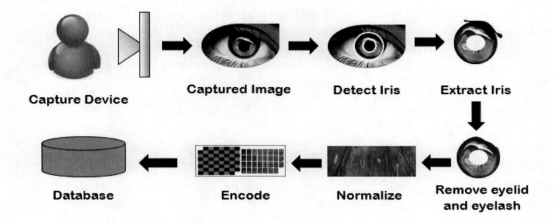

Figure 7.5 – Preparing the iris

As shown in the preceding screenshot, the process is as follows:

1. The subject positions themselves in front of the capture device.

2. The device captures the image.

3. Algorithms isolate and detect the iris.

4. The iris image is extracted.

5. Any non-iris artifacts, such as eyelid and eyelashes, are removed.

6. The image is normalized.

7. The iris image is encoded into a template.

8. The template is stored in the system database.

One of the first steps in iris recognition is obtaining a high-quality image, as we'll learn in the next section.

Obtaining the iris image

To be recognized in the system, iris recognition begins by obtaining an iris image. The image is captured using ordinary or visible light, along with **infrared** (**IR**) light. For best results, the system must be able to obtain a high-quality image, without overly inconveniencing the subject. The capture must have proper illumination along with sufficient contrast, and should clearly show the entire eye, especially the iris and pupil.

Today's cameras are able to capture the iris at a comfortable distance. In most cases, the subject only needs to look at the capture device. The iris scanning process is very fast, lasting about 2–6 seconds. To have an effective sample to process, the system must be able to acquire over 50% of the iris area. In some cases, the subject may have to open their eyes wider so that enough of the iris can be captured.

Today, nearly all iris recognition systems utilize IR light. Let's discover what makes IR ideal when capturing an iris image.

Improving detail using IR light

In an iris recognition system, visible light can be used to illuminate the eye. However, IR light is better at revealing the complex patterns of the iris. IR, also called **near infrared** (**NIR**), is a safe method of scanning the eye as it is closest in wavelength to visible light. An IR light can pass through glasses and plain contact lenses and works even in the dark. IR light has a slightly longer wavelength and helps improve visualization of the iris. It does not cause discomfort, nor will it harm the subject's eye.

Scanning an iris using only visible (or ordinary) light is not recommended as it is unable to capture tiny, complex details of the iris. More importantly, visible light can't pick up the nuances of a heavily pigmented or dark-brown iris. In addition, using visible light can be uncomfortable as it can cause pupil contraction during an iris scan.

In the past, it was necessary to have a specialized camera or sensor that used IR light and was specifically designed to scan the iris. However, as technology has improved, cameras are more readily available, at a reasonable price. In fact, several mobile device manufacturers are capable of capturing and processing an iris image.

After obtaining the image, the system localizes and extracts the iris, as outlined next.

Detecting and extracting the iris

When looking at an annular-shaped iris, you will see a rich source of detail. Everyone's iris is complex and unique, even between twins. In fact, your right-eye iris is different from your left-eye iris.

Each iris has many wavy, complex patterns that radiate outward from the pupil. As shown in the following screenshot, we see a small segment of an iris, enlarged to show the detail:

Figure 7.6 – A segment of an iris

After capture, the next step is to isolate the iris—a critical step, as discussed next.

Isolating the iris

Once the system captures the eye image, it will need to obtain the iris to create the sample. This process is referred to as Daugman's algorithm. The process seeks to localize the curvilinear boundaries of the lower and upper eyelids. It then excludes any non-iris artifacts, such as eyelashes and eyelids, and targets the circular iris. This is a critical step; if this is not properly done, the biometric sample will be unusable.

Once the iris is obtained, the image will move through a process of compliance checks, to determine whether or not the sample is of an acceptable quality. The algorithms will assess any of the following: contrast, sharpness, and the presence of extraneous artifacts. What is left is the true biometric, or the iris of the eye.

After passing the quality check, the isolated iris then moves to normalize the image, as outlined next.

Normalizing and encoding

Normalization occurs after acquiring the image and isolating the iris. This step first seeks to stabilize the captured image with the appropriate sample size. This process is done so that the image has the same constant dimensions, even when the iris image is obtained under different conditions. In addition, normalization will correct distortion and smooth the intensity of each pixel.

After balancing the dimensions, the algorithm will prepare the normalized iris image. As shown in the following screenshot, the process will divide the iris into sectors to produce segmented sections. The features are extracted and then moved to be encoded into a sample, to be compared:

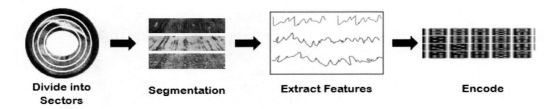

Figure 7.7 – Preparing the iris

As shown, the first step is to divide the iris into sectors. Prior to segmenting the circular iris, the iris is unrolled or flattened, and then segmented. Once the iris is divided and segmented, the next step is to extract the features, as outlined next.

Extracting the features

The iris has a great deal of information in the form of textures, waves, and spots. When extracting features, one approach is to use Gabor filters. Gabor filtering detects and enhances the edges and improves visual textures. Another approach is to use Gaussian filters, which give more weight to the center of the filter and less to the edges and help pull the features under different illumination conditions.

Once the features are extracted, the algorithm creates a feature vector. A feature vector is a set of numeric values that represent the significant characteristics of an object. The values are then used to generate an encoded template.

> **Important note**
> Think of a feature vector as a record in a database. For example, a database record contains the attributes that uniquely represent a person, place, or thing.

The last step is to either store or match the template, as we'll learn next.

Matching templates and preventing spoofing

Once the encoded template is created, the system will either identify or authenticate, according to the design.

The template is compared against a record in search of a match. As with any biometric, the match will never be 100%. Matching occurs as a result of whether or not the threshold is acceptable.

One way to evaluate whether a sample matches a template is by calculating the Hamming distance. The Hamming distance is the result of comparing two binary values, as we'll see next.

Calculating the Hamming distance

The Hamming distance is a comparison of two binary values. To calculate the Hamming distance, we use an **exclusive OR (XOR)** operation on both values. When complete, count the number of bits that are equal to 1, and that will be the Hamming distance.

> **Important note**
>
> An XOR operation is a logical operation that compares two values. In an XOR operation, if A =1 and B =1 but not both, the output is 1.

For example, as shown in the following screenshot, the result of using an XOR operation on the two values A and B will show that there are three values that are equal to one (1). The result is a Hamming distance of three (3):

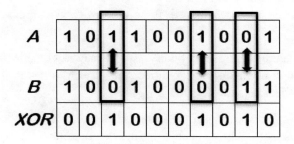

Figure 7.8 – Hamming distance = 3

A Hamming distance of zero (0) is a perfect match. However, a perfect match is not likely as we are dealing with biometric data, and it is rare to return this result.

> **Important note**
>
> If the system returns a perfect match, the sample should be discarded as this can indicate a replay or spoof attack. This attack can occur if someone obtains the template on file and then presents the template as the sample to the system.

Therefore, we look to find an acceptable value for the sample to be considered a match. For example, the Hamming distance must be < .2 to be a match.

As iris recognition gains popularity and is used in large-scale applications, it's important to prevent presentation attacks. In the next section, let's take a look at spoofing and ways to avoid this type of attack.

Avoiding spoofing

A presentation attack will spoof the system to try to obtain a positive match, in order to gain access to the system. While not common, there are a few methods malicious actors use to spoof an iris recognition system. Let's take a look at these.

Imitating an iris

Depending on the quality of the system, there may be a way to spoof the system into accepting a replicate iris.

One way to spoof a system is by using a high-quality image. Instead of a live subject, a photograph is presented to the system for comparison. Because most systems currently use 2D imaging, this type of attack is possible.

Another type of spoof attack uses a custom-made textured contact lens. Most contact lenses are clear. Some lenses have a tint of color and can be used as either a corrective or cosmetic lens. A textured contact lens is designed to have a visual texture that mimics the appearance of an iris.

While using a texture contact lens may be possible, it may not be effective. The reason is that the contact lens will move on the eye during capture. As a result, the IR camera will pick up a mixture of the lens and iris.

As you can see, spoofing a system is conceivable. However, there are methods to detect and prevent imposters from gaining access to the system, detailed as follows:

- Some systems are able to detect textured or printed contact lenses.
- Another way to prevent spoofing is by adding another biometric such as a fingerprint, which would provide an additional test.
- Another method to prevent spoofing is by assessing the liveness or realness of a subject when using iris recognition, as outlined next.

Detecting liveness

Liveness detection is a method to determine whether or not the subject engaging with the biometric system is a real person or not.

A few methods to determine liveness can include the following:

- **Capturing pupillary oscillation**: An individual's pupil will oscillate slightly even with steady illumination. This is an effective method to detect spoofing, as this will only occur with a live subject.

- **Monitoring retinal light reflections**: This is where light reflects off of the retina and the eye appears red. This is also effective, as this will only occur with a live eye.

While spoofing a system is an ongoing issue, there have been advances in techniques to avoid this type of attack. However, we must be aware of the presentation attacks that are possible.

In the next section, we'll see the many ways we can use this technology.

Reviewing iris recognition applications

The iris provides an optimal biometric for many reasons. As technology improves, the use of iris recognition is becoming more available and popular. One of the uses of iris recognition is to ensure our safety, as discussed next.

Ensuring public safety

Iris scanners have come down in price; as a result, iris recognition is being used to provide access control for organizations. The technology is also being used to manage our borders to securely identify or verify individuals.

Iris recognition may be appropriate in highly secure areas, such as a military base. Using this method to verify friendlies is ideal when individuals do not have ID cards.

Some countries are enhancing their national citizen ID programs to include the use of biometrics, such as fingerprint, facial, and iris recognition.

In addition, law enforcement agencies are employing iris recognition to identify individuals. By using a handheld device that is mounted to a mobile phone, the application can quickly obtain biometrics such as facial recognition or fingerprints and iris scans.

Iris recognition is also enhancing our everyday experiences, as we'll learn next.

Streamlining experiences

We know that passwords and pins can be stolen. Using iris recognition provides a way to gain access to systems while providing an additional layer of security.

Financial institutions are employing iris recognition to provide a more secure way to interact with the **automated teller machine** (**ATM**) and prevent losses for the consumer as well as the bank.

Retail establishments use a **point-of-sale** (**POS**) terminal to accept and process payments. To prevent theft and unauthorized transactions, retailers can require staff to use iris recognition technology in their POS terminals. Using a secure login method will restrict access to only approved staff members and help isolate the individual if there are any unauthorized charges.

Iris recognition is finding a home on mobile devices. Specially designed IR cameras authenticate only authorized individuals, to keep the contents of your phone safe from prying eyes. Once you have authenticated to the device, the system provides a **single sign-on** (**SSO**) technology, allowing you to traverse the contents of your phone and quickly and safely log in to accounts.

Iris recognition can also improve the travel experience, as we'll see next.

Traveling with ease

Within many airports, iris recognition may be used to move through the terminal, providing accurate identification for borders during entry and exit and allowing travelers to board a plane or enter an airport lounge. Iris recognition can replace credit cards and boarding passes.

In addition to airports, some hotels are incorporating iris recognition into the check-in process. Instead of a key, you would use the iris-sensing camera to identify and authenticate to gain access to your room. Once you have checked out of the hotel, the biometric data will expire, preventing someone from posting unauthorized room charges to your account.

While it's obvious there are many applications for iris recognition, we'll want to take a minute to compare the pros and cons of using this technology, as outlined next.

Comparing benefits and limitations

With the wide range of applications that can benefit from iris recognition, we can clearly see many advantages. However, it's important to understand the limitations to using this type of technology.

Let's start by listing some of the benefits of using iris recognition.

Listing the benefits

One of the key benefits of iris recognition is that the iris is unique, and its pattern remains stable, even as we age. In addition, iris recognition is highly accurate, as it has low false acceptance and false rejection rates.

Most systems are fast, and can obtain a sample and determine a match within seconds. Iris recognition systems are easy to use. With advanced software and cameras in use today, a system can obtain a sample from a subject from a normal distance, much like taking a photograph.

The subject requires minimal engagement and only has to look at the camera. Iris recognition is not intrusive, as no physical contact with the device is necessary. A sample can be obtained even if the subject is wearing glasses and normal (not textured) contact lenses.

Although some forgery is possible, iris recognition is more resistant to spoofing.

Iris recognition can be used on a small-scale or large-scale system, such as government biometric authentication programs.

While we can see the many advantages of using iris recognition, there are some disadvantages. Let's take a look at these.

Dealing with the drawbacks

An iris recognition system must use an IR camera to be effective. While obtaining the image, it's important to have the correct amount of illumination, as the system must have enough light to visualize the eye. However, excessive glare or extreme visible light will interfere with the quality of capture.

Iris recognition is being offered to consumers for online transactions—for example, while shopping and banking. This will provide a more convenient and secure method to authenticate than using a password. However, to use the system, customers will need to have an appropriate capture device.

Obtaining an image can be difficult if there are excessive eyelids or eyelashes. In addition, if the subject has cataracts or is blind, they may not be able to use this method to authenticate.

The use of contact lenses—specifically, toric lenses for astigmatism, or lenses with embedded logos or lettering—can negatively impact the match rate.

Although an iris recognition system is contactless, the subject should be cooperative, in that excessive movement will influence the ability to properly capture the iris. However, even if the subject is cooperative, they may suffer from a fairly rare condition called nystagmus, which causes uncontrolled movements of the eye. As a result, a subject with nystagmus may not be able to use iris recognition technology.

As you can see, iris recognition is an extremely versatile technology that is finding a purpose in many different areas.

Summary

The next time you look into someone's eye, you will be able to better appreciate how the iris can be used to identify and authenticate.

In this chapter, we reviewed the evolution of iris recognition, from the early days of Alphonse Bertillon dabbling into using the eye as an identifier in the 1880s, to John Daugman's studies in the 1980s, to today's modern systems. You now can see how the iris provides an optimal biometric that can be used in a wide range of applications. We took a closer look at the eye itself, and, more specifically, the colored portion or uvea. In addition, we evaluated some diseases and conditions that could affect iris recognition.

We then stepped through the process of iris recognition. We learned how using IR light enhances the ability to obtain an iris image with greater detail. We saw how the Hamming distance can be a metric for determining a match, and we covered some ways an iris recognition system can be spoofed, along with ways to counteract spoofing. Finally, we covered the many uses of iris recognition technology, and evaluated the pros and cons of this amazing biometric.

In the next chapter, we'll take a look at another popular biometric: voice recognition. You'll see how voice recognition works, and what it means when you say, *My voice is my passport*. We'll cover the process of enrollment and matching. We'll then look at how systems determine a match. Finally, you'll appreciate the many uses of voice recognition software such as access control, and issuing commands to mobile devices and smart homes.

Questions

Now, it's time to check your knowledge. Select the best response to the following questions and then check your answers, found in the *Assessment* section at the end of the book:

1. Iris recognition provides an effortless way to obtain biometric data, as cameras can obtain a high-quality image at a comfortable distance. This relates to the desired biometric feature of _____.

    a. Universal

    b. Permanent

    c. Collectability

    d. Performance

2. The colored portion of the eye area is called the _____, which comprises three structures: the iris, the ciliary body, and the choroid.

    a. Uvea

    b. Retina

    c. Sclera

    d. Cornea

3. When dealing with diseases of the eye, _____ is where the shape of the pupil is altered from a normal round appearance.

    a. Coloboma

    b. Synechia

    c. Dyscoria

    d. Corectopia

4. One way to evaluate whether a sample matches a template is by calculating the _____ distance, which is the result of comparing two binary values.

    a. Uvea

    b. Universal

    c. Collectable

    d. Hamming

5. In an iris recognition system, using a _____light will reveal the complex patterns of the iris, even with darker eyes.

    a. Retinal

    b. Infrared

    c. Hamming

    d. Gaussian

6. One method to detect liveness and prevent spoofing of an iris recognition system is by monitoring _____ light reflections. This is where the eye appears red and would only occur with a live eye.

    a. Gaussian

    b. Retinal

    c. Coloboma

    d. Infrared

7. The process known as _____ algorithm seeks to localize the curvilinear boundaries of the lower and upper eyelids. It then excludes any non-iris artifacts such as eyelashes and eyelids and targets the circular iris.

    a. Daugman's

    b. Hammer's

    c. Gaussian's

    d. Neola's

Further reading

- Compare and contrast iris recognition scanners with fingerprint scanners by visiting the following web page: `https://www.bayometric.com/iris-recognition-scanners-vs-fingerprint-scanners/`.

8
Using Voice Recognition

The use of biometric technology is expanding into our homes, lives, and businesses. Voice recognition is no exception and is an attractive biometric for many reasons. Currently, voice recognition is the only biometric that you can use on the phone to verify your identity to a company. Using your voice to prove who you are, instead of going through lengthy security questions, can simplify your life. As a result, many are seeing how voice recognition is especially beneficial when using Fintech.

This chapter provides an overview of a rapidly expanding biometric. We'll compare two related technologies: voice recognition, which can identify and authenticate, and speech recognition, which converts speech to text. We'll step through the evolution of both and see how technological advances have opened a wide range of potential applications. We'll also generate a voiceprint by using the **Windows Tool for Speech Analysis (WASP)**. By using WASP, you will better understand what a *voiceprint* looks like when used for identification or authentication.

We'll then cover the process of enrollment and matching. You'll understand the difference between text-dependent and text-independent systems. So that you better understand how a voice recognition system compares voiceprints, we'll compare two matching methods. You'll be able to see the differences between template matching versus feature analysis. By the end of this chapter, you'll understand what it means when you say, "*My voice is my passport.*" In addition, you'll appreciate the many uses for voice recognition software to simplify our lives.

In this chapter, we're going to cover the following main topics:

- Understanding voice recognition
- Enrolling and matching
- Employing voice recognition

Understanding voice recognition

While there are many different biometrics, using our voice to identify and authenticate is becoming more commonplace. Voice recognition is gaining in popularity because the technology required to input and transmit voices is already in place. Technologies include the telephony infrastructure, along with components such as speakers and microphones that are built into mobile devices.

In this section, we'll outline voice recognition and the history that shaped the ability to recognize speech, along with an explanation of how our voices are digitized.

First, let's take a look at what defines voice recognition.

Defining voice recognition

Voice recognition, also called speaker verification, uses a person's voice to either identify or authenticate into a system. Voice recognition systems are capable of differentiating between individual voices.

There are many things that can influence the way we speak. A person's voice can change slightly from day to day, because of a medical condition, their emotional status, or their energy level. However, the subtleties in an individual's voice remain the same. As a result, using voice as an identifier is a behavioral biometric, as it represents the manner in which a subject speaks.

Let's next look at what shapes the way we speak.

Babbling to verbalizing

Our ability to speak starts at a young age. Babies begin to babble at as early as 4 months old. In response to their parents' reaction, they experiment with inflection, squeals, and sounds.

Even though voice recognition is a behavioral biometric, there is a great deal of physiological elements that can influence the way we speak. Those include the physical structures that allow us to form words. The elements in a vocal tract include the tongue, airway, vocal cords, soft tissues, and jaw. In total, there are over 70 parts of the human body that contribute to our ability to speak.

How we speak is an individual characteristic, in that this not only involves the physical components but also how the various parts work together to produce sound. How our voice sounds is dependent on these physical structures but involves other elements as well.

Let's explore what other factors help to make our voice unique.

Influencing speech behavior

Each and every one of us will learn a native language in a different way. In addition to the physiological structures involved, there are other factors that can alter the way we speak, such as environment, education, and socio-economic status.

Behavioral attributes include the way we pronounce certain words, along with inflection, speed, pitch, and rhythm. These behavioral attributes are developed over time and include the influence of our parents, regional factors, and even climate. All totaled will be instrumental in creating an individual's unique voiceprint.

Voice Recognition Technology (VRT) is used mainly by adults for identification and/or authentication.

> **Important note**
> Although VRT can be used for children, it may not be as effective. The main reason is that many times, a child's voice changes as they grow, which might require them to periodically re-enroll into the system.

Another closely related technology is speech recognition. Speech recognition is a set of technologies that are capable of interpreting what a subject is saying; however, it is not used as a biometric identifier.

In the next section, let's take a look at the evolution of both technologies.

Stepping back in time

Voice recognition has had rapid advances in recent years. However, the early stages of the technology we use today started over 70 years ago, with the development of systems capable of recognizing speech. In this section, we'll see how both VRT and speech recognition are tightly coupled, and how the evolution of speech recognition has branched out into VRT.

Let's start with some of the systems developed from 1950 through 1990.

Chronicling early efforts

Efforts to teach computers to synthesize and recognize speech began in the 1950s. Bell Laboratories developed the *Audrey* system, which was only capable of understanding the numbers zero to nine. A decade later, IBM introduced Shoebox, which was able to recognize and respond to 16 English words.

Early experiments into VRT began in the 1960s, as law enforcement sought ways to verify the identity of criminals by using their voice. Concurrently, researchers began investigating ways to develop speech recognition systems, as discussed next.

Understanding speech

Throughout the 1970s, scientists at the **United States Defense Advanced Research Projects Agency (DARPA)** developed the **Speech Understanding Research (SUR)** program. This significant project resulted in numerous advances in the field of speech recognition. The report of findings on SUR can be viewed here: `https://apps.dtic.mil/dtic/tr/fulltext/u2/783507.pdf`.

Interest in computerized speech recognition systems expanded, as researchers and industry developed and improved systems. In 1976, **Carnegie Mellon University (CMU)** developed a speech system called *Harpy* that was able to recognize over 1,000 words. Other industry leaders and universities developed systems to have a greater vocabulary, along with the ability to understand different voices.

During this time, the evolution of technologies to understand speech led to research in distinguishing or verifying an individual's voice, as we'll see in the following section.

Verifying an individual's voice

In 1976, the **National Security Agency (NSA)** presented the work of several scientists in speech recognition. Participants included *George Doddington* and *Barbara Hydrick* of Texas Instruments, who had developed a speaker verification system. Another group, from the Speech Recognition Group at IBM, used statistical modeling to train the system and improve accuracy. You can view a summary of some of the findings here: `https://asa.scitation.org/doi/pdf/10.1121/1.2003005`.

Advances and interest in speech processing continued into the 1980s. Although the systems and technologies of the time had challenges, scientists continued to improve the algorithms. During this time, speech recognition systems made significant advances in the ability to recognize words.

One of the main drivers was a result of employing a **Hidden Markov Model (HMM)** in analyzing speech. Next, let's take a look at a high-level explanation of how an HMM works.

Predicting the next value

An HMM is a statistical method that works by looking for predictive patterns, and then changes the state accordingly. The model begins with an observable input or Markov process (X) and the subsequent hidden states (Y). The state changes according to the next most likely change. The HMM learns about one value by observing another, the final analysis will be determined by the most recent value.

When using an HMM, the next possible value is determined by the probability of what might be next. For example, in the graphic we see the HMM starts with an observable input, **ba**, which is the Markov process (X). The subsequent hidden states (Y) are shown below the dashed line, and represent the transition probabilities:

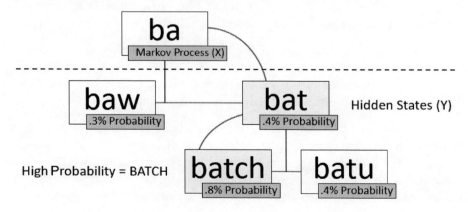

Figure 8.1 – HMM process

In this case, the process might go as follows:

1. First, the **ba** Markov process (X) input will most likely be followed by the **bat** transition which has a higher probability than **baw**.

2. Next, the **bat** input will most likely be followed by the **batch** transition probability, which has a higher probability than **batu**.

3. Finally, the result is that there is a high probability that the final value will be **batch**.

With advances in technology and improved algorithms, speech recognition vocabularies expanded from a few words to thousands of words.

At this point, scientists began to see the value in using our voice to control automated and computerized systems. While still in its infancy, the technology evolved fairly quickly in the late 1990s to the present day, as we'll see in the next section.

Moving into the 21st century

In the 1990s, we saw a rise in the use of personal computers. Over the next three decades, the improvements in processing, along with more complex memory management, allowed voice systems to be more efficient.

Just as scientists predicted, the journey for our voice to control our automated and computerized systems would become a reality, as we'll see next.

Providing assistance

Every year, computing processing power improved, which made it possible for systems to quickly convert text to speech, and vice versa. Companies began developing tools to improve our workflow, such as the Dragon speech recognition software. In addition, BellSouth introduced the concept of an **Interactive Voice Response (IVR)** system. IVR systems interact with callers and provide contactless call routing, and are still in use today.

In the early 2000s, Google began using speech recognition technology for searching websites. Because of the millions of people that use voice search, the system was able to collect and learn billions of words used when searching. The database of words was refined and optimized to predict what someone is actually saying.

Similar to Google's Voice Search, Apple began to implement Siri in their products. In addition, we saw the release of many other voice recognition apps. Today, the popularity of products such as Alexa and other home apps has proven that consumers are comfortable talking to machines. Speech recognition technology has expanded to cars, retail establishments, and even appliances. The accuracy of systems has improved with time, along with a perception of personality.

After seeing such successes in speech recognition, the next logical step is to expand the technology to provide voice recognition, to control access. Let's take a look.

Enhancing access control

VRT is implemented to provide logical access control, and in some cases as part of a **Multi-Factor Authentication (MFA)** solution. Companies are seeing the benefits of using our voices to prevent fraud and secure transactions. Voice recognition has many other uses and benefits, which includes personal identity management solutions, as we'll learn later in this chapter.

Although speech recognition is different from VRT, the two have similar characteristics, along with hurdles to overcome. In the next section, let's take a look at the technology that drives the ability to digitize, transmit, and understand our voice.

Digitizing voice

When using VRT, there are many considerations we must take into account that enable us to effectively use the technology. Some of the factors that influence the success of VRT include the following:

- The ability to digitize our voice
- Method of transmitting the data
- Amount of available bandwidth along the data channels

Let's first take a look at how we convert our voice so that it can be used in a computerized system.

Converting a signal

Most of the world has moved from the **Public Switched Telephone Network (PSTN)** to **Voice over Internet Protocol (VoIP)** to transmit phone calls and other forms of information.

> **Important note**
> VoIP is also known as **Internet Protocol (IP)** telephony.

PSTN is primarily an analog system, and VoIP uses digital transmission. As a result, when using IP telephony to make a call, devices may use a **Voice Interface Card (VIC)**.

A VIC provides the **Digital Signal Processing (DSP)** required to make the appropriate conversion. This conversion is necessary when inputting a human voice because when we speak, we create an analog signal, and a computer must input a digital signal. In addition to providing a way to convert signals to be used in the telephone system, a voice card enables the user to input signals for speech and voice recognition.

As shown in the following diagram, an analog signal is represented as a waveform, and a digital signal is shown as a discrete value of either an on or off binary digit (bit):

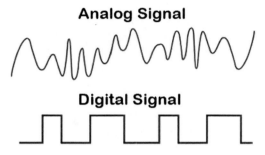

Figure 8.2 – Analog and digital signal

When using a VIC or other voice or sound input, the signal generally passes through the DSP to appropriately convert the signal.

In order for a system to understand our voice, there must be a way to input or record the sound. In addition, the system must be able to output or play back the sound. As shown in the following diagram, we see how our voice is converted from analog to digital and then from digital to analog:

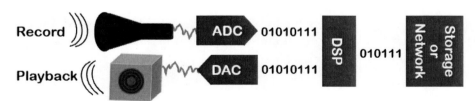

Figure 8.3 – Analog-to-Digital converter (ADC) and Digital-to-Analog converter (DAC)

The process is as follows:

1. The user inputs (or records) their voice using a microphone.

2. The analog signal, as shown as a wavy line, passes through an ADC to convert the analog signal to a digital signal.

3. The digital signal passes to the DSP, which performs the proper encoding, possibly to MP3, voice, or text format.

4. The encoded data is saved to memory or sent across a network.

5. To play a sound, the process is reversed. On playback, however, the digital signal must be converted to an analog signal so that the user can hear the sound.

> **Important note**
>
> To see and hear an example of converting text to speech, visit `https://text-to-speech-demo.ng.bluemix.net/`.

Digitizing speech is only one of many considerations when using VRT. Another factor we must consider is how the signal is transmitted, as we'll learn next.

Transmitting voice traffic

When using VRT on a standard phone or mobile device, many times the signal must travel to a remote location, such as a server across the state or across the country. Once there, the VRT system provides the backend processing to identify and/or authenticate the subject.

Whenever voice traffic travels across a network, a number of factors can influence the quality of the sound. In some cases, the received signals can have errors during transmission, which can be the result of many things. Factors that can influence transmission include the following: inferior microphone; electromagnetic and/or radiofrequency interference; latency; and jitter.

Errors during transmission can result in a distorted voiceprint. The distorted signal can alter the true pattern of someone's voice, emotions, and speaker traits. If the voiceprint is distorted significantly, this can result in a failed match.

The internet has seen significant improvements in recent years. This is as a result of the explosion of voice-controlled, cloud-computing, and **Internet of Things** (**IoT**) devices. Accordingly, while there is a chance of errors in transmission, various compensation techniques have been implemented within the internet backbone that have helped to improve voice traffic.

There are many factors that can affect the quality of voice transmissions. However, one crucial element in accurately transmitting voice is bandwidth, as discussed next.

Influencing the quality of speech

With most of the world using VoIP for telephone calls, the internet has adjusted to this change and optimized communication channels. Along with the equipment that drives traffic on the internet, bandwidth plays a major role in the quality of telephony communication.

When transmitting VoIP, bandwidth represents the spectrum of frequencies a voice signal moves through in a communication channel. The frequency range can be represented in **kilohertz (kHz)**, **megahertz (MHz)**, or **gigahertz (GHz)**. The two main frequencies when describing a communication channel are identified as narrowband and wideband.

When speaking, our voice can range from 50 **hertz (Hz)** to 8 kHz. If voice traffic travels over a communication channel that limits the bandwidth, this restricts or flattens out the signal and can make the signal unintelligible. When using VRT and sending the signal using VoIP, the limited frequency can affect whether or not the voiceprint is a match.

Let's investigate these concepts starting with narrowband, and its effect on voice traffic.

Restricting using narrowband

For over 100 years, most voice traffic traveled over the PSTN or an **Integrated Services Digital Network (ISDN)**. Both limited the frequency range from 300 Hz to 3.4 kHz. Although the frequency range is restricted, in most cases we can still understand what someone is saying.

However, when using narrowband to transmit voice, this removes the richness of the voice and can be less than optimal for the listener, as they may have to strain to hear what someone is saying. The narrow frequency range, coupled with background noise and errors in transmission, may influence the ability to make a match when using VRT.

Most phone systems have begun gradually improving transmissions using wideband. Let's examine why using wideband improves VoIP transmission and will improve the effectiveness of VRT.

Enriching using wideband

Wideband transmission expands or widens the frequencies from 50 Hz to 7 kHz. Because the frequency is double the range of narrowband, this improves the sound quality. Wideband voice is also called **High Definition (HD)** voice. When using HD voice, the full richness of someone's voice is transmitted.

When available, VoIP is transmitted over wideband, and improves the intelligibility of phone conversations. Because HD voice transmission uses nearly the entire range of frequencies of a human voice, this helps assure a greater match rate when using VRT.

Everyone has subtle differences in the way we speak, in our inflection, pitch, and frequency range. So that you can see the unique pattern of your voice, let's create a voiceprint in the following section.

Creating a voiceprint

When using VRT, we want to evaluate the voiceprint of someone. We use the voiceprint to compare with a template and decide whether or not there is a match. To generate your own set of voiceprints, you can use WASP.

> **Important note**
>
> You can download and install WASP on your computer by visiting the following web page: `https://www.phon.ucl.ac.uk/resource/sfs/wasp.php`.

When you launch the program, you will see a screen as shown in the following screenshot:

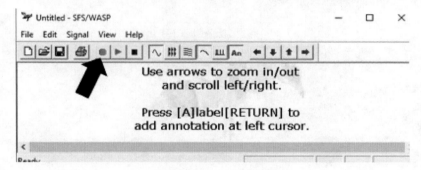

Figure 8.4 – Using WASP

When you are ready, select the red button, which will bring up a screen where you can modify the settings for recording, as shown in the following screenshot:

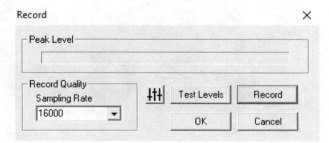

Figure 8.5 – Recording in WASP

Once in this dialog box, you can modify any settings, test the voice levels, or select **Record**. For a simple test, accept the defaults and select **Record**, speak into the microphone, and recite *My voice is my passport*. The recorded voice will then be displayed.

With WASP, you can display various characteristics of a voiceprint, which include metrics such as the amplitude, frequency, and the fundamental frequency. You can modify your own view by going to the **View** menu choice, as shown in the following screenshot. However, for this simple example, I have only displayed the **speech waveform**:

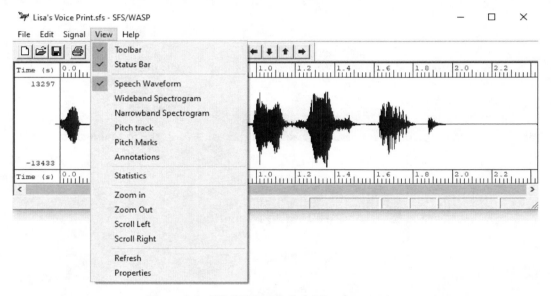

Figure 8.6 – WASP View Speech Waveform option

To show the differences in speech waveforms, we can compare the voiceprints of two subjects. Here, we see the voiceprint of test subject L, as shown in the following screenshot:

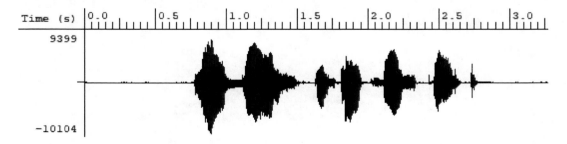

Figure 8.7 – "My voice is my passport" test subject L voiceprint

Next, we see the voiceprint of test subject M, as shown in the following screenshot:

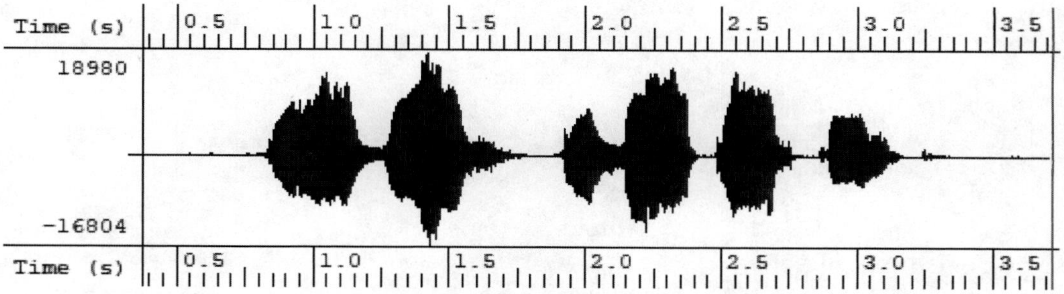

Figure 8.8 – "My voice is my passport" test subject M voiceprint

WASP has several more metrics; however, at a high level, we can see subtle differences. For example, test subject M has a slightly greater inflection when saying *voice*, as we see the pattern expands more than with test subject L.

We have taken a look at the advances in voice recognition over the years and how a voice is digitized and transmitted. Next, let's outline what happens through the voice recognition process.

Enrolling and matching

As with any biometric, the process begins with enrolling the subject. Once the subject is enrolled, the system can obtain the voice sample of the subject and determine whether or not there is a match.

In this section, we'll step through the process of what happens from enrollment to matching. We will compare the different types of systems, either text dependent or text independent. Then, we'll look at matching methods that use either template matching or feature analysis.

Let's start with the enrollment process.

Registering with a system

A voice recognition system goes through the phases shown in the following screenshot:

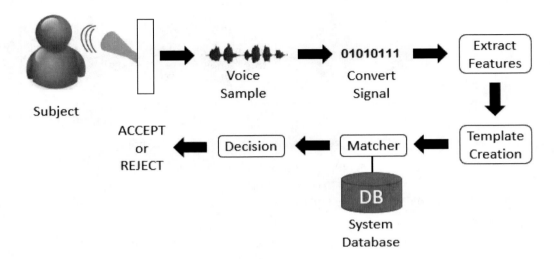

Figure 8.9 – Voice recognition process

To enroll in a voice recognition system, the process goes through the following steps:

1. The subject is prompted to repeat a short passphrase or sequence of numbers.

2. The voice must pass through an ADC, and then the algorithm extracts the features.

3. After the features are extracted, the data then moves to create a template to be stored in the system database.

4. Once the template is stored, the subject can then be identified and/or authenticated.

> **Important note**
> VRT can employ various audio-capture devices such as a telephone, mobile device, or a PC microphone. As a result, the performance of the VR system will depend on the quality of the audio signal.

When using VRT, feature extraction can be done using either text-dependent or text-independent methods. Let's compare the two.

Extracting features

Voice recognition begins with a subject uttering a short passphrase or sequence of numbers. To extract the features of the voice, the system can be either text dependent or text independent.

First let's outline a constrained—or text-dependent method.

Constraining text

When using a text-dependent system, the subject must repeat a fixed phrase. The system can interact with the subject in one of two ways, as follows:

- The system can use a pre-programmed phrase. In this case, the subject might be prompted to recite the following: *My voice is my passport.*

- The subject selects a personal question and then provides the answer, which adds an additional verification factor. For example, the system might prompt the subject by asking: *What is your favorite vacation spot?* The subject might answer: *The beach.* The match is text dependent as the speaker must say the correct phrase.

Text-dependent systems are constrained to a predefined phrase and use HMMs to represent the various states of each sound made by the subject. When using text-dependent mode, the sample is generally matched using template-matching techniques that detect specific patterns.

Next, let's describe using an unconstrained or text-independent method.

Unconstrained input

In contrast, a text-independent system provides an unconstrained mode, which can recognize the speaker no matter what is being said. These systems use a **Gaussian Mixture Model** (**GMM**), which generates various states that characterize the individual sounds and represent the unique speech behavior of the individual.

As shown in the following screenshot, we see the characteristics of the speech patterns of three subjects. Using a GMM, the unique characteristics such as loudness, pitch, and inflection present as a unique pattern:

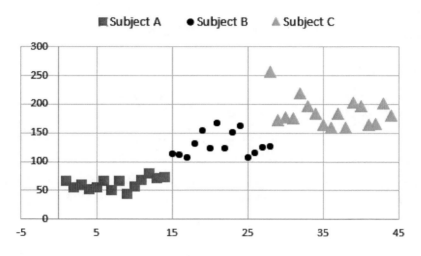

Figure 8.10 – GMM

Although text-independent systems are unconstrained, they can be challenged when dealing with a variety of inflections and accents.

Some advanced systems will use a combination of both text-dependent and text-independent input, which might work in the following manner:

- The system will first present the subject with a text-dependent login to answer a personal question for verification.

- The subject will then be presented with a text-independent phrase to determine liveness.

After the subject inputs their voice sample, in either a text-dependent or text-independent manner, the system will extract the voice features. Afterward, the data then moves to create a template to be stored in the system database.

Now, let's take a look at how systems match the templates to determine whether there is a match.

Matching the samples

When the subject enrolls, he or she can then use the system to identify or authenticate. VRT can use either template matching or feature analysis.

Template matching is the least complex method and is used in text-dependent systems. After the subject supplies a sample to the system, the sample is compared against a stored template in the database. If the threshold for a match is met, the speaker is then verified. Using template matching has an accuracy rate of about 98%; however, this is limited to the template that must be matched.

Feature analysis is a more advanced matching technique that is used in text-independent systems. Using this method pulls the unique features of the voice by using methods such as GMMs, and then comparing the sample with the template. Using feature analysis has a lower accuracy rate than template matching; however, it is not constrained to match a predefined template.

The submitted sample is compared with the stored template. If there is a high degree of similarity, the sample will be considered an acceptable match.

Over time, VRT and speech recognition have shown promise. As a result, governments, academia, and industry leaders all work together to improve the technology, as described next.

Improving the technology

Over time, VRT has improved, and efforts have been made to encourage development and interoperability. In VRT, technology developers can use the **Speaker Verification Application Program Interface (SVAPI)** to provide interoperability amongst vendors and applications.

In addition to standards, the **National Institute of Standards and Technology (NIST)** speech group actively promotes the study of speech processing technology. Since 1996, NIST has been hosting an annual Speaker Recognition Evaluation to evaluate and quantify select systems. This annual program has been instrumental in propelling advances in technology and improvements, in the algorithms used in speech processing.

Next, let's explore the many ways VRT might be used in our world today.

Employing voice recognition

Voice recognition provides an attractive alternative to other access-control methods. A password, token, or **personal identification number (PIN)** can be lost, forgotten, or stolen. However, when using VRT, if you need to gain access into a system, just utter the suggested dialog when prompted, and, if approved, you are granted access.

In today's complex environments, fraud prevention is a necessary element to prevent unauthorized access to data and resources. Let's review some of the ways VRT can minimize fraud.

Preventing fraud

When accessing resources over the internet, we generally provide a way to identify and authenticate. Many organizations require MFA. MFA requires two or more authentication factors, such as a password and a biometric scan, and can improve the security of a transaction.

Let's examine how using VRT can help establish your identity and secure transactions.

Proving identity

In most cases, when we interact with our phone or Fintech to reach a company for assistance, we must prove our identity in some way. For example, when calling a credit card company to check a balance, the credit card company will need to determine whether you are a customer. To prove that you are a customer, you may be required to enter a PIN or a password. Using VRT can provide a higher level of security than using a password or PIN, both of which can be forgotten or stolen.

In addition to ensuring identification and authentication, VRT can provide proof of life when identifying the speaker. Using voice recognition with Fintech is ideal, as a mobile device has all the necessary components to capture a voice, and no additional hardware is required.

Many of us are using Fintech for mobile banking, which has improved the customer experience. However, with this convenience comes added risk. Let's next look at how VRT can help secure our online transactions.

Securing transactions

Using a client's voice as an identifier holds the promise of enhanced security. Large companies are improving their systems to authenticate thousands of clients a day, in several different languages. In addition, using VRT as part of an MFA solution can satisfy regulatory requirements such as the **Payment Services Directive 2** (**PSD2**) and the **Payment Card Industry Data Security Standard** (**PCI DSS**).

Some companies are starting to implement VRT as a *voice signature*, to create a legally binding document and authorize financial transactions. Similar to a digital signature, a voice signature provides non-repudiation, and will authenticate a financial transaction.

We can use our voice to establish our identity or make a payment, but there are other benefits, such as saving time. Let's see how VRT can save time and improve our workflow.

Saving time

When calling a company to get assistance, most organizations require a process called **Identification and Verification (ID&V)**. The process can take as little as under a minute, to a longer and more complex ID&V taking a minute and a half.

Next let's outline how VRT can let you bypass the lengthy security questions from an agent.

Streamlining authentication

Businesses are finding voice recognition attractive as, instead of an agent, they only need an IVR. The customer must first register with the system. Then, when they call, the IVR gathers the required information, authenticates the user, and then connects the user to the appropriate department.

For example, a contact center is used by companies to assist their customers with one of the following:

- Queries related to payment issues
- Technical assistance
- Complaints or compliments
- Complex issues related to a product or service they have purchased

Using voice recognition for ID&V will save time and money, for both customers and the agent. In addition, VRT can improve the customer experience, as the client will have less frustration in answering numerous questions before actually getting assistance.

Using VRT can also be used to manage a large workforce, as we'll see next.

Managing the workforce

Managing numerous employees in a large organization can be challenging. Using voice recognition can provide an optimal solution in workforce management, to confirm not only identity but also presence.

For example, instead of using a badge to check in and out of rooms and buildings, employees can use their voice to verify they have arrived and are ready to begin work. In addition, once an employee's location is verified, they can easily be located in case of an emergency.

In a large distributed workforce, VRT can also improve personnel absenteeism because someone must identify using their voice, and hence VRT can also reduce fraud. VRT prevents the ability to cover for a coworker who clocks in using a time card on someone's behalf.

Using voice recognition in healthcare facilities can improve and secure a patient's experience, as outlined next.

Obtaining healthcare

Similar to a call center, patients must provide ID&V when calling a doctor's office or other healthcare facility.

In these facilities, guidelines are stricter, as most healthcare facilities must adhere to regulations. Regulations include the **Health Information Technology for Economic and Clinical Health (HITECH)** Act, and the **Health Insurance Portability and Accountability Act (HIPAA)**. Any violation of privacy can result in hefty fines.

Using voice recognition for ID&V in the healthcare arena will provide an additional layer of security. In addition to patients using voice recognition, the technology can also be used by healthcare professionals—for example, when calling a pharmacy to order medication. VRT can enable doctors and nurses to identify themselves by voice and provide a secure, efficient experience for all parties.

As with any biometric, there are benefits along with drawbacks. Next, let's take a look at some of the positive and negative factors to be considered when considering VRT.

Examining the pros and cons of VRT

Using our voice as a biometric identifier seems almost natural, and there are no negative connotations associated with voice recognition. Some of the industry leaders using VRT include financial services, healthcare providers, and governments. With the benefits of any technology, we must also consider the drawbacks.

Let's compare some of the pros and cons of voice biometrics, starting with the benefits.

Comparing advantages

Using our voice to gain access to systems has several advantages. In most cases, the use of additional hardware or software is not required. Most of what is needed for VRT is currently in place, such as the speakers and microphones that are built in to mobile devices.

The user does not need to touch any special equipment, making VRT non-invasive. Using your voice to authenticate feels natural, as in most cases, you only need to speak into the phone. As opposed to fingerprints, which may be associated with law enforcement, voice biometrics currently has no negative connotations.

VRT is an easy-to-use, emerging technology that can be used while online and on mobile devices, and has a high level of user acceptance. The use of voice biometrics is beginning to find a home in many environments as a safe, contactless alternative to high-touch biometrics such as fingerprint scanners.

Along with the positives, there are a few other issues we must consider when using VRT, as outlined next.

Considering the drawbacks

Although voice recognition is becoming a popular biometric, there are some concerns. One is in regard to one of the optimal biometric characteristics—permanence. A biometric that has permanence does not change, or changes only minimally over time. The human voice does not have permanence. Voice recognition is a behavioral biometric, which generally changes over time as we age.

The voice can be affected by illness, fatigue, or other factors that can lead to slurred or garbled speech. In addition, background noise can affect VRT, along with issues during data transmission.

VRT is not recommended for physical access control to a facility. One reason for this is because of environmental issues, such as extraneous sounds that can interfere with the sound quality. Another concern is the potential for someone to eavesdrop during the process, and hear your secret passphrase.

If the voice template is stored, there may be additional storage requirements, as a voice template can be large.

Voice biometrics is effective with identification and authentication on a small scale, such as using VRT to gain access to a mobile device. However, voice biometrics has a lower accuracy than other biometrics. In addition, when using VRT, you can become a victim of a presentation or spoofing attack, as described next.

Spoofing the voice

When spoofing someone's voice, an attacker uses one of several methods. Methods to spoof or mimic someone's voice include the following:

- Using a pre-recorded voice or imitating someone

- Using specialized software to convert or synthesize speech

> **Important note**
>
> Voice conversion or speech synthesis software is freely available. An example can be found here, where you can try a couple of samples: `https://www.descript.com/lyrebird-ai`.

Being able to duplicate someone's voice would negate any of the benefits of VRT. To prevent spoofing attacks, vendors use liveness detection to determine whether the subject is alive or is a recording. To prevent someone from using a pre-recorded voice sample, the subject may be required to repeat a randomly generated phrase, such as *apple—orange—grape*.

Other detection algorithms can monitor the natural or dynamic inflection in your voice, which can't be easily recreated by a computer. Here is one solution that provides biometric authentication along with robust liveness detection: `https://www.aware.com/knomi-mobile-biometric-authentication/`.

Summary

We have taken a look at how using a voice as an identifier is a behavioral biometric, in that it represents the manner in which a subject speaks. We then reviewed the many things that can influence the way we speak, such as medical conditions and aging. We examined the advances of VRT over the years and its similarity to speech recognition. We saw how to use statistical methods such as HMM, which helps recognize speech by looking for predictive patterns to change the state.

We reviewed how a voice is digitized and transmitted and learned how performance can be impacted by transmission errors and inferior equipment. We then stepped through the process of what happens from enrollment to matching. We compared text-dependent versus text-independent methods, and then compared matching methods that use either template matching or feature analysis. Finally, we saw how using VRT to quickly provide identification and authentication can streamline the overall experience and enhance workflow. As the technology matures, the applications of voice biometrics will only continue to grow.

In the next chapter, we'll take a look at some of the lesser-known biometrics that are in use today or have the potential to be used in the future. We will evaluate biometrics such as hand measurements, along with keyboard dynamics and signatures, which all provide measurable unique characteristics. You'll see how using gait recognition can be a viable biometric for large venues such as the Super Bowl, as it is a passive biometric. Although not used as much, you'll see why using **deoxyribonucleic acid** (**DNA**) and the retina provides a strong spoof-proof biometric when security is imperative. Finally, you'll learn how other identifiers such as tattoos, scars, and ears can also be used to identify individuals.

Questions

Now, it's time to check your knowledge. Select the best response to the following questions, and then check your answers, found in the *Assessment* section at the end of the book:

1. Even though voice recognition is a behavioral biometric, there is a great deal of _____ elements that can influence the way we speak.

    a. analog

    b. spectral

    c. physiological

    d. discrete

2. When we speak, we create a(n) _____ signal, which is represented as a waveform.

    a. analog

    b. spectral

    c. digital

    d. discrete

3. Using the Hidden _____ Model statistical approach in analyzing speech improves the ability of the algorithm to recognize words.

    a. analog

    b. spectral

    c. digital

    d. Markov

4. Wideband transmission expands or widens the frequencies from 50 Hz to _____ kHz.

   a. 3.4

   b. 7

   c. 11

   d. 20

5. A (n) _____ voice recognition system is unconstrained and can recognize the speaker no matter what is being said.

   a. analog

   b. spectral

   c. text-independent

   d. Markov

6. Since 1996, _____ has been hosting an annual Speaker Recognition Evaluation to evaluate and quantify select systems.

   a. NIST

   b. IEEE

   c. SANS

   d. Markov

7. Some companies are starting to implement VRT as a "Voice _____" to create a legally binding document and authorize financial transactions.

   a. signature

   b. template

   c. spectrum

   d. Markov

Further reading

- *Texas Instruments, Inc. Speech and Image Understanding Lab* report: `https://ntrs.nasa.gov/archive/nasa/casi.ntrs.nasa.gov/19890010509.pdf`

- A report on how to use a voice to predict fatigue: `https://www.frontiersin.org/articles/10.3389/fbioe.2015.00124/full`

- The online version of WASP: `https://www.speechandhearing.net/laboratory/wasp/`

- Report from the *2018 NIST Speaker Recognition Evaluation*: `https://www.isca-speech.org/archive/Interspeech_2019/pdfs/1351.pdf`

9
Considering Alternate Biometrics

Many of us are familiar with the more common biometrics, such as face, fingerprint, and iris recognition. However, each of us has other unique features we can explore as alternate biometrics. In this chapter, we'll take a look at the lesser-known biometrics that are in use today or have the potential to be used in the future.

We'll learn how we can use other elements of the hand as a biometric identifier. In addition to using our hand to obtain fingerprints, we can also use palm prints, hand geometry, and palm veins. We'll then cover how we can use gait recognition, or the way we walk, as a viable biometric. You'll see how gait recognition is a passive biometric that is optimal for threat management in large venues such as malls and arenas.

Although not used as much, you'll see why using **deoxyribonucleic acid (DNA)** and the retina provides strong spoof-proof biometrics when security is imperative. We'll also see how keystroke dynamics and an individual's signature can be evaluated to provide identification and authentication, as both have unique characteristics. Finally, we'll learn how our ears can be a possible, yet lesser-known biometric, and we'll see how law enforcement uses tattoos and scars to aid in identifying individuals.

In this chapter, we're going to cover the following main topics:

- Using our hands to authenticate
- Measuring an individual's gait
- Comparing DNA and retinal scans
- Viewing keystroke and signature biometrics
- Using tattoos, scars, and ear biometrics

Using our hands to authenticate

When asked, most of us would gladly lend a hand to help someone in need. In the near future, you may need to present your hand to authenticate into a system.

Every human hand is unique and provides a rich source of details to aid in identifying someone. Along with using fingerprints, a well-known biometric identifier, scientists have identified other areas of the hand that can be used to identify or authenticate a subject. These methods include the following:

- Palm print technology
- Hand geometry
- Palm vein recognition

Let's start with a lesser-known biometric, palm print recognition.

Scanning the palm

Scanning a palm obtains the print of a subject's palm. The technique is similar to obtaining a fingerprint, because the skin on a palm has the same type of skin as the fingertips. Once a palm is scanned, the device obtains the various features, such as ridges and valleys, along with minutiae points and textures.

Everyone's palms are unique. Each palm has several different areas, as outlined next.

Isolating regions of the palm

Although we look at our palm as a whole, there are actually different parts that make up a palm, as shown in the following screenshot:

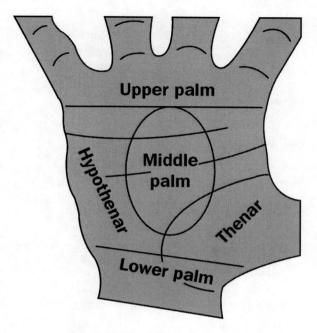

Figure 9.1 – The palm regions of the hand

The different regions of the palm include the following:

- Upper palm
- Middle palm
- Lower palm
- Hypothenar (area beneath the little finger)
- Thenar (area adjacent to the thumb)

Palm prints can provide a great deal of detail, as we'll see in the following section.

Obtaining a palm print

When a whole palm print is obtained, there are generally enough distinct details to be pulled for a sample. Using the palm provides more details when comparing a template for identification. More details can improve the accuracy of the match. However, when using palm prints, there may be problems with dryness, roughness, moisture, or scarring of the palm.

Palm prints can be used for several applications—for example, for providing access control in securing a door, or to register with an organization's attendance system. To obtain a palm print, the subject will actively scan their palm. Palm scanning devices are fairly straightforward, and work in the following manner:

1. The subject places his or her hand on a scanner.

2. The scan will capture as much of the hand as possible, including the entire palm and fingers, and create an image.

3. Once the print is obtained, the captured image is prepared to be compared with a template.

Palm prints are generally not the best choice for identification and authentication, as these systems require a fast, accurate, and reliable method for personal identification. In addition, palm print scanners are more expensive when compared with finger scanners.

However, law enforcement uses palm prints in criminal investigations. When used in conjunction with fingerprints, this can help provide a match in identifying a criminal. For serious offenses, law enforcement will capture the **major case prints** (**MCPs**). This captures all friction ridges on the hand, to include fingertips below the nail. To see an example, visit `http://www.clpex.com/images/Articles/PZ-Code.jpg`.

Another potential way to identify someone is by using hand geometry, as discussed in the following section.

Measuring the hand

Hand geometry is a physiological biometric that is based on measurements of parts of the hand to verify a person's identity. This biometric only obtains the measurements of the hand and discards other details, such as palm prints or scars.

Interest in hand geometry began in the 1980s, when commercial systems started to become available. Over the next decade, devices were put in place to restrict access to buildings, rooms, and other secure locations. A notable application was in 1996, when hand geometry was used to gain access to the Olympic villages in Atlanta.

The process for using hand geometry is as follows:

1. The subject places his or her hand on a surface or device.

2. The subject may also be required to enter a **Personal Identification Number** (**PIN**) or swipe a smart card so that the system can locate the subject's template, or as a second validator as part of **Multi-Factor Authentication** (**MFA**).

3. The image of the hand is then captured using scanning technology. In most cases, the device obtains a 3D image of the hand.

4. Once scanned, the system will measure the length, width, and height of the hand and fingers, at various measure points.

5. After the sample is obtained, the results are then compared against the stored template in the database. If the sample is a match, the subject can gain access.

Hand geometry is fast and generally takes only a few seconds. The technology is used in a variety of applications that include gaining access to factories, office buildings, and construction sites. To see an example of a hand geometry system, visit `https://www.bayometric.com/hand-geometry-recognition-biometrics/`.

Hand geometry systems generally have a high user acceptance, and can be either a peg or freeform system. These are detailed as follows:

- A peg or constrained system provides guided hand placement. When the subject interacts with the system, the pegs in the surface will restrict the ability of the hand to move about the device.

- A freeform or unconstrained system allows the subject to place their hand on the scanner in a natural manner during image acquisition.

Hand geometry is a mature technology that is non-intrusive and convenient. Studies show an individual's hand can provide enough distinct characteristics to be used for personal identification.

However, most feel that it is not considered accurate enough to satisfy the requirements of modern biometric security systems. There are other concerns related to the use of hand geometry. One drawback is that a person's hand can change due to aging or disease. In addition, hand geometry can suffer from spoofing attacks.

Both palm recognition and hand geometry systems require full contact with a scanning system; that is, someone has to place their hand on a device. Many individuals are averse to a full contact system, unless it is their own personal device. Palm vein technology offers a no-touch solution to identification, as outlined in the following section.

Using the palm veins

Underneath the skin on your palm are numerous veins. Each of our palms has a unique vascular pattern. A palm vein scan uses **near-infrared** (**NIR**) wavelengths to identify the veins in a subject's palm.

In addition to having a nearly 100% accuracy rate, using palm veins to identify and authenticate has one other key benefit. A palm vein scan is a contactless biometric solution.

While biometrics is becoming more popular in providing access control, we must be aware of user acceptability. Contactless biometrics provides a more hygienic solution, as users do not have to touch a device.

A contactless solution should be considered in applications where a large number of individuals are using the system. Applications such as biometric time clocks or doors to a facility would benefit from a palm vein reader, as the user does not have to touch anything.

To use a palm vein scan, the subject places his or her hand over the device, as shown in the following screenshot:

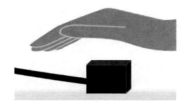

Figure 9.2 – Using a palm vein reader

Scanning the palm veins is fast, and the reader captures your vein pattern to be compared with a template in the system.

Aside from being a contactless, easy-to-use biometric, there are a few other advantages to using our palm veins as an identifier. The advantages include the following:

- Palm vein readers are able to adapt to environmental changes, such as sweating in hot humid environments.

- Because the palm vein is read and not the palm itself, this type of biometric does not have a problem with palm dryness, roughness, or scarring.

- A palm generally does not have hair or other artifacts to contend with the capture.

- Nearly 100% of individuals using palm vein technology are able to be enrolled into a system.

- Palm vein technology is contactless. As a result, it has a higher acceptance rate.

- The template for a palm vein is relatively compact, so storage requirements are not excessive.

- Using palm vein technology is spoof-resistant, as someone cannot recreate the vein pattern by using a photograph.
- Over time, there is minimal change to the palm veins. However, they can change due to injury, disease, or age.

Our hands provide several ways to identify and authenticate into a system. Along with our fingerprints, we can use our palm prints, hand geometry, and palm veins.

Another biometric that is showing signs of promise is gait recognition, which examines the way we walk, as described in the following section.

Measuring an individual's gait

Gait recognition is a behavioral biometric that identifies the manner and style of how we walk. Using a gait to identify an individual is an unobtrusive biometric that does not require the cooperation of the individual. In this section, we'll outline how gait recognition works and how this biometric can aid law enforcement in threat management.

Let's start with how we define and assess a subject's gait or stride.

Characterizing a gait

Gait recognition is a unique biometric that measures the various parameters involved when we walk. The gait cycle consists of several iterations of foot-to-surface (or heel strike) contact for the same foot.

Let's first outline what is measured when assessing our gait.

Measuring our stride

When we walk, we move through various phases, according to the position of our feet and legs. All of these movements can be measured. Phases range from the stance, through the resultant swing, acceleration, and heel strike, as shown in the following diagram:

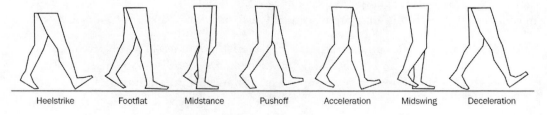

Figure 9.3 – Phases of a normal gait

The following outlines what happens during some of the phases:

1. **Footflat**: One of the subject's feet is on the ground, and the opposing foot is brought back into alignment from an extended position.

2. **Midstance**: One of the subject's feet is on the ground, and the opposing foot is lifted to begin the stride.

3. **Pushoff**: The subject's heel that was on the ground is lifted, and the opposing foot is well into the stride.

4. **Acceleration**: The subject's foot that was on the ground is lifted off the ground, and the opposing foot now begins the heel strike.

The algorithm analyzes the various movements of the stride, such as how the heel hits the ground or the angle of the leg when it is in mid-swing, in preparation of the next step. Also assessed are other elements of the gait, which include the following:

- Pace or rhythm of the stride
- Height of the foot during pushoff
- Speed and movement of the body
- Length of the stride
- Angle of the foot and hip

Prior to using gait recognition, the subject must be enrolled onto the system. The enrollment process goes through a series of observing and analyzing the pattern of foot pressure and placement. Enrollment can be active, whereby a subject is aware of the process, or passive, where a video of the subject walking is used to enroll the subject.

In order to identify someone by the way they walk, there must be a way to evaluate the stride. Next, let's see how a gait is modeled.

Modeling the characteristics

Gait recognition is more complex to evaluate, as the system must consider multiple images in sequence. Gait recognition systems generally use one of two approaches, as follows:

- **Model-based** relies on discrete gait characteristics and uses the measurements of the body, such as limb lengths, and other elements of the human structure. This method requires more processing power, as it must model and track the body.

- **Model-free** assesses the characteristics of the gait while the subject is moving. In this case, there is no model to compare. Model-free is better able to deal with elements that can affect the gait, such as footwear or carrying a large bag.

Of the two, a model-free approach is preferred, and this is more commonly used for gait recognition. The approach is simple and has improved results over a model-based approach.

With gait recognition there are some limitations on accuracy, as discussed next.

Limiting accuracy

Because gait recognition observes an individual's stride, there are certain environmental elements that can negatively affect the recognition process. These elements can include the following:

- Walking on unstable surfaces, such as grass or ceramic tiles, can result in a significant variation in the way someone walks.
- The subject is carrying something heavy, such as a purse or backpack.
- Clothing that limits the view of the gait, such as a long gown.
- Footwear that is different from the registration, such as registering in sneakers and then wearing heels on a subsequent analysis.

However, existing algorithms are sensitive to different types of clothes, illumination, and speed, and are able to adapt the analysis.

Environmental elements can affect our gait and influence the match rate. However, there are physiological changes that can alter the way we walk as well, which can affect the accuracy of the result. The following can affect the gait:

- Aging, which can cause the subject to slow his or her stride.
- A leg or back injury, as the subject may walk more carefully to avoid pain.
- Fatigue can slow the gait and affect the posture.
- Experiencing joy or excitement can quicken the gait.

As you can see, gait recognition can evaluate many elements of an individual's stride. Currently, scientists are evaluating the use of gait recognition to observe changes in a medical condition—for example, using the technology in a senior home to monitor when someone is in distress or has fallen.

Gait recognition can recognize individuals at a distance, and it is difficult to hide or spoof. As a result, law enforcement is using this for threat management, as we'll learn next.

Identifying threats

Facial recognition requires a close-up of an individual's face in order to properly identify someone. In contrast, gait recognition is a passive biometric that can observe people without their cooperation—for example, during surveillance.

Observing a gait during surveillance allows someone to be identified, even if their face is concealed. Individuals can cover their face or part of their face in several ways: by using a hat, decorative make-up, or a surgical mask.

Consequently, law enforcement is using gait recognition as a surveillance tool to monitor for threats, and is optimal in large venues such as malls and arenas.

> **Important note**
>
> To see how gait recognition is used for surveillance, visit `https://apnews.com/bf75dd1c26c947b7826d270a16e2658a`.

The benefits to using gait recognition for threat management include the following:

- Law enforcement can identify individuals from a distance of approximately 165 feet away, using low-resolution cameras.
- It is difficult to spoof by modifying the way the subject walks.

Although gait recognition shows promise, using this biometric identifier alone isn't the most reliable way to prove someone's identity. However, combining gait recognition with another biometric can help improve the recognition process, as outlined next.

Combining methods

In order to verify the identity of known criminals, agencies use a fusion of gait recognition and other biometric modalities, when available. Other biometrics can include facial recognition, tattoos, or iris recognition.

Another related technology is body recognition, which is a newer method that identifies a subject by their shape and clothing. Using body recognition can allow law enforcement to track someone's movements, even when their face becomes completely obscured.

On its own, body recognition is not an accurate identifier. However, when paired with another biometric such as gait recognition, this can be a valuable way to improve the identification of a subject.

> **Important note**
>
> To learn more about body recognition, visit `https://www.ncbi.nlm.nih.gov/pmc/articles/PMC5375891/`.

User acceptance on gait recognition for threat management is mixed. Law enforcement benefits as it aids in the apprehension of criminals; however, the public feels this is another form of surveillance.

Gait recognition has several benefits. It is an unobtrusive, contactless biometric that can be used to identify an individual. Law enforcement is seeing how the technology can aid in threat management and counterterrorism. In addition, the medical profession is seeing some value in assessing health conditions. As a result, we'll most likely see more uses of gait recognition in the future.

When the stakes are high and there is a need to accurately identify someone, the biometrics of choice are to use either a subject's DNA or a retinal scan. Let's take a look at them in the following section.

Comparing DNA and retinal scans

Two highly accurate methods to prove someone's identity are by evaluating a subject's DNA or using a retinal scan. In this section, we'll uncover just what is involved in these two forms of biometrics, along with some of the reasons we might use them.

Let's start with seeing how DNA is used to identify an individual.

Using our DNA

DNA is what makes up our genetic code. Every living being has DNA, which holds all the information required to build and maintain an animal, plant, or single-celled life form.

When evaluating DNA to identify someone, a key indicator is called a **Short Tandem Repeat (STR)**, which is examined and then compared between individuals. The **Federal Bureau of Investigation (FBI)** uses 13 core STRs, which are used in the **Combined DNA Index System (CODIS)**, a government-managed DNA database. During an evaluation using DNA, the core 13 (or more) STR sequences are chosen for comparison, as they vary from person to person.

DNA as a biometric is highly accurate. Because evaluating someone's DNA requires specialized equipment that is not available to everyone, it is difficult to spoof. When working with DNA identification technologies, the most practical applications are those dealing with providing a solid method to prove someone's identity.

Applications where DNA is used as a biometric include the following:

- Confirming or denying blood relationships, in cases such as paternity and maternity testing

- Helping aid disaster victim identification, missing persons, and human trafficking cases

- During a forensic exercise to prove whether or not someone might have been present at a crime scene

Using DNA to identify whether or not a suspect was involved in a crime is commonly done, as we'll see next.

Conducting a forensic investigation

During a forensic exercise, investigation begins by collecting evidence related to the crime scene. Evidence includes carpet fibers, tire tracks, computers, footprints, and fingerprints. In addition, investigators will also collect any biological evidence left at the scene, such as blood, hair, saliva, and skin cells, which can contain DNA evidence.

Similar to fingerprints, DNA is something a criminal might leave behind. When collected, forensic scientists can obtain DNA from the biological evidence left at a crime scene. The investigator might choose to run the sample results through CODIS, to see whether there is a match. Keep in mind that when searching CODIS, if the sample is not in the database there will not be a match.

On television and in the movies, using DNA to link a suspect to a crime is shown as a fast, simple, and foolproof method. The reality is that the process of analyzing DNA to prove someone's identity is not always simple or foolproof. However, over time, DNA technology has evolved, and scientists have created a more rapid test to establish the unique patterns of DNA. What used to take several days in a laboratory setting to obtain results can now be achieved in under 2 hours on a portable desktop unit.

Another highly accurate biometric identifier is the retina. Next, let's see why retinal scans are used to provide absolute identification.

Scanning the retina

The retina is a highly vascular area in the back of your eye. This area accepts light as it enters the eye through the pupil. The light is then converted into signals that are sent to the brain, to be interpreted as patterns and shapes.

Using the retina can provide robust identification. Much like a fingerprint, the retina is unique, even between identical twins, and remains stable throughout most of your life.

Next, let's see how we obtain an image of the subject's retina, in order to identify someone.

Obtaining a retinal image

A retinal scan uses an **infrared** (**IR**) light. The light must pass through the pupil so that the scanner can visualize the retina.

To obtain the retinal image, the subject must do the following:

- The subject must remove any glasses and situate the eye very close to the scanning device.
- Once in place, the subject must focus on a dot that is generally in the center of the visual field and remain still.
- The scanner will then capture the retina pattern. The process generally takes only a few seconds.

After the system obtains the retinal image, the algorithm determines whether there is a match in the database. If there is a match, the subject is positively identified.

Problems with retinal scans can occur if the system is unable to obtain an image of sufficient quality. Until the system captures an appropriate image, the subject may be rejected. An individual may have to try several times before getting a match.

Now, let's see how and where we use retinal scans.

Using retinal scans

Retinal scans are highly accurate and have been in use since the 1980s. Over the last several decades, numerous US government agencies have used retinal scans. Agencies include the **National Aeronautics and Space Administration** (**NASA**), the FBI, and the **Central Intelligence Agency** (**CIA**). Currently, this biometric is reserved for high-security areas and applications. Other appropriate uses can include access control for power plants, correctional facilities, and military stations.

Aside from being highly accurate, retinal scans have other benefits. Due to the nature of how the scan is obtained, this biometric is resistant to spoofing. In addition, in most cases, everyone can use a retinal scan, and the template is small, so storage requirements are easily met.

When selecting a biometric, users need to feel comfortable, and the modality must be accepted by nearly everyone. A retinal scan is one of the least used scans, as it is perceived by many to be invasive. For example, while users may feel comfortable using iris recognition, they may not agree to a retinal scan. The reason is that the two work completely differently when collecting a sample for comparison, as detailed here:

- An iris scan uses a camera at a comfortable distance.

- A retinal scan requires the user to be very close to the scanning device.

In addition to being intrusive, examining the retina can potentially identify diseases such as hypertension, diabetes, and malaria. The possibility that a medical condition may be exposed is another deterrent, and is a reason retinal scans are rarely used.

Using a subject's DNA or retinal scan is on the extreme side of biometric identification, as they are invasive and can be costly. Therefore, they are only used only on a limited basis.

In the next section, let's evaluate how typing on a keyboard or writing your signature can be used as a biometric identifier.

Viewing keystroke and signature biometrics

Many of us work on our computer, and interface with various entities in our digital world. In some cases, there is a need to verify someone's identity while working online. Two methods that can be used to verify an identity are keyboard or keystroke recognition, along with signature verification.

First, let's see how we can use our keyboard to prove our identity.

Using a keyboard

Whenever you type a string of characters, you have a unique way of hitting the keys. Keystroke dynamics is a behavioral biometric that evaluates how you type on a keyboard. This biometric identifier measures several aspects of the typing process, including the following:

- The time it takes you to press a key

- The latency between each keystroke

- How long it takes to type a string of characters

To use keystroke dynamics, the subject must first register into the system by typing between 60–180 characters. The algorithm will then build a profile of the subject for comparison. Then, when the subject is required to log in to a system, they only need to enter a short text, such as an email address, to be verified.

Keystroke dynamics is a non-invasive, natural biometric that is widely accepted. To use this biometric there is minimal training involved, and the verification process is transparent to the user.

While not universally accepted or recognized, using typing patterns to authenticate into a system can be beneficial, in a few niche applications. For example, if an office worker needs to log in to an online system, keystroke dynamics can offer a spoof-resistant method to provide a second way to identify and authenticate.

Other uses include the following:

- E-learning to verify a student is taking a test or completing lessons
- Logging in to check a bank account

Benefits to using this biometric include that there is no additional hardware required. In addition, as long as the subject has a standard keyboard, the system can be used as part of someone's normal workflow.

Drawbacks of using keystroke dynamics as a biometric include the fact that accuracy is low, and there is a limited range of applications. In addition, when using a keyboard to provide authentication, a different keyboard may influence the match rate.

Next, let's look at signature recognition, which is another method to provide authentication when online.

Analyzing a signature

Signature recognition is a biometric based on the way you sign your name. This identifier measures several aspects of the unique way you create your signature.

Two methods of signature recognition are the offline and online methods.

Offline or static signature recognition is a simple method to verify a signature, which does not assess the dynamic nature of signing your name. With an offline verification system, the subject enrolls in the system by signing his or her name. The signature, as shown in the following screenshot, is scanned and then used for comparison:

Figure 9.4 – Lisa Bock signature

Online or dynamic signature recognition extracts the more salient features of the way someone signs their name. This method takes into account variables such as the timing, pressure, velocity, and acceleration that occur when you create your signature.

> **Important note**
>
> Online signature recognition relies on the way the signature is written, instead of simply comparing the sample to a template. By analyzing the behavioral aspects of composing a signature, this provides a more robust method to provide verification.

Using a signature to authenticate is non-intrusive and difficult to forge, especially when using an online verification method. Similar to signing a check, this biometric could strengthen document authentication and minimize fraud.

As with keystroke dynamics, using a signature can provide a second authenticator, such as using a password and then a signature. This can ensure an advanced level of privacy and protection for online accounts.

Signature verification can provide an adaptable biometric identifier that can be beneficial in a variety of different applications. Applications can range from commercial use, such as signing financial documents, to using a signature to access government resources.

The costs to deploy this biometric would depend on whether or not specialized hardware is required to create the signature. In addition, signature verification can run into problems with inconsistent or trivial signatures, and the template can be large, which can result in storage concerns.

In this last section, we'll see how existing identifiers on a body can provide a few more ways to complement the identification process.

Using tattoos, scars, and ear biometrics

Today, there are several biometrics in use to identify and/or authenticate an individual. In addition to the common biometrics such as fingerprint, iris, and facial recognition, there are a few other unique features that can help positively identify someone.

In this section, we'll take a look at how tattoos, scars, and birthmarks can also be used in the identification process. In addition, we'll cover ear biometrics, a novel way to uniquely identify someone.

Let's start with a discussion on ways we can use tattoos.

Visualizing tattoos

A tattoo is a visual design or marking on the skin. To obtain a tattoo, dyes or pigments are imprinted into the dermis layer of the skin. Tattoos have been in existence for centuries, dating back to Egyptian times.

Today, over one-third of the world's population has a tattoo. Individuals that have them range in age, socio-economic status, and nationality. In addition to the diversity in the population, there is a wide range of designs, colors, and patterns.

Tattoos are obtained for a variety of reasons, including the following:

- As a result of a dare
- To recognize membership in a gang
- To honor someone they love
- For religious reasons

Tattoos can be a valuable identifier, as for the most part they are permanent. Over time, the color will fade, but the essence of the tattoo will remain. Even if the tattoo is removed, the area where it was will have a scar, which can then be used as an identifier. In addition to the tattoo itself, the location is another key factor.

Tattoos can be used to identify someone during a forensic examination. The medical examiner will search the body for identification marks, which will include scars, tattoos, and birthmarks.

In some cases, someone will provide an image of a tattoo as part of an investigation. Without more information to identify the subject, there may be a need to expand the search to locate the owner of a tattoo. Let's see how this can be accomplished.

Locating a tattoo

Because a tattoo is an image, locating the owner can be accomplished by searching for an image of the tattoo. One way to accomplish this is by comparing the work of tattoo artists. Many times, a tattoo artist will take a picture of their completed work and post the final product online, either on a web page or social media site.

Locating a tattoo using a search engine can be done with an image-based or a textual search. Once run, the search engine will display a set of images found on the internet. After the images are displayed, you can visually search for a match.

Over time, law enforcement has added tattoos to repositories that can be searched and compared to identify a suspect. The **Next Generation Identification** (**NGI**) system has expanded capabilities from fingerprints to other biometric identifiers, and includes tattoos. In addition, the state of Florida has a database with nearly a half a million tattoo records. You can download the Access database by going to this page: `http://www.dc.state.fl.us/pub/obis_request.html`. Once there, you will find a download link in the first paragraph.

Searching for a tattoo is considered an investigative lead, rather than a method to prove identification. In addition, on its own, a tattoo is not enough to verify someone's identity. However, when coupled with another identifier, such as face or fingerprint, this can be enough to prove someone's identity.

Another way to confirm someone's identity is by examining scars and birthmarks, as we'll see in the following section.

Observing scars and birthmarks

Most of us have either a scar or a birthmark somewhere on our body. Both can be enough of a distinguishing feature to help identify someone.

A scar is a mark on the skin where someone has had some type of trauma. This can be the result of an accident, burn, wound, or past surgery.

During someone's lifetime, it's not unusual for someone to get a scar. If the subject was hospitalized, there may be a record of an individual's scars that will end up on the patient's medical records. That is because, many times, when someone goes to hospital, a medical professional will mark the location of the scar on areas of the body.

Birthmarks are markings that are present at birth or develop shortly after someone is born. These distinctive marks can be found anywhere on the body and can range from small marks to large spreading birthmarks, and can also range in color. It is common for physicians to photograph a large or elaborate birthmark for later comparison. In some cases, the birthmark is easily recognized, such as a port wine stain on someone's face. In other cases, the scar is concealed, in a less-than-obvious location on someone's body.

Both scars and birthmarks can be used in combination with other identifiers, such as DNA or fingerprints, to positively identify someone.

When we think of what uniquely identifies us, we may not consider the ear as a biometric identifier. However, researchers feel there are enough specific and unique features of the ear to be used to identify someone, as we'll see in the following section.

Assessing the ear

The shape of someone's ear is a physiological biometric that is not widely recognized. However, the ear has many of the desired qualities of a biometric, including the following:

- **Uniqueness and universal**: Every one of our ears is unique, and nearly everyone has at least one ear.

- **Permanent**: The ear changes in size and shape in children up to around 8 years old, and then again in adults over 70. Other than these two times, the ear doesn't change that much.

- **Performance**: Ear biometrics can be evaluated using similar algorithms used in facial recognition and can provide reliable and consistently correct results.

- **Collectable**: Ear biometrics can suffer from issues related to lighting, head position, and artifacts such as hair and jewelry. However, the ear is not very large and will result in a small template, with minimal storage requirements.

- **Acceptable**: Obtaining an image of an ear is similar to taking a picture. It's fairly non-invasive; however, the subject may need to cooperate by holding their hair back or removing jewelry.

- **Able to avoid circumvention**: Depending upon the method, a high-quality image could be used as a presentation attack. However, with 3D imaging available, this can result in less effective spoofing attacks.

The study of using the ear as a biometric began in 1948, when *Alfred Iannarelli*, a forensic science consultant, began to study the ear. Iannarelli proposed each human ear was unique and could be included in the identification process. In 1964, he published a book, *Ear Identification (Forensic Identification Series),* that described his classification method. Over time, he amassed a collection of over 10,000 ear images and published a second edition in 1989.

Using the ear has advantages, which include the following:

- **Position**: The ear is centered in the middle of the side of the subject's face, so it is easy to obtain an image without requiring the subject to move in line with the camera.

- **Passive capture**: An image of the ear can be obtained from a distance, in some cases without the cooperation of the subject.

In most cases, the ear is generally uniform in color, with minimal variations. Once the ear image is captured, the algorithm will derive the features. When looking at the ear, you'll see that it has a couple of interesting parts, such as the outer ear and ear lobe. But in general, the system will attempt to identify the ear as a whole.

Common features in ear shape identification include the helix, foseta, antitrago, and the lobe, as shown in the following diagram:

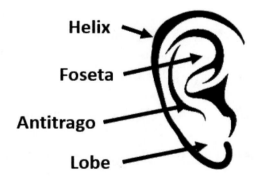

Figure 9.5 – Anatomy of the human ear

When used as a biometric identifier, the ear image is captured using a camera, and then processed to be compared with a template. As with the face, accuracy can suffer when there is variation in lighting or angles.

The shape of the outer ear can provide a unique biometric. However, the inner ear canal can also be used as a way for a subject to be identified, as discussed next.

Using sound as an identifier

As an alternative to an image of the outer ear, researchers have found a way to identify a subject by using sound waves generated by the ear canal.

The ear canal is the channel from the outer ear to the ear drum. This technique uses a 1-second sound that is inaudible to humans, to determine the unique shape of a subject's ear canal. The method works in the following manner:

1. The sound is generated into someone's ear.

2. As the sound waves move through the ear canal, this produces a unique signature.

3. The sound wave signature is captured by a microphone. This then becomes the subject's biometric identifier.

This identifier can be used in place of a password or fingerprint to unlock a mobile device.

> **Important note**
> To learn more, visit `https://www.sciencedaily.com/releases/2019/09/190918184504.htm`.

As you can see, the ear has a couple of unique features. However, as a single biometric, the ear may not be a viable solution, but a complement to other biometrics.

Summary

In addition to the commonly known biometrics, such as iris or fingerprint recognition, we can now see that each person has many other unique identifiers. In this chapter, we learned how several elements of a hand, such as the palm and hand geometry, can be used to provide identification. We then saw how palm vein recognition can provide a more robust, contactless biometric that can be used in a variety of applications.

By now, you can see how gait recognition can assist in identifying someone, even if we can't see their face. As a result, gait recognition can be used as a passive biometric that is optimal in large venues such as malls as a tool for threat management.

We then saw how using two biometrics, DNA and retinal scans, are strong methods to identify someone when security is imperative. In addition, you can now appreciate how using keystroke dynamics and signature verification can complement a PIN or password when interacting online. Finally, we saw how law enforcement uses tattoos and scars to aid in identifying individuals. We also saw how our ears can be a possible, yet lesser-known biometric.

In the next chapter, we move from learning about the various biometrics to what should be considered when implementing a biometric solution. We'll apply our knowledge of biometric technology to see why it's important to provide a practical biometric solution that is acceptable and also has appropriate hygiene. We'll then evaluate some of the factors involved when selecting a biometric (including price, accuracy, affordability, speed, and efficiency) in a large-scale implementation.

Questions

Now, it's time to check your knowledge. Select the best response to the following questions, and then check your answers, found in the *Assessment* section at the end of the book:

1. Interest in hand geometry technology began in the _____ when commercial systems started to become available to the general public.

    a. 1930s

    b. 1960s

    c. 1980s

    d. 2000s

2. A _____ scan uses NIR wavelengths to identify the veins in a subject's palm.

    a. palm print

    b. fingerprint

    c. palm vein

    d. retinal

3. When assessing a gait, there are several phases. _____ is when one of the subject's feet is on the ground, and the opposing foot is lifted to begin the stride.

    a. footflat

    b. acceleration

    c. pushoff

    d. midstance

4. When evaluating DNA to identify someone, a key indicator is called a(n) _____, which is examined and then compared between individuals.

    a. STR

    b. midstance

    c. CODIS

    d. retina

5. _____signature recognition takes into account variables such as timing, pressure, velocity, and acceleration. This method is capable of extracting the more salient features of the way someone signs their name.

    a. offline

    b. online

    c. coded

    d. marked

6. Common features in ear shape identification include the _____, foseta, antitrago, and the lobe.

    a. helix

    b. marley

    c. outer ring

    d. Markov

7. In addition to being intrusive, a(n) _____scan can potentially identify diseases such as hypertension, diabetes, and malaria.

    a. palm vein

    b. ear

    c. palm print

    d. retinal

Further reading

- To read more on hand geometry, visit `https://www.fbi.gov/file-repository/about-us-cjis-fingerprints_biometrics-biometric-center-of-excellences-hand-geometry.pdf`.

- To get more information on gait recognition, check out this article: `https://arxiv.org/pdf/1903.10744.pdf`.

- Visit the following to read a study on a potential application of ear biometrics: `https://bmcmedinformdecismak.biomedcentral.com/articles/10.1186/s12911-019-0833-9`.

Section 3 – Deploying a Large-Scale Biometric System

In this section, we'll analyze a biometric system for usability and accuracy, and step through the process of implementation, through testing and deployment. We'll also learn about the many practical applications of biometrics in use today, and wrap up with a discussion of privacy concerns.

This part of the book comprises the following chapters:

- *Chapter 10, Selecting the Right Biometric*
- *Chapter 11, Integrating the Biometric System*
- *Chapter 12, Testing and System Deployment*
- *Chapter 13, Discovering Practical Biometric Applications*
- *Chapter 14, Addressing Privacy Concerns*

10
Selecting the Right Biometric

Any decision where multiple stakeholders are involved requires a holistic approach. Deciding on what type of biometric solution to implement is no exception and can be a difficult process. In this chapter, we'll outline the importance of focusing on the clients that will use the system and their needs, throughout the selection process. We'll cover why it's important for the team to gather system requirements, in order to determine what is necessary for the system to be successful. We'll also outline why it's important to select a biometric solution that focuses on the end user, and how they interface with the system. By doing this, you'll learn how making the right choice can improve the overall efficiency, effectiveness, and successful adoption of the system.

While biometrics can be instrumental in providing access control and improving security, there is also value in implementing a practical solution. You'll understand that there are many different types of biometric systems. You'll appreciate why selecting a contactless biometric system that provides a more sanitary solution can be a better option. We'll then cover why it's important to select a biometric system that can accurately determine a match and prevent spoofing.

We'll also cover the importance of selecting a biometric that is both acceptable and has no negative connotations and that can accurately and effectively identify a broad range of individuals. We'll then outline, in addition to accuracy and affordability, why it's important to provide speed and efficiency in a large-scale authentication environment. Finally, you'll get a better understanding of how different technologies can vary in price, and also learn ways to make an appropriate selection while adhering to your budget.

In this chapter, we're going to cover the following main topics:

- Ensuring usability

- Guaranteeing accuracy

- Providing speed and efficiency

- Selecting a cost-effective solution

Ensuring usability

With the ongoing threat of cyber-attacks, many businesses are continuously seeking to strengthen their security posture. Organizations enforce policies to control access for anyone that interacts with their system resources.

To prevent unauthorized users from gaining access to a resource, most systems will require individuals to identify and authenticate themselves in some way.

The methods for doing this include using passwords, PINs, smart cards, and biometric authentication. Many organizations feel that using one solution is not enough and choose to implement **multi-factor authentication** (**MFA**) to improve the security of their system resources. MFA requires two or more authentication factors, such as a password and a biometric scan, or a PIN and a smart card.

Companies seeking solutions to reduce the risk of a data breach are discovering the value in using biometric technology as part of an overall security solution. To make the most appropriate decision, a necessary step is to gather requirements. Conducting a requirements analysis exercise will define the nature of the application, as well as the reasons for its implementation.

It's good practice for an organization to follow a structured plan when implementing a biometric solution. In this section, we'll outline the steps to take to develop a usable system, as well as the importance of clearly defining the business requirements. We'll then take a look at focusing on the end user's needs, such as age, experience, and average body type, while selecting a system. Let's start by exploring the process of developing a system.

Developing the system

When planning a system, it's common to meet with all the stakeholders that may be involved with the development and the subsequent use of the application. Stakeholders include IT staff, managers, users, and vendors. They generally move through a process called the **system development life cycle (SDLC)**. As shown in the following diagram, the main phases of the SDLC are **Plan**, **Analyze**, **Design**, **Implement**, and **Maintain**:

Figure 10.1 – The SDLC

The general purpose of each of these stages is as follows:

1. **Plan**: Once the project has been given the green light to proceed, the planning phase begins. Generally, this phase goes through a couple of key steps:

    a. Gather the functional and desired requirements of the proposed system from all key stakeholders, such as software, hardware, and training.

    b. Outline the SDLC management plan, from inception to implementation.

2. **Analyze**: This phase takes a closer look at the system requirements in order to determine possible limitations and details. This step helps stakeholders get a better perspective on what was in place so that they can clearly define how things will be improved by a new system.

3. **Design**: This phase translates the requirements into an appropriate solution. All the different aspects of the system are outlined with as much detail as possible. These details describe the methods used to input and store data, processing requirements, and ways to output the information. Other considerations include how to interface with existing systems, onboarding and training new users, and documentation on how to use the system.

4. **Implement**: The new or enhanced system is installed in the production environment. This phase will go through a couple of steps, as follows:

   a. Prior to fully implementing the system, a series of tests are performed with a small group of users. At this point, any bugs or outstanding issues are addressed.

   b. After successful testing is complete, the process moves to the full implementation of the system. This step will include training the users, importing data, and outlining the security and recovery procedures.

5. **Maintain**: Once in place, ongoing maintenance is required to keep the system functional, secure, and up to date with the latest software.

While all these phases are equally important, the one process that will allow all stakeholders to have a voice in this decision is describing the requirements. Let's take a look.

Outlining requirements

Once the decision to implement a biometric system has been approved, a key step is to discover what requirements must be met in order for the system to be successful.

Requirements can be either functional or non-functional, as described in the following points:

- A **functional requirement** defines a task or function a system must be able to complete. For example, the system must be able to obtain the fingerprint of a client's right index finger.

- A **non-functional requirement** defines how something should work in terms of variables such as performance or reliability. For example, a match decision must be returned within 3 seconds.

Non-functional requirements *complement* the functional requirements and should be fully outlined as they can impact the quality and effectiveness of the system. If the non-functional requirements are not properly defined and/or met, this can adversely impact the **total cost of ownership** (**TCO**).

Requirements analysis is an exercise that establishes what is necessary for the system to be successful. Any requirements must be relevant, measurable, and provide enough detail so that they can be implemented properly.

Gathering system requirements can take anywhere from a few months to over a year. However, completing this important step prior to making a decision about whether to purchase will ensure you select a solution that is in line with the needs of the business. To read more on gathering requirements, visit `https://www.jamasoftware.com/blog/how-long-do-requirements-take/`.

So that you can view the many considerations and elements of the SDLC, we'll review a high-level example of a project plan in the next section.

Stepping through a sample project

When planning a biometric implementation, the project will move through several phases. The following figure represents a scaled down, high-level plan used to develop a biometric system:

ID	Task Name	Duration	Start	Finish	Predecessors
1	Sample Biometric Project Implementation	166 days	Mon 07/13/20	Mon 03/01/21	
2	Initiation	11 days	Mon 01/04/21	Mon 01/18/21	
3	Develop Project Charter	10 days	Mon 01/04/21	Fri 01/15/21	
4	Scope Statement	3 days	Mon 01/04/21	Wed 01/06/21	
5	Milestones	2 days	Thu 01/07/21	Fri 01/08/21	4
6	Business Case	2 days	Mon 01/11/21	Tue 01/12/21	5
7	Funding Details	3 days	Wed 01/13/21	Fri 01/15/21	6
8	Stakeholder Identification	1 day	Mon 01/18/21	Mon 01/18/21	7
9	Planning	14 days	Mon 01/18/21	Thu 02/04/21	
10	Project Management Plan	2 days	Mon 01/18/21	Tue 01/19/21	3
11	Requirements	5 days	Wed 01/20/21	Tue 01/26/21	10
12	System Design	5 days	Wed 01/27/21	Tue 02/02/21	11
13	Test Plan	2 days	Wed 02/03/21	Thu 02/04/21	12
14	Training Plan	1 day	Wed 01/27/21	Wed 01/27/21	12SS
15	Implementation and Cutover Plan	1 day	Wed 02/03/21	Wed 02/03/21	12
16	Support Plan	1 day	Thu 02/04/21	Thu 02/04/21	15
17	Execution	166 days	Mon 07/13/20	Mon 03/01/21	
18	System Build and Directory Integration	10 days	Fri 02/05/21	Thu 02/18/21	9
19	Factory Acceptance Testing	1 day	Fri 02/19/21	Fri 02/19/21	18
20	Issue Remediation	3 days	Mon 02/22/21	Wed 02/24/21	19
21	On-Site Installation	2 days	Thu 02/25/21	Fri 02/26/21	20
22	Site Acceptance Testing	1 day	Mon 03/01/21	Mon 03/01/21	21
23	Training	2 days	Mon 07/13/20	Tue 07/14/20	
24	Authentication Enrollment	3 days	Wed 07/15/20	Fri 07/17/20	23
25	User Acceptance Testing	2 days	Mon 07/20/20	Tue 07/21/20	24
26	Issue Remediation	2 days	Wed 07/22/20	Thu 07/23/20	25
27	Cutover or Begin Parallel Operations	1 day	Fri 07/24/20	Fri 07/24/20	26
28	Closing	5 days	Mon 07/27/20	Fri 07/31/20	
29	Lessons Learned Documentation	3 days	Mon 07/27/20	Wed 07/29/20	27
30	Transition to Support	1 day	Thu 07/30/20	Thu 07/30/20	29
31	Close Implementation	1 day	Fri 07/31/20	Fri 07/31/20	30
32	Operational Support	1 day	Mon 08/03/20	Mon 08/03/20	
33	Analyze Thresholds and Adjust	1 day	Mon 08/03/20	Mon 08/03/20	31
34	Begin Maintenance and Monitoring	1 day	Mon 08/03/20	Mon 08/03/20	31

Figure 10.2 – Sample biometric project plan

In this example, you can see that the column headers are as follows:

- **Task Name**: This is the name of the assigned job. When planning a project, you will take a large, complex project and break it into smaller, more manageable tasks. For example, if we look at the task, **Develop Project Charter**, we will see several related tasks listed underneath, each of which must be completed:

  a. **Scope Statement**

  b. **Milestones**

  c. **Business Case**

  d. **Funding Details**

- **Duration**: This is a best guess estimation regarding how long it will take to complete the task.

- **Start**: This is when the task begins.

- **Finish**: This is when the task must be completed.

- **Predecessors**: These identify what must be complete before the task can be started. For example, the **System Design** task has **11** as a predecessor. This means that before you can begin the task, you must complete task **11**, which is specified as **Requirements**.

Keep in mind that, when implementing an enterprise solution, there may be 300 or more tasks. However, this is a good example of what might be involved when you're planning to implement a biometric system within an organization.

> **Important Note**
>
> This sample plan was provided by *Roger Konecny*, senior director of Biometric Systems Integration and Delivery at *NEC Corporation of America*.

When designing a solution, the user is key in the ultimate success of the system. Not keeping the user in mind can result in improper use and errors. In the next section, we'll take a look at the importance of focusing on the user when selecting a solution.

Focusing on the end user

Many times, the focus of selecting a system is based on technical aspects such as reliability, speed, and accuracy. However, an appropriate system selection should include the user. Users respond well to an intuitive, user-friendly system that allows them to move through the process with ease.

If you focus entirely on the technical aspects, you are missing nearly half of the equation. Careful consideration needs to be given to the end users as they are the ones that will interact with the system.

A properly implemented system that is universally accessible and can be used by all audiences can improve user satisfaction. While we can't tailor a solution to everyone, we can focus on the greatest needs for the demographics of the cohort.

A user-centered design includes several considerations. Let's start with the age, experience, and ability of the average user.

Considering age and experience

When assessing user needs, you'll want to take the average age of the user into consideration. Is the population that will use the system mostly older or younger? Younger adults tend to adapt more readily to technology, with minimal modifications. In contrast, many older individuals can be resistant to using new technology, for fear of making a mistake. In addition, some older individuals may take longer to move through the system.

Education and experience will be a factor as well. Inexperienced users may struggle with or fear new technology. For example, migrant or temporary workers, who have not had to use any form of access control in the past, might struggle with, or be wary of the process.

To overcome the limitations that can occur because of age and experience, you'll want to provide adequate feedback. Let's explore this concept.

Providing feedback

The system should provide adequate feedback that is clear, intuitive, and uses symbols, colors, and icons so that it is easily understood by all.

While evaluating the system, think about the following questions:

- When approaching the system, will users understand what actions they should take?
- Will the user instinctively know how they should position themselves?
- How will the user know when the capture has completed successfully?
- What happens if the scan or capture fails?

As these are real concerns, make sure the design provides sufficient feedback. This feedback will help the user know what steps to take during the capture process. Types of feedback can include the following:

- Posters or signs with simple, easy-to-read instructions should be placed in the proper location and at an appropriate height.

- Feedback for a complete or incomplete scan should be a combination of audio and visual prompts.

Age and experience are important factors. In addition, you'll want to make sure the system provides the appropriate methods so that you can easily access and interact with the system across a wide population. We'll explore this next.

Designing for the body

When creating things where people will interact with objects such as cars, buildings, and furniture, a good design takes *anthropometrics* into account, or the study of standard bodily measurements. *Anthropometrics* are used so that users can interact effectively with objects and systems. For example, if we take the height of a facial recognition system and think about where this will be used, we might consider the average height of the local user.

If we compare the average height of an adult male in two countries, we will find the following:

- In the United States, the average height of a male is 5'9".

- In Bahrain, the average height of a male is 5'5".

Taking that information into consideration could be instrumental in where to place the camera.

Another consideration in good design is accessibility. This examines what provisions are necessary to address the needs of all individuals. Accessibility means that most users will be able to successfully interact with the system.

This can include the following:

- Someone who is visually or hearing-impaired

- An individual that has a language barrier

- A person who uses a wheelchair

When incorporating these characteristics, there is a better chance the system will be more universally acceptable, effective, and efficient. This will, in turn, increase throughput and reduce errors.

In addition to designing for the body, we must also look at the psychological aspects of the system and provide for the user's sense of wellbeing. One of the considerations when deploying a large-scale biometric system should include the user's perceived sense of security in providing a contactless solution. We'll discuss this next.

Providing a contactless solution

Today, more and more individuals are concerned about getting a disease from touching an object, such as a countertop, doorknob, or handrail. This is a realistic concern as ordinary objects may have the residuals of an infectious agent, such as a virus, bacteria, or fungus, on them. As a result, when deciding on a biometric solution, many feel a more desirable option is a contactless solution.

Several options for contactless biometrics are available and include the following:

- Facial and iris recognition
- Finger and palm vein
- Voice and gait recognition

Contactless biometrics provide a minimally intrusive, sanitary solution, and are appealing in several ways. Because the device does not need to be touched, a contactless solution protects the health of the subject. In addition, there is less upkeep. This is because this type of biometric, such as a hand geometry system, must be cleaned and adjusted often as a result of everyday use.

Contactless biometric solutions are already making inroads in several industries, such as the airline industry and healthcare:

- The airline industry has been utilizing biometrics for several years to streamline the passenger experience.
- The healthcare industry is seeing value in providing a secure authentication solution for the care providers.

For a biometric solution to be practical, it must be designed with the user in mind. However, we must also ensure that the system will return accurate results. We'll explore this concept in the following section.

Guaranteeing accuracy

When selecting a biometric, the design decision is based on a number of factors. When looking over the product specifications, you'll see a list of the benefits and features. Details can include how it interacts with the users, system requirements, and product capabilities.

One key factor is to determine how accurate the selected system is under varying conditions. It's important to provide acceptable error rates, but also be resistant to spoofing. The team should review the product specifications to understand the true nature of the product. In addition, the specifications should provide reassurance that the quality and standards are in line with the business requirements. This is particularly important if the biometrics are intended for government **identification** (**ID**) solutions, such as the **International Civil Aviation Organization** (**ICAO**).

Let's start by discussing the ways a biometric system provides the correct decision when determining a match.

Ensuring precise results

When selecting a biometric solution, precision is a primary concern for many. Biometric devices go through rigorous technical testing to ensure a high degree of accuracy. During recognition, the process will determine how correct the device was in determining a match. After testing, the report will list the error rates.

When looking at the possible results, there will be values in several ranges, as shown in the following diagram:

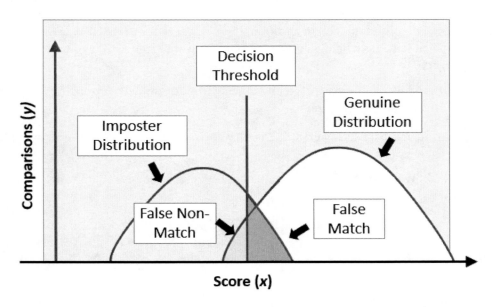

Figure 10.3 – Decision matching threshold

As we can see, the y-axis represents the number of comparisons, while the x-axis represents the score. The higher the score, the higher the probability for a match.

The results during the decision matching process can fall into one of the following ranges:

- Genuine distribution will be the expected range of a subject matching their own sample on file. This range should ideally be greater than the imposter range.

- Imposter distribution is the range of subjects not matching a sample on file.

- The decision matching threshold is some value in between genuine and imposter.

On either side of the decision matching threshold, you will see two outliers:

- **False Non-Match Rate (FNMR)** (also known as False Negative) is when the system incorrectly determines the subject's sample did not match their own template.

- **False Match Rate (FMR)** (also known as False Positive) means an imposter was able to match someone else's template.

During the matching process, verification works by comparing the sample to the template using a one to one comparison. If the sample is within an acceptable threshold, the system will provide a positive match (yes) decision. If the sample is not within an acceptable threshold, the system will return a no match (no) decision.

> **Important Note**
>
> When comparing the sample to the template, the algorithm will assess a value based on the similarity between the subject's sample and the template on file. A higher score means that there is a greater level of confidence that the given sample matches the template.

The metrics that directly relate to the security of the system are FNMR and FMR. System tuning can modify these values. Prior to tuning the system, there are a few key considerations to be made:

- If you set the threshold higher, this will help ensure the system will match fewer imposters. Keep in mind that a higher threshold will most likely have a higher number of FNMR, which means genuine subjects may be rejected.

- If you set the threshold lower, this will lighten the restrictions so that nearly every authorized subject will be matched. However, a lower threshold can lead to a higher number of FMR.

Adjusting the threshold should be done according to the use case and risk profile. Prior to modifying the threshold, careful consideration should be made to determine whether security or convenience is the primary factor.

For example, in a low security setting, such as a gym or club setting, the system may not have to be as stringent. In this case, convenience is more important, and if some imposters slip through the system, this can be included in the cost of doing business.

> **Important Note**
>
> If rigorous security is required, the organization should think about using a multimodal approach, which requires a second biometric authenticator. For example, the user will need to provide their palm vein, along with an iris scan, prior to authenticating to a system.

The performance of a system takes other metrics into account as well, which can include the following:

- **Failure to Capture (FTC)**: This means the system could not capture the sample, which could be the result of an issue with the sensor.

- **Failure to Acquire (FTA)**: This means the system was unable to distill or extract the features, which may be because of a problem with processing.

- **Failure to Enroll (FTE)**: This means the biometric sample was captured and acquired but lacks the necessary details to create a template for future comparisons.

It's also worth noting that all biometric solutions will be affected by the operational environment or environments. For example, performance may be affected in the following situations:

- In extreme cold or heat, vascular biometrics such as finger and palm vein may not perform as well.

- In full sunlight or shadows, a process that captures images may not work as expected.

- In noisy environments, any biometric that involves voice will not work well as the software will have difficulty capturing the subject's voice.

When assessing accuracy, having a robust system with a high rate of performance provides assurance that the system is functioning correctly. Another performance concern is preventing fraud, as outlined next.

Preventing fraud

An important consideration when selecting a biometric is that the system is resistant to impersonation or spoofing attacks. Malicious actors use various methods to try and spoof a biometric system into thinking they are someone else, in order to gain access to the system.

A number of standards organizations and industry leaders in biometric technology are concerned about presentation attacks and are actively developing methods to prevent spoofing.

There are several ways to spoof a biometric system. For example, because of the vast number of images and videos available from users, it may be possible to spoof a facial recognition system. Spoofing techniques for facial recognition can include using the following:

- **Two-dimensional (2D)** technology, such as an image or video
- **Three-dimensional (3D)** technology, such as a lifelike mask

As a result, it's important to employ methods to prevent imposters from using various techniques to trick the system into falsely recognizing them.

A predominant technique to prevent someone from spoofing a biometric system is using liveness detection. Liveness detection is generally specific for each biometric. For example, you could use any of the following:

- During facial recognition, the system could use algorithms that detect subtle facial movements of the lips or eyes.
- To check for liveness during iris recognition, the system could capture pupillary oscillation. This is an effective method as an individual's pupil will oscillate slightly even with steady illumination.

Even with liveness detection, there can still be methods that can be used to spoof a system. As technology evolves, advanced methods to spoof a system are becoming available.

High-quality images have been in existence for many years. However, 3D lifelike silicon masks are available, and are very realistic. You can read more on lifelike masks here: `https://www.technology.org/2019/11/24/can-you-tell-between-a-real-human-face-and-a-hyper-realistic-mask-it-is-becoming-more-difficult/`.

The masks are expensive as they are generally made by hand. However, if someone is determined enough to spoof a system, this could pose a threat by allowing an imposter to be granted access.

The concern for accuracy is important to ensure a secure system. However, there is also a need to ensure that the users can move through the system with ease and efficiency. We will explore this concept in the next section.

Providing speed and efficiency

When deciding on a biometric solution, another consideration is to make sure the system is intuitive, easy to use, and can quickly move the subject through the process. If the system is clumsy, difficult, and slow, users will avoid interacting with the system. Next, we'll examine some considerations we should take into account when selecting an efficient system.

Expediting the process

A biometric system must be robust so that it can efficiently move subjects through the system. This is especially true when dealing with a large-scale authentication environment. Users interacting with a biometric system expect a smooth process that gets them through it in a timely manner.

Ensuring the speed and efficiency of a biometric system is important. One of the main reasons for this is that, because of our digital, always-on society, many individuals become impatient during mundane activities, such as the following:

- Waiting for a traffic light to change
- Being on hold when calling technical support
- Watching a complex web page load

This concept is outlined in the following study on the impatient nature of today's society: https://www.studyfinds.org/hurry-up-modern-patience-thresholds-lower-than-ever-before-survey-finds/. As a result, it is imperative to select a system that moves individuals through the biometric process in a timely manner.

An individual may be more tolerant with a process that is moving along; for example, during activities such as going through a checkout line at the grocery store or the security line at the airport. As long as we are taking a step further every few seconds, we are less prone to becoming impatient.

As shown in the following diagram, this might be a typical timeline of a *pause and go* or *stop and go* process. This type of system requires the subject to stop and present a biometric, such as a fingerprint or static face capture:

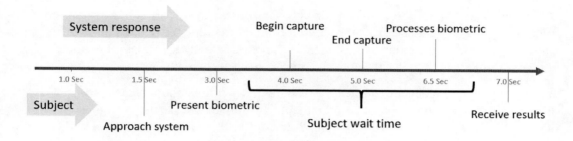

Figure 10.4 – Moving through the biometric capture process

When moving through a system, the biometric process generally involves several steps.

The subject completes the following steps:

1. Approach the system.
2. Present the biometric.
3. Wait for the results.

While the subject waits for the results, the system will do the following:

1. Start the capture.
2. End the capture.
3. Process the biometric.

At the end of successfully processing the biometric, the system will display a notification that the subject has been positively identified. However, in some cases, the system is not able to identify the subject, and they must repeat the process.

The whole operation should have a natural flow, with intuitive directions or symbols to move the subject through the process; for example, using a green light to indicate a successful match, or an orange light with lettering, and *See agent* if there is a problem.

In some systems such as facial recognition, there can be a *frictionless* or *free-flow* process. In this model, the subject simply walks through the process, and is only stopped if they fail to authenticate or the system fails to capture.

A biometric system must be able to efficiently move subjects through the system. However, there are other variables that can influence the throughput, as described next.

Considering the throughput

A system's throughput represents how quickly subjects can move through the system to identify and/or authenticate. This throughput should be acceptable to most individuals, for example, within the range of 8 to 10 subjects per minute. In most cases, a biometric system can move individuals through the process in a timely manner.

Throughput will also depend on the type of system. If we think about someone who is using a personal biometric scan on their laptop or mobile device, they will most likely interact with that device more quickly. In contrast, a newer system that is in the organization will most likely have some users who are hesitant and/or nervous, which can slow down the overall throughput.

In addition, the subject may have to complete other non-biometric-related processes, which can affect the total throughput. Some examples include the following:

- Entering another authenticator such as a PIN or filling out traveler information such as a passport card and/or customs declaration.

- Swipe a smart card when authenticating into the system as some systems house the biometric information on a subject's smart card.

- Removing or adjusting clothing or artifacts; for example, removing a glove to use vein recognition, which can slow down the process.

Total throughput can also be dependent on a couple of other factors. You will also want to consider the time it takes to initially enroll into the system. This process should be efficient, and acceptable to most individuals, in a range of under 2 to 3 minutes.

In addition to providing a system that has speed and accuracy, we also need to think about the bottom line. We'll explore this next.

Selecting a cost-effective solution

When deciding on what type of biometric system to select, we know that there are many details to consider. One of the factors is the cost of the system. Different biometric technologies can vary in price. Often, the price will depend on the required features, such as the following:

- **Type of sensor**: Such as optical, capacitive, or ultrasonic.

- **Specific property**: For example, weather-resistant nature or minimal energy requirements.

- **Hardware**: Some biometric modalities require more processing power for the best performance.

- **Speed**: This represents how fast the system can provide a match. A system that can provide results in 1-2 seconds will cost more than a system that takes 8-10 seconds.

- **Manufacturer**: Such as an established versus new vendor or a large or a small niche company.

While doing your research, you may find that iris recognition can be more expensive than a fingerprint system. In addition, within the same family of technologies, pricing can have a wide variable. A simple fingerprint scanner can be under $100; however, for a more complex system that is networked and has several advanced features, the cost can be much higher.

The good news is that, today, the drive to move to biometric authentication has resulted in lower prices. For example, if we look at fingerprint technology, we'll see that in the time period between 2016-2020, the cost of fingerprint scanners has gone down by more than 50%.

So that you can make a more informed decision when considering costs, we'll explore some of the factors your team should consider. We'll also look at offloading some of the costs by using **Biometrics as a Service** (**BaaS**) and what's involved when you move to the cloud.

Let's start with ways to calculate the total cost of ownership when selecting a biometric system.

Considering the total cost

Although many purchases have an initial one-time price, you should also think of the total cost of ownership. This amount will include other factors, such as operating and personnel expenses.

Some of the factors you can use to calculate the total cost of a system includes variables such as the following:

- What existing system or process is being replaced? In some cases, a new system, such as an automated password reset using voice biometrics, can provide cost saving benefits, often within a single quarter.

- How often does the IT staff have to update the system? This may involve time for the IT staff to manage the updates.

- When will we need to upgrade the system? A full upgrade cycle will involve additional costs.

- Can the system be upgraded? In some cases, a poorly designed biometric system won't allow you to upgrade the algorithm. In that case, if you need newer features, you may have to replace the system, which can be costly.

- What type of additional hardware will be required? A standard biometric system will have the necessary hardware and software. However, there may be additional modules so that the system can integrate with the directory.

- Is technical support included in the costs? Will there be a license that includes support, or will we be billed for each ticket?

- Evaluate whether the licensing model for the biometric system is per enrolled person, match, use case, or server, which will help determine the TCO.

- Will the vendor provide initial training? In some cases, training is included, while other times, there are costs for on-site or online training.

Carefully thinking through the entire purchase is important as the total cost of ownership can easily outpace the initial purchase.

Another key consideration when adopting a new system is whether the equipment is purchased outright or owned by the biometric company. Whenever you implement a biometric solution, you will still need to monitor and manage the system, even if you do not own the equipment.

To avoid much of the additional burden of managing a biometric solution, the organization can choose a cloud solution, as outlined next.

Moving to the cloud

In today's world, there are many choices when it comes to implementing a biometric solution. One option is **BaaS**. Similar to **Software as a Service** (**SaaS**), this model can reduce the burden on IT for the majority of issues that can arise.

BaaS reduces the need to maintain the server and update the matching software. The processing and backend components are in the cloud, where they are managed and updated, as shown in the following diagram:

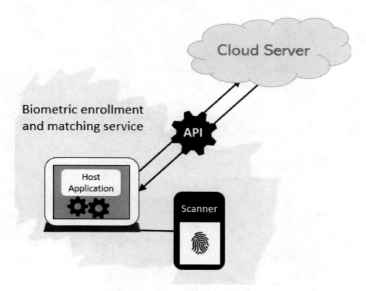

Figure 10.5 – BaaS model

When using BaaS, the IT staff will only need to manage the local interface, such as the hardware used to obtain biometric modality. Moving much of the biometric system to the cloud alleviates the need to store and process the biometric data.

Other benefits include the following:

- An always-on solution with 24-hour support coverage
- The ability to support multiple languages
- A flexible system that can be scaled up or down
- Being able to securely send and save the biometric data
- No need to maintain a physical server
- Support for multiple operating systems

As you can see, there are choices when selecting a biometric solution. The bottom line is that while cost is a consideration, it's important to select the biometric of choice for your organization.

Carefully researching all aspects of the system, while involving all stakeholders, will ultimately lead to the success of the system as a whole.

Summary

In this chapter, we reviewed the complexities of selecting an appropriate biometric system. We stepped through the SDLC and recognized that, when selecting a system, it must be in line with an organization's needs. We then saw the importance of gathering system requirements. We also examined why it's common to meet with all stakeholders that may be involved with the development and subsequent use of the application.

By now, you understand that a key factor when determining what biometric to select is a system that is optimal for the majority of users. We also looked at the importance of providing an accurate solution that prevents someone from spoofing the system. During the selection process, we saw how soft factors such as user comfort should also be part of the equation. We outlined the value in providing a system that quickly and efficiently moves users through the process.

Finally, we covered the cost factors to consider when selecting a system, and how it's important to consider the total costs involved. In addition, we saw how moving to the cloud can decrease the burden on IT, along with several other benefits.

In the next chapter, we'll take a look of some of the aspects that must be considered when integrating a biometric system into an organization. You'll see how transferring biometric data over the network may have additional bandwidth and device requirements. We'll also cover the importance of protecting biometric data while it's in transit or in storage. You'll then recognize the importance of how integrating with the network directory will make the system more efficient and secure. Finally, you'll appreciate the importance of having a solid plan in place in case of disaster or disruption.

Questions

Now, it's time to check your knowledge. Select the best response and then check your answers, which can be found in the *Assessment* section at the end of this book:

1. _____analysis is an exercise that establishes what is necessary for the system to be successful.

   a. Cloud

   b. Threshold

   c. Requirements

   d. Spoof

2. _____ are applied to the ergonomics of objects such as furniture and machines so that users can interact effectively with the system.

    a. Anthropometrics

    b. Genuine marks

    c. Requirements

    d. Deployments

3. If the results during the decision matching process fall into the range of a _____, this means the system incorrectly determined the subject's sample did not match their own template.

    a. genuine distribution

    b. **False Match Rate (FMR)**

    c. **False Non-Match Rate (FNMR)**

    d. decision matching threshold

4. Performance of a system takes into account other metrics as well. Failure to _____ may be the result of problems with the sensor.

    a. acquire

    b. capture

    c. distribute

    d. deploy

5. _____ techniques for facial recognition can include using 3D technology; for example, a life-like mask.

    a. Acquisition

    b. BaaS

    c. Ransom

    d. Spoofing

6. In today's world, there are many choices when it comes to implementing a biometric solution. One option is _____, which can reduce the burden on IT for the majority of issues that can arise.

   a. acquisition platform

   b. smart card technology

   c. deployed technology

   d. BaaS

7. In some cases, users may have to swipe a(n) _____when authenticating into the system, as that is where the system houses the biometric information.

   a. smart card

   b. anthropometric

   c. threshold monitor

   d. cloud metric

Further reading

Please refer to the following links for more information:

- To learn more about biometric pricing, visit `https://www.bayometric.com/biometric-devices-cost/`.

- To view a report by Spiceworks on biometrics in the workplace, go to `https://www.spiceworks.com/press/releases/spiceworks-study-reveals-nearly-90-percent-businesses-will-use-biometric-authentication-technology-2020/`.

- To see projections on biometric use through 2024, visit `https://www.thalesgroup.com/en/markets/digital-identity-and-security/government/inspired/biometrics`.

- To see where more and more companies are seeking contactless biometric solutions, visit `https://www.pymnts.com/authentication/2020/covid-19-spurs-biometric-innovations-contactless-global-society/`.

- To see how biometrics can save an organization money, visit `https://www.veridiumid.com/blog/mobile-devices-the-last-mile-to-enterprise-biometrics/`.

- Understanding performance rates: `https://precisebiometrics.com/wp-content/uploads/2014/11/White-Paper-Understanding-Biometric-Performance-Evaluation.pdf`.

- For a discussion on fear of technology as we age, visit `https://www.sciencedaily.com/releases/2018/03/180312091715.htm`.

- Although written in 2008, this article provides some solid examples of causes of biometric implementation failures. This will help reinforce why it's important to take time and properly plan a biometric implementation: `http://www.secureconsulting.net/Papers/secmgmt-biometrics.pdf`

- You can read more on usability and biometrics in this report by NIST: `https://www.nist.gov/system/files/usability_and_biometrics_final2.pdf`.

11

Integrating the Biometric System

Once you determine the need to fully integrate a new biometric system within an organization, the next step is to outline how best to move through the process. To ensure a successful implementation and avoid major complications, the team should carefully plan and think through all critical aspects. In this chapter, you'll get a better grasp of some of the planning that must be done prior to deploying a biometric system.

Today, there are several ways to integrate a biometric system within an existing environment. In some cases, the organization will opt to use an out-of-band, proprietary system. However, in other cases, the system will integrate with a central network directory, and the biometric data will need to travel over the network. In that case, one of the considerations when deploying a biometric system in an organization is to evaluate the network.

Sending biometric data over the network may have additional bandwidth and device requirements. We'll see why understanding the logical data flow is important prior to implementation, to avoid bottlenecks. We'll review several areas where biometric data might be stored, including a database server, portable device, or in the cloud. We'll then outline why it's important to secure and protect the biometric data while in transit or in storage.

So that you can have a better understanding of a network directory, we'll outline the concept and cover some well-known directories. You'll come to better understand ways of using a network directory that will make the system more efficient and secure. Finally, you'll understand that even with careful preparation, a system can fail or suffer from a cyberattack. You'll understand the importance of responding to incidents and having a solid plan for disaster recovery and business continuity in place in case of disaster or disruption.

In this chapter, we're going to cover the following main topics:

- Sending biometric data over the network
- Securing biometric data
- Integrating with the directory
- Ensuring business continuity

Sending biometric data over the network

Once the decision is made to provide a networked biometric solution, the information technology team must begin the process of planning the implementation. To ensure a successful transition, the team must think through the process, and carefully consider all aspects of the network.

Each business is different. The goal is to meet the needs of the organization. Therefore, while planning the integration, it's important to have a clear idea of the objective of the biometric system.

Some of the questions to address are as follows:

- What is the goal of the system; identification and/or authentication?
- Where will the biometric capture device(s) be located?
- What are some of the security threats?
- How many concurrent users will access the system during an average day, and how many can be expected during peak usage times?
- Will the system need to be integrated into an existing or legacy system?
- Will there be a secondary use for the biometric, for example, using a photo of a face on an identification card, or embedding a fingerprint on a smart card?
- Will this be a single or multimodal solution?

Once these and other questions are addressed, the team can move forward with implementation.

In this section, we'll see why it's important to understand the logical data flow prior to implementation. We'll take a look at how networked devices communicate with each other, and why it's important to identify possible areas of network congestion. And finally, we'll see why baselining our network prior to installation will help you better assess issues while troubleshooting the network after the system is operational.

Let's first begin by getting a better understanding of the various topologies on a **Local Area Network (LAN)**.

Understanding network topologies

When planning to integrate a biometric system and send data over the network, it's important to consider the response time of the system.

Today, the most common design for a biometric solution is a centralized, networked system that serves all clients. During the process of identifying and authenticating someone, the network needs to be fast and responsive, with minimal downtime. In an enterprise network, the system generally consists of many devices that send and receive data.

When planning to integrate a biometric system, it's important to have a basic understanding of network topology. To help all stakeholders get a better idea of what's involved, the network administrator should briefly outline the network layout. The overview should be done early on, for example during the planning meeting. This knowledge will give everyone a better understanding of the complexities of the network, so they can understand why slow response times may occur.

Let's outline some common topologies in the next section.

Connecting devices

The topology of the network shows how the network devices are all physically interconnected, so they can communicate with one another.

Common types of network topologies in a local area network include star, mesh, and hybrid, as shown in the following graphic:

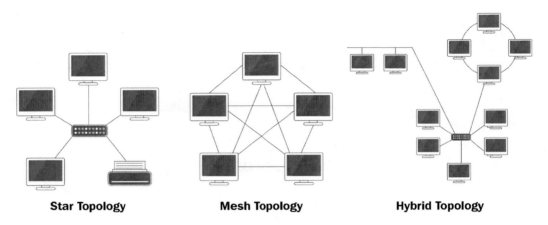

| **Star Topology** | **Mesh Topology** | **Hybrid Topology** |

Figure 11.1 – Common network topologies

These common topologies have advantages and disadvantages as follows:

- **A star topology** is where all devices are connected to a central device, such as a switch. This type of configuration allows the administrator to easily add or remove hosts and provides a central device that can make troubleshooting easier. The downside is that because there is a single device, this could represent a single point of failure.

- **A mesh topology** is when all devices are connected to one another and there is a common configuration for a wireless network. The advantage is that, when used with a wireless LAN controller, users will have a seamless handover and be able to roam freely throughout the organization's network. The disadvantage is that, with a wireless mesh, you'll need more careful configuration in order to keep the signal strength consistent.

- **A hybrid topology** is a combination of two or more different network topologies; for example, using a star topology that extends to a wireless mesh topology. Hybrid configurations are common on LANs today, as they are scalable and flexible. However, the downside is that the administrator must document and maintain multiple types of networks.

> **Important note**
> To see an example of the different types of network topologies, visit the page at `https://www.dnsstuff.com/wp-content/uploads/2019/08/network-topology-types-1024x536.png`.

Next, let's take a look at how the data flows through a network.

Modeling the data flow

In most cases, a biometric system is a networked solution, using a client-server configuration that works within a domain.

In a client-server configuration, the following takes place:

- Clients send requests to a central server.
- The server stores the biometric system database and responds to client requests.

During a transaction, when a client requests resources, the data must travel through many devices on the network to reach the server. As a result, when using a networked solution, it's imperative to ensure network stability.

To achieve this, the network administrator will provide redundancy, in the form of additional pathways and devices within the network infrastructure. That way, if there is a failure in one device, the traffic will continue to flow with minimal downtime.

Within a network, data travels between devices and hosts over a communication channel, also called a transmission medium. This can be in the form of either a cable or a radio wave over the air. Network devices can include switches, routers, and wireless access points, all of which transfer the data, as shown in the following diagram:

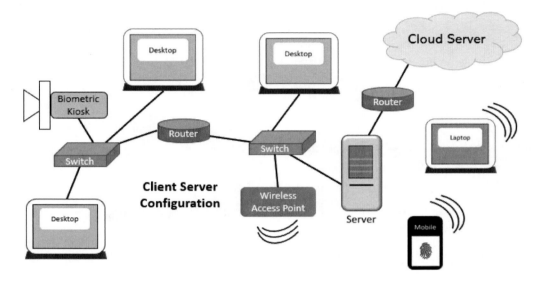

Figure 11.2 – A networked client-server configuration

For example, a transaction in a standard networked biometric solution might go as follows:

1. A client presents their biometric sample using a device with dedicated hardware, such as a biometric kiosk, laptop, or mobile device.

2. The biometric sample can be converted to a template at the source; if not, then the data must be sent across the network and converted on the biometric system server.

3. The server can be on the LAN, or in the cloud. On its journey, the biometric data can travel over the network through any number of devices, such as switches and routers, to get to the server.

4. Once at the server, the comparison template is then input into the biometric system for comparison to the client's template on file.

5. The results of the comparison (either **ACCEPT** or **REJECT**) are then sent back through the network to reach the client.

When data is sent from one host to another, it is broken down into smaller units called packets. The packets travel through the network to their final destination. Once there, the packets are reassembled and sent to the appropriate application.

In a network, the communication channels can vary in bandwidth, which is the amount of data that can be transmitted at any given time.

In some cases, biometric data such as images must be transmitted over a narrow-bandwidth communication channel to a server. To send data more efficiently, we use compression, as discussed next.

Compressing the data

In a networked solution using a client-server configuration, biometric data such as the source image, template, or associated metadata may need to travel over the network. What is transported is dependent on the system and objective:

- If authenticating the subject, creating the template on the device and then sending the template over the network to the server is a good strategy.

- If identifying the subject, sending the image over the network to the server may be more appropriate. That is because, in some cases, human analysis may be required to identify the subject.

When thinking about bandwidth utilization, it's also important to determine the resolution of the images. Data compression is removing redundancy to make a file smaller and helps reduce storage and data transmission requirements.

> **Important note**
>
> When referring to digital image or video quality, we use the term **Pixels Per Inch (ppi)**, which represents the number or density of pixels per inch when displayed on a monitor. Images that have a higher ppi will have better quality.

Next, let's take a look at a couple of compression algorithms, and how they are used.

Selecting an algorithm

Two well-known compression algorithms are **Joint Photographic Experts Group (JPEG)**-2000 and **Wavelet Scalar Quantization (WSQ)**, which differ in the following manner:

- **JPEG-2000** is used to compress iris, fingerprint, and facial images at 1,000 ppi and can effectively pull features and resolutions while preserving image quality.

- **WSQ** provides compression at 500 ppi, which in most cases provides sufficient quality.

The type of algorithm used will depend on the biometric and how the image is used. For example, when dealing with fingerprints in the United States, most law enforcement agencies use WSQ for storage and transmission, which provides an acceptable level of detail. However, if the image is used for latent fingerprint examination, JPEG-2000 is the preferred method. That is because a higher quality image will provide better visualization of the third-level details of a fingerprint, such as the position of the pores, and the shape of the ridges.

When using data compression, there is some loss of the fine details of an image. Let's explore this concept next.

Reducing the pixels

When an image is compressed and then expanded, there is some loss of quality. In order to achieve minimal degradation, some parts of the image can be compressed at a lower rate.

As shown in the following diagram, the main part of the subject's face will be compressed at a lower rate than the perimeter of the face, which can use a higher compression rate:

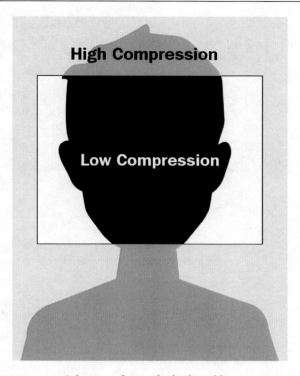

Figure 11.3 – Selection of areas for high and low compression

When sending data to the server from all over the organization in an enterprise network, it's common to have multiple requests throughout the day. So that the server does not get overloaded, the network administrator should configure load balancing, as outlined next.

Sharing the load

Once the biometric system is operational, the transactions should be monitored. The goal is to apply fairness in the processing of server requests. In a large organization, the transactions can be voluminous. If one server receives too many requests, this can overload the **Central Processing Unit (CPU)** and cause a system failure.

If the organization is large and spread across several locations, the biometric readers might be placed at various, strategic locations. If there are login requests from multiple locations, the load should be distributed and balanced so that one server doesn't get all of the requests. Services can be balanced evenly, or on a weighted scale.

As shown in the following diagram, one load balancing host is configured to accept 40% of the requests, and the other host will accept 60% of the requests:

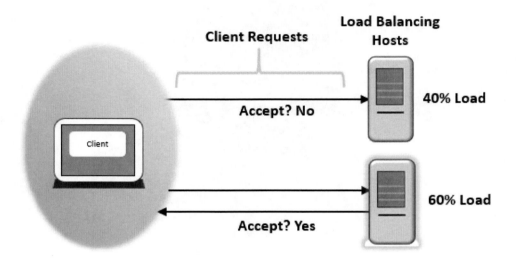

Figure 11.4 – Load balancing scenario

For example, when using load balancing in an identification system, the biometric databases (or galleries) are duplicated across several servers. Identification requests are then load balanced to provide fairness in request handling.

In addition to balancing the load, there should also be failover clusters put in place, so that if one system fails, the other system will continue to respond to requests.

The overall system design needs to be evaluated to ensure there are no bottlenecks, and that all clients can access the server(s). Any delays in response time could have widespread effects, and negatively affect throughput.

So that you have a way to compare network performance over time, the networking team should gather some baseline traffic prior to implementation, as discussed next.

Baselining the network

In most cases, a company's infrastructure represents a critical asset that allows members across the organization to communicate and share resources. Networks have evolved, and boundaries have become blurred as a result. **Internet of Things (IoT)** devices are talking to us, and to each other. Clients are watching videos, downloading emails, and searching content on the internet. As a result, more and more traffic travels over our networks.

To provide this communication infrastructure, organizations have an internal LAN, as well as cloud computing deployments, **Wide Area Network** (**WAN**) connectivity, and mobile devices.

So that biometric transactions occur within a few seconds, the network must have sufficient capacity and throughput, with no bottlenecks.

To keep the traffic flowing, the administrator should observe the network for changes. Let's explore this concept.

Monitoring the data flow

A part of a network administrators' job is to manage and monitor the network. Because of the quantity of traffic exchanged on a daily basis, it's important to take a proactive approach in ensuring the network is up and operational.

For example, one component of network traffic is the phone system, in the form of **Voice over Internet Protocol** (**VoIP**). VoIP traffic is sensitive to time delays, and performance can suffer if the voice traffic does not travel in a timely manner. If the network becomes sluggish and traffic does not move efficiently, users will complain about the poor quality of calls.

Prior to adding a new application that can affect the entire network, it's important to gather some sample traffic in the form of a baseline. Let's discuss this concept next.

Setting a baseline

A baseline is a snapshot in time when traffic is flowing well and there are no major issues.

Some of the beneficial things that baselining allows us to do include the following:

- Observe the protocols that are in use on the network.
- Assess the round-trip time.
- Determine bandwidth usage.

The one key benefit to doing a baseline before a major system implementation is to be able to compare the baseline with current traffic to see what changes have occurred. Changes can include bandwidth utilization, possible security issues, and slow response times.

By comparing the network to a baseline, the administrator will see clearly any problems present, such as slow response times or dropped packets. This will allow the administrator to take a proactive approach and apply corrective actions to prevent further degradation of the network.

Baselining provides us with something that we can use to compare with the state of the network after the new implementation. We really can't be sure if a network is sick unless we know what it looks like when it is healthy.

While it's important to keep the data flowing on the network, another consideration is keeping data secure, as discussed next.

Securing biometric data

The use of biometric technology is expanding into smartphones, government facilities, and financial institutions. In addition to the growing popularity, there are also concerns about the level of security associated with biometric systems, along with the repositories that hold biometric data.

In recent years, there have been a number of high-profile data breaches on systems that contained sensitive data, passwords, and biometric data.

Some of those notable cyberattacks were as follows:

- 2019 – BioStar 2 suffered a breach of a database containing 28 million fingerprint and facial recognition records.

- 2016 – The Philippines' **Commission on Elections (COMELEC)** was the victim of a compromised website. The hackers were able to gain access to the **Personally Identifiable Information (PII)** and biometric data of 55 million registered voters.

- 2015 – The United States' **Office of Personnel Management (OPM)** suffered a breach of 5.6 million scanned fingerprint records.

While this list is not conclusive, it does illustrate that there is a real threat that biometric data can be compromised in some way.

> **Important note**
> Unlike a password that can immediately be changed if lost or stolen, a biometric identifier is permanent, in that it does not change significantly over time. In contrast, if someone were to steal a biometric template (or record) this has limited use in the real world. That is because many times, templates are only able to be used on the same system. In order to use the stolen template, this would require physical access to the system. However, in time this could change.

With data privacy laws, organizations face the need to be more responsible when managing their data. A data breach could have widespread implications, and the organization might suffer hefty fines.

Because of the increasing reports of compromised biometric data, along with possible risks to systems, careful consideration must be made to secure the biometric data. Next, let's take a look at ways we can reduce the risk of exposure.

Reducing the risk of exposure

When thinking about protecting data, a common security tenet is called the **Confidentiality, Integrity, and Availability (CIA)** triad.

The CIA triad goals are intended to ensure the following:

- **Confidentiality** is keeping private data private. Data should be protected so that only authorized individuals have access to view that data.

- **Integrity** is maintaining the condition of the data. To provide integrity, only authorized individuals should be able to make modifications to the data.

- **Availability** is the assurance that authorized individuals are able to access their data when needed.

Data loss prevention is ensuring there is no data exfiltration, which is data that leaves the organization without authorization. Data loss can occur either by accident, or as a result of a cyber-attack, and can cost a company millions of dollars.

In an organization, there are many attack vectors, or methods, by which vulnerable data can be compromised. Vectors can include storage devices, emails, missing or improper access controls, cloud storage, and malware. As a result, the network administrator must be aware of the many ways data exfiltration can occur and seek ways to prevent data loss.

The different types of biometric systems that can store biometric data include the following:

- A hardware-based system or kiosk can store the data locally and does not require any external response. To gain access to the system, the subject presents their biometric identifier, and the comparison is made locally. This is a simple, secure solution; however, its use is generally restricted to that single device.

- A smart card or token can house biometric data. When using a system to identify and authenticate, the subject presents the token and then their sample. The comparison is made locally, without having to send data over the network.

- Mobile devices are common today and store a user's biometric data on the device itself. Similar to using a smart card or token, the matching process is performed locally. Once a positive match is made, the system will grant the user access to the device.

- A biometric server is a shared resource that allows clients to access the stored biometric data remotely. In a client-server configuration, the server is a central device that can be managed, monitored, and secured more easily. However, because it is a central device that is housing sensitive information, it can be a vulnerable target.

Today, one of the most common locations to store biometric data is on a server. To reduce the threat of an attack, the network administrator should take steps to lock down and secure the server(s).

Some best practices for this include the following:

- Use the principle of least privilege, and limit access to the server(s) only to authorized individuals.

- Disable any unnecessary services.

- Apply security patches when available.

In addition, make sure to store PII and biometric data on separate servers. That way, if one system is compromised, it won't be as damaging, as an identity without biometric data is less useful, and vice versa.

When using a server in a biometric system, the data is the most important element of the system. As a result, it should be protected when traveling over the network or while in storage, by using encryption. Let's explore this concept next.

Encrypting biometric data

Encryption scrambles or encodes data by using a key or a pair of keys. The encrypted data is meaningless unless you have the key to decrypt the data.

For example, let's create a simple example by going to `https://encode-decode.com/aes256-encrypt-online/` and encrypting the following text:

A biometric system inputs an identifier, such as a fingerprint or face, and determines whether or not the characteristic is authentic to the individual.

Using AES 256-bit encryption, along with the `orangekitten` secret key, will result in the following output:

```
oIUzft6Pw1a3B8EJPm9wDfr/iZ/
LwauPGiFolQVN8RjhwYQhAvr8d0A9QxlWoM8d0H2QulktUNuoCFO5CrcV/
oGaiiUl+tRCHV8+IFalsaOlnC374N/
JSM5u0UyF0ZCxNtfs7v7Ktm3brYmS54zDphB
rgabfpKCQI0JlgqxCcYdVftdb27Ose/
hCmMckvw+ZNKPycCz1TP2um+ZxdGucyA==
```

As you can see, the only way the data will make sense is if you have a key. As a result, when using encryption, an organization can enjoy the reassurance that the biometric data is secure.

The two main types of encryption are symmetric and asymmetric encryption. The differences between symmetric and asymmetric encryption are as follows:

- Symmetric encryption uses a single shared key to encrypt and decrypt data. Common algorithms include **Data Encryption Standard** (**DES**), **International Data Encryption Algorithm** (**IDEA**), and **Advances Encryption Standard** (**AES**).

- Asymmetric encryption, also called public-key cryptography, uses two keys, a public and a private key. Asymmetric algorithms include **Rivest–Shamir–Adleman** (**RSA**), Diffie Hellman, and **Elliptic-Curve Cryptography** (**ECC**).

The type of encryption algorithm used will depend on the application.

Data can be secured with encryption while at rest or in motion:

- For data at rest, encryption can be applied to an entire drive, or to individual files and folders, a database, or just to individual records in that database. Securing data at rest is primarily done using symmetric encryption, however, some applications do use asymmetric encryption.

- For data in motion (as it's traveling over the network), data can be secured using a **Virtual Private Network** (**VPN**) tunnel. VPNs commonly use either the **Secure Socket Layer/Transport Layer Security** (**SSL/TLS**) or **Internet Protocol Security** (**IPSec**) protocols.

When using encryption, the administrator must consider how the keys are to be managed. Encryption keys must be stored properly, and only a limited number of individuals should have access to the keys.

Another way to secure the biometric data is by integrating the system with a central network directory. In the next section, let's outline the concept of a network directory, which can help ensure that only authorized individuals have access to the system.

Integrating with the directory

A directory, or directory service, is a centrally managed database that holds objects and forms an integral part of a client-server configuration.

When using a biometric system that provides identification and authentication, integrating with the directory will restrict access to network resources and reduce the possibility of a cyberattack.

In this section, we'll take a look at defining the concept of a directory, and how it allows the network administrator to more easily manage the objects on a network. We'll then discuss how we can integrate a biometric system with the directory.

Let's first explore the concept of a directory.

Understanding the directory

A directory service provides an efficient way to customize the ability of objects in the network domain to interact with one another. Objects on a network include users, groups, computers, printers, servers, and shared folders. The centralized format allows the network administrator to easily manage the objects and their attributes.

This is achieved by granting permissions or restricting access, by applying policies that govern the behavior of the objects on the network. Today there are a few popular network directories, as discussed next.

Recognizing well-known directories

A directory service provides authentication and authorization services to objects on a network. Some well-known directory services include the following:

- **Microsoft Active Directory (AD)**
- **Azure Active Directory (Azure AD)**
- **Lightweight Directory Access Protocol (LDAP)**

AD is a directory service that is part of the Microsoft Windows Server family of operating systems. Azure AD provides an interface to cloud resources, such as Office 365. LDAP provides a similar function and works within a Linux environment. However, LDAP can be configured to integrate with a Windows environment, and can access AD.

When using a directory service, objects can locate and request resources that are distributed throughout the network. Next, we'll see that in order for objects to be able to interact with one another, the directory must be configured correctly.

Configuring directory objects

The directory holds all the objects on the network so they can communicate with one another and access resources.

Prior to interacting with other objects, a given object must be in the directory with the appropriate permissions to access network resources. When configured correctly, this provides an additional layer of security.

For example, if a user logs on to the network, the process works as follows:

1. The client logs in and requests access to network resources.
2. The server checks the credentials of the client, and once authenticated, grants access to the network resources they have permission to access.

When clients use a biometric identifier to gain access to the network, they will go through the process of identification and authentication, just as they would if they were using a password. Once authenticated, the system allows them to access network resources.

Prior to using the system, the network administrator will need to integrate the biometric system into the directory.

Managing the integration

Integration into the directory can be a complex process and can take some time. To ensure a smooth transition, the team needs to manage all aspects of the project.

In some cases, integration with the directory is done with vendor assistance, as part of the contract. In other cases, this will be done in house by the IT staff.

In order for the directory to be set up properly, the team will need to know the function of the biometric system.

For example, the team needs to know whether the system is intended for the following:

- Providing single sign-on functionality for the network
- Providing physical access to a facility
- Being part of a time and attendance system

Once the integration is underway, the team needs to develop a plan to ensure business continuity in case of disaster or disruption. Let's explore this concept next.

Ensuring business continuity

In most cases, the networking team works hard to keep all systems operational and adhere to the rule of five-nines. The rule of five-nines means the network must be available 99.999 percent of the time, which allows for downtime of approximately 5 minutes. However, even in the best of circumstances, a system can fail or suffer from a cyberattack, and be down for more than 5 minutes.

> **Important note**
> Even if there isn't a disaster, it's important to ensure business continuity. For example, in a large-scale government biometric solutions, one best practice is to build discrete subsystems. The systems can be swapped out or upgraded without impacting other systems, or interrupting network production.

A biometrics system failure can have a serious effect on an organization, especially if the system provides identification and authentication. In that case, you could have hundreds if not thousands of employees unable to gain access to network resources. By working together as a team and communicating with one another, businesses can more quickly keep systems up and operational.

In this section, we'll take a look at what to do immediately after an incident. We'll also see the importance of having in place solid plans for disaster recovery and business continuity in case of disaster or disruption.

Let's start with the importance of managing incidents.

Responding to incidents

An incident is an unplanned event that temporarily interrupts network activity. Incident management involves responding to a disruption in network services or business processes. If the organization is the victim of a system failure or malicious activity, the team needs to move quickly to prevent further damage.

When a biometric system is networked, incident management is important, as they go hand in hand. As shown in the following diagram, there is an evolution of events that generally takes place after an incident:

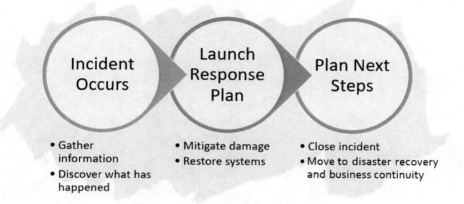

Incident Occurs
- Gather information
- Discover what has happened

Launch Response Plan
- Mitigate damage
- Restore systems

Plan Next Steps
- Close incident
- Move to disaster recovery and business continuity

Figure 11.5 – Evolution of an incident

The progress of an incident generally takes the following path:

1. The incident occurs and the team gathers information about the incident.

2. The team launches its response plan with the goal of limiting the damage to systems.

3. After taking steps to mitigate the incident, the team either closes the incident, or moves to the **disaster recovery** (**DR**) and **business continuity** (**BC**) modes.

The first step is to gather information on the event, as outlined next.

Gathering information

Immediately after someone reports an incident, one of the first steps is to gather information. The team needs to discover what actually happened. The discovery can include the following questions:

- Who reported the incident – a manager, end user, customer, or an other individual? It's important to gather this data, as you may have to check back with the individual to get more information on the incident itself.

- What happened? Ask whoever reported the incident to step through the event, encouraging them to try to recall even the smallest detail.

- Where did this occur, outside or inside the facility? Did it just affect the individual, or everyone in the department? Here, you are trying to determine the scope of the incident.

- When did this occur? Train your users to report an incident as soon as they become aware of an issue that could possibly affect the network or the system.

For example, someone might report the following: "*I received a suspicious email and immediately moved the message to the trash, however, my coworker opened the same email, and now she can't access any of her files.*"

Take notes so you can document the details later. Once you have sufficient information on the incident, the next step is to mitigate the damage. Let's discuss this.

Mitigating damage

There are several reasons why a system can fail. Common events include a power disruption, malware, or even user error. Whatever has occurred, remain calm and put the team into action to reduce the damage. The goal is to restore the system as soon as possible. One thing to remember is, if left unchecked, an incident can lead to disaster.

While the team works to restore the system, communicate with the clients so that they are aware that there is a failure that might interrupt their workflow. The team will continue to manage the incident until the network is back up and all systems have resumed normal activity.

At some point, you will either close the incident or move to DR and BC mode. Let's outline this next.

Planning the next step

After moving through the process of gathering information and mitigating the damage, the team should make a decision as to whether they have reached the natural end to the incident, or whether the incident has escalated to a disaster.

If there is a natural end, the team should document the entire event and take steps to prevent a repeat incident by mitigating any vulnerabilities.

If the incident has escalated to a disaster, the team must go into DR mode. Let's see what's involved in this process next.

Recovering from disaster

Even if you have a strong incident response team, an incident may be immediately classified as a disaster. A disaster is a serious event that causes a major disruption in services for a prolonged period of time. A disaster has widespread effects and can involve monetary losses, hardship, and injury.

Disasters can include the following:

- **Natural**: Such as a flood or earthquake

- **Technological**: Such as a ransomware attack

- **Man-made**: Such as accidently causing a fire

If the incident has escalated in status to a disaster, there may be a sudden loss of communications and an interruption to network services. DR involves the steps necessary to regain control of business operations. That includes restoring all data, hardware, software, and communications back to a near-normal state as soon as possible. The key focus should be on protecting the data and quickly restoring critical operations.

The organization should have a DR team in place. While a disaster is a more serious event, the amount of success will depend on how prepared the team is to deal with a disaster. Each team member should have a clear role, with specific tasks that should be completed. Additional best practice guidelines include the following:

- Have a backup strategy along with a data restoration plan for all digital assets.

- Outline a communications plan to disseminate information and coordinate the recovery strategy.

After addressing the more critical needs of dealing with a disaster, steps should be taken to ensure BC, as outlined next.

Planning business continuity

Once the team engages in the DR stage, a natural evolution to this process is to ensure BC. When a system suffers a major interruption, the business must get back in operation as quickly as possible, preferably within a week to 10 days. The reality is, if the business does not resume operations within 2 weeks, this may very well lead to the business failing.

BC moves through the process of restoring operations such as the network, communication systems, and other vital business functions.

Disasters can occur, many times through no fault of our own. To get through a disaster with minimal downtime, the team should take steps to plan for a disaster. Meet periodically to review roles and assignments and conduct tabletop exercises so that your team is better prepared and can respond confidently and quickly.

Summary

By now, you can appreciate the complexities in moving from the procuring of a biometric system to the integration phase. In this chapter, we took a look at considerations on how to interface with existing systems. We reviewed network topologies and outlined the importance of understanding and managing the data flow, so that the data moves efficiently through the network.

We covered the importance of baselining the network, to help with troubleshooting. Then we discussed ways to protect the biometric data and reduce the risk of exposure. We outlined the concept of a directory and saw how, when we integrate the biometric system with the directory, this will provide a more efficient and secure system. Finally, we covered how incidents and disasters can occur. We then learned why it's important to move quickly after a disaster to restore services to ensure BC.

In the next chapter, we'll take a look at the process of moving to the deployment phase. We'll see why it's important to test the system prior to using the system. Because we want a successful deployment, you'll learn how providing education and awareness will help promote user acceptance. We'll then review key considerations during the enrollment process. Finally, we'll evaluate what modifications we can make, so the functioning of the biometric system is in line with acceptable parameters.

Questions

Now it's time to check your knowledge. Select the best response, then check your answers with those found in the *Assessments* section at the end of the book:

1. On a network, a _____ topology is where all devices are connected to a central device, such as a switch.

    a. mesh

    b. ring

    c. hybrid

    d. star

2. On a network, the communication channels can vary in_____, or the amount of data that can be transmitted at any given time.

   a. bandwidth

   b. compression

   c. Central Processing Unit

   d. baseline

3. A _____ is a snapshot in time when traffic is flowing well and there are no major issues.

   a. bandwidth

   b. compression

   c. Central Processing Unit

   d. baseline

4. _____ is about keeping private data private and protected, so that only authorized individuals are able to access the data.

   a. Integrity

   b. Availability

   c. Confidentiality

   d. Compression

5. For a client to access network resources, they must be in the directory and have been assigned the appropriate _____.

   a. folders

   b. permissions

   c. scanning device

   d. compression algorithm

6. A(n) _____ is an unplanned event that temporarily interrupts network activity.

   a. incident

   b. baseline

   c. disaster

   d. switch

7. A (n)_____ is a serious event that causes a major disruption in services for a prolonged period of time.

a. incident

b. baseline

c. disaster

d. switch

Further reading

- For more information on biometric compression, visit `https://www.nist.gov/programs-projects/biometric-compression-information`.

- To see a graphic on market share percentages of different network operating systems, visit `https://global-uploads.webflow.com/5d71c5b5ed21579fe7c3535a/5e4b3d5264f7f54d7b331ac2_server-operating-system-market-share-2018.png`.

- To read more on JPEG-2000, visit `https://jpeg.org/jpeg2000/`.

- For guidelines on how to handle an incident, visit `https://csrc.nist.gov/publications/detail/sp/800-34/rev-1/final`.

12
Testing and System Deployment

At some point, the system will be ready for the final phase of implementation, and the team will put the biometric system into operation. In this chapter, we'll take a look at moving through this phase, and some of the tasks that the team will need to complete. We'll discuss the different strategies of implementing a system, such as running in parallel, cutover, and the hybrid approach.

You'll see that testing before full deployment will identify any problems that might adversely affect the current system. We'll first take a look at how industry conducts rigorous trials, and then we'll outline some of the testing that should be done within the organization. You'll also see the value of providing documentation for the users and team members and then, when everything is ready, moving to full deployment.

We'll also see the importance of including training as part of the transition. We'll outline how education and awareness helps manage this change in a positive way and promotes user acceptance. We'll then take a look at selecting an appropriate training format, as well as ways to customize this training format so that it is specific to the audience. We'll review the enrollment process and outline some of the considerations when adding a new user to the system. In addition, we'll cover some troubleshooting techniques for the problems that might occur when working with the system. Finally, we'll evaluate what modifications we can make, such as upgrading the biometric template and tuning the acceptance threshold, so that the biometric system is in line with acceptable results.

In this chapter, we're going to cover the following main topics:

- Testing the system
- Providing education and awareness
- Enrolling the users
- Fine-tuning the decision process

Testing the system

During the deployment phase, the new or enhanced biometric system is installed in the production environment. Prior to fully deploying the system, the team will perform a series of tests with a select group of users. This will help determine if there are any outstanding issues to resolve. Once testing is complete, the process will move on to the full implementation of the system, which includes training, enrolling users, and fine-tuning the decision process.

In this section, we'll take a look at some of the steps to complete prior to deployment. We'll discuss the planning process and outline the different strategies the team can take to set up the new system. Then, we'll outline testing, providing documentation, and then moving to full deployment.

Let's start with getting the team ready for the new system.

Preparing for deployment

Deploying a new system can be complex. As a result, the team should start planning as soon as possible. In some cases, it may be best to begin the planning meetings soon after making the decision to procure the system.

Early planning meetings will help identify any unique needs that may have been overlooked when selecting the system. In addition, taking time to plan will help avoid failures.

When managing a deployment project, there can be several departments involved. So that everyone is aware of the process, gather the stakeholders that will be included in the transition to the new system. Once gathered, you'll want to outline the project.

We'll discuss the planning process next.

Planning the process

Process planning will take time. However, careful consideration of all aspects of deploying a new system will help ensure a smooth transition, with a high rate of user acceptance.

When planning the deployment, you'll want to gather the team and get a feel as to how they envision the system in production. The facilitator can use a whiteboard and list the key elements of interacting with the system.

Have the team talk through the scenario as if they were going through the process, which can help them think of all possible variables that might occur. During the exercise, the team should think about the type of biometric in use and identify what might cause delays.

In addition, as you move toward deployment, don't assume that certain elements will be in place. By using a checklist, you can periodically review the list and do a gap analysis to see what is missing. For example, if you are using a smart card that has the biometric template on the card, along with a palm vein reader, you might want to check the following:

- Will the users have to take the time to remove their work gloves?
- Is the reader at an appropriate height?
- Will the system administrator receive an immediate alert if the user is denied access?

Keep the culture of the organization in mind. Some users will be quick to adopt the new technology. Others may get frustrated easily if the process doesn't work as expected. In addition, if the organization has a large, diverse culture, there may be a need to create separate teams for system deployment and user training.

Some examples of the variables you may encounter include the following:

- Providing support for multilingual clients
- Adjusting training schedules for a department where the shift begins at midnight

Customized site support may be required to accommodate these unique needs.

Throughout the planning process, the team should stay agile, regularly review the deployment plan, and make adjustments as needed. Keep the goals realistic, but have go/no-go decision points that will prompt a rollback if the progress runs into critical issues.

For example, a finger vein recognition system that controls entry into a warehouse should work in the following manner:

- The users walk up the device and place their finger on the capture device.
- Once the user has been authenticated, the warehouse door is released and the user can enter the warehouse.

If, when testing the finger vein recognition system with a small group of clients, the warehouse door does not open for anyone, the testing should stop, and the team will need to identify why the door is not opening as expected.

One of the considerations the team must make during the planning process is how to manage this transition. We'll take a look at some choices in the next section.

Making the transition

When determining how you will deploy a new system, there are a few methods we can follow for its implementation:

- If there isn't an existing system in place, the team can make a decision to begin operating a new system at some point.
- If the team is replacing an existing system, more planning will be required to minimize problems during the transition.

When replacing an existing system, the transition can be made by running both systems in parallel, performing a complete cutover, or even using a hybrid solution.

Now, let's take a look at what's involved when running the existing and new systems concurrently.

Running in parallel

When running in parallel, both systems will be operational. As shown in the following diagram, the team will determine a start date to phase in the new system and an end date for the existing system to retire:

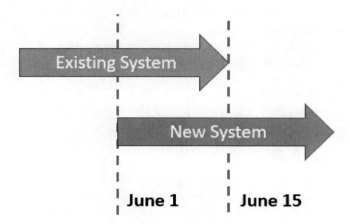

Figure 12.1 – Phasing in a new system

The team should carefully choose an end date for the existing system. You'll want to give everyone enough time to monitor the transactions and make any necessary adjustments that can improve functionality. Once the team is confident that everything is working properly, they can safely disconnect the existing system.

Some of the advantages of running in parallel include the following:

- The ability to provide a more stable transition. If there is a major failure, you can simply return to the existing system.

- An opportunity to compare accuracy and throughput against the existing system. The data can provide a clear return on investment that you can share with the stakeholders.

However, the downside to this option is that is more expensive as your team will need to manage both systems.

Another way to make a transition is by doing a clean cutover. Let's see what's involved when using this method.

Cutting over to the full implementation

In some cases, an organization will choose to immediately cut over to the new system. This could be a viable option if the team is fully confident about the success of the new implementation.

The downside to this method is that the team will have to take down the existing system. This will suspend operations for a few hours or even a few days, depending on the type of system and what needs to be transferred during deployment.

When using this method, the team needs to double-check all the configuration settings to prevent any mishaps and ensure a seamless transition. Timing is important. It's best to do the cutover when the least number of clients are interacting with the system. That way, if the system fails, fewer clients will be negatively affected.

In some cases, the organization will do a hybrid implementation to retain parts of the existing system, while gradually introducing the new system. We'll explore this concept next.

Using a hybrid transition

If the organization is complex, it may be better to adopt a hybrid approach. In this case, the existing system can remain operational, and the team can do a small rollout by doing a site by site implementation. That way, a small subset will be affected in case of failure, instead of the entire organization.

Once the planning and preparation is complete, the next step is to test and then deploy the system, as we'll learn next.

Testing and deployment

When implementing a new biometric system, testing is an important step. In this section, we'll take a look at how industry conducts rigorous trials, and then we'll outline some of the testing that should be done within the organization. We'll discuss why you should prepare documentation that describes how to use the system. We'll then see that once all the testing is complete, it will be time to move to the deployment phase.

Let's start with an overview of how the government and industries test their systems.

Outlining industry testing

Most government agencies and large enterprises regularly test their systems for accuracy, performance, and other variables using a three-phase testing procedure. This testing procedure includes the following phases:

- **Factory or Laboratory Acceptance Testing (FAT/LAT)** is conducted in a controlled environment to validate accuracy, throughput, and the overall process.

- **Site Acceptance Testing (SAT)** is performed in the production environment to ensure the system will function in the end state environment, just as it did during FAT/LAT testing. Site acceptance testing will flush out any issues that occur within the production environment, such as lighting and response times.

- **User Acceptance Testing (UAT)** is done before cutover or during parallel operations and can validate FAT/SAT by the users in real-world conditions. This exercise will pick up any capture problems that can occur from the rigor of a varied user population and situations. During UAT, any issues around failure to enroll will become evident.

When evaluating a system prior to fully deploying a new system, you'll test many of the same variables, along with other organizational-specific issues.

Let's start by looking at what's involved when testing the system.

Running the tests

Even when purchasing a system from a reputable vendor, there may be issues or bugs. In addition, although the team has finished preparing, testing will identify any problems that might adversely affect the current system. Therefore, prior to the system's full implementation, the team should outline a streamlined testing and deployment plan that includes the appropriate documentation for all clients.

During testing, you'll want to take into consideration the specific nuances for each type of system. Next, we'll outline what we might test when using a facial recognition system.

Testing a facial recognition system

When using a facial recognition system, there might be glare from lights or the sun that can adversely impact the system's ability to properly capture the facial features. In that case, the team should conduct testing at various times of the day and in the locations where the system will be implemented. This exercise will evaluate the system's performance under actual conditions, as well as whether the camera placement is correct.

It's best to run a series of simulations with a small group of users. After testing the facial recognition system, the team might observe the following:

- First-time users could not tell where to look during the capture phase.

- The system was unable to properly capture individuals whose height was less than 5'6".

- In several locations, the late afternoon sun cast a glare on the subject's face, which interfered with the capture.

This exercise will help flush out any issues that might impair the functionality of the system or cause any failure. Afterward, the team should make the appropriate modifications so that all users are able to effectively use the system.

Knowing that the goal is to minimize disruption for the clients, the team should do the following:

- Create a worksheet that outlines what the team should check to make sure the system is ready for integration and deployment.

- Complete all system backups and double-check that all operational and environmental conditions are performing properly.

- Communicate with the vendor to answer any questions and validate any contractual agreements.

Your team should also include throughput testing, which evaluates how quickly the transactions move through the system. In addition, if the system is tied to the directory, you'll want to check and make sure the system is responding to requests. During the initial evaluation, write notes on any issues that arise so that the team can resolve these issues.

While testing the process will make an easier transition to deployment, you'll still need to provide documentation to the clients, as described next.

Preparing documentation

If the system is used in a large diverse organization, you'll want to make sure that you hold regular meetings prior to full deployment to obtain input from stakeholders.

In most cases, the team should prepare documentation that outlines how to handle any issues that arise. For any system, there are generally a few main groups that will interact with it. The documentation should be appropriate for each group, as follows:

- **End users**: Includes anyone that will use the system. The users should have a simplified user guide.

- **System administrators**: These are the individuals that interact with the system on a day-to-day basis. The administrator should have a user manual and backup procedures.

- **Technical support staff**: These are the individuals that help with system-related issues, once the system is operational. The documentation includes commonly asked questions, user documentation, and procedures that will outline the conditions that require escalation.

Everyone should have contact information on whom to call in case of system failure. During the first month of implementation, you may need to update the documentation. These updates can provide information on issues that may change the way users interact with the system.

Once the team is ready to move forward, it's time to deploy the system, as outlined next.

Moving to full deployment

After passing all internal testing, and the team is confident that everyone is ready to move forward, it's time to announce the deployment.

When crafting the announcement, take time to reiterate the benefits of the system and how it will affect the users. In the announcement, stress that the team will make every effort to minimize disruption and that, shortly, everyone will be trained on how to use the new system.

Once the system has been deployed, the team should continue testing during this early operational phase and report any issues as soon as possible.

Whatever method the team uses to make the transition, at some point, the new implementation will be in a reliable state. It will then be time to retire the existing system.

One of the ways to ensure a successful deployment and continued use of the new system is by providing training to all users. We'll explore some of the ways we can train our clients in the next section.

Providing education and awareness

Deploying a new system in an organization can have a major effect on the population. Training users on a new system can be challenging. However, education, training, and awareness should be part of the transition. Not only does this help everyone get up to speed on the new system, but it helps manage change in a positive way.

During the training process, the team should provide an overview of the basics of how the biometric system works, along with some of the benefits. In addition, the team will need to make the clients aware that, before using the system, they will need to be enrolled.

In most cases, the transition team has made everyone aware of the new system. As the time gets closer to deployment, the team needs to begin the training phase. In this section, we'll take a look at selecting an appropriate format, as well as ways to customize the training so that it is specific to the audience.

Training can be done in a variety of ways. It's important to select the right format, as we'll see in the next section.

Choosing a training format

Training users on a new biometric system may not be necessary for everyone as some individuals are more comfortable with change and technology. However, it is strongly recommended to require training for everyone, for a couple of reasons. One reason is that all employees will receive the correct information on how to use the system. In addition, this can be a time to reinforce why the new system is of benefit to the entire organization.

Training can be done in a number of different formats. You might choose an interactive format with a live trainer or use an online, asynchronous approach with short interactive videos.

Regardless of the format, the team should evaluate the ways to get the best value from the training process. Some best practice advice includes the following:

- Think about what is really required for training. Learning should be dynamic and fun, and too much information can overwhelm the learner. Offer only what is required to get users up and running with the new system.

- Add an incentive for completing the training, such as light snacks for live training or a gift card to a coffee shop when training online. This small gesture shows that you value the employee's time and helps to reward their efforts.

One format you can use to introduce your users to the new system is by using prepackaged training from the vendor. We'll explore this concept next.

Training the trainer

When purchasing a new system, the vendor may offer an on-site training package. The package is generally in a well-planned format that contains all the knowledge necessary to efficiently and effectively train your employees. In some cases, training comes as part of the purchase, or it may be an additional cost.

If the organization obtains a package with the vendor, they will send an instructor to review the training material. The instructor will generally spend 1 to several days at the facility helping the team make the transition by educating the clients on the new system.

The trainer may need to instruct everyone in the group at a large meeting. Or, in some cases, the organization may opt for a "train the trainer" program. When using "train the trainer", the vendor trains a single individual in the organization. That individual then trains the rest of the organization. If the organization selects this option, they will need to identify someone internally to conduct the sessions.

The individual that's selected as a trainer should have a solid idea of the way the new system works. In addition, it will be helpful if that individual was part of the initial testing. That way, if issues arise, they may have an idea of how to deal with the problem.

In many cases, training can be offered on-demand in video format, as outlined next.

Microlearning and video simulations

Video training is an option today where the client goes through a series of interactive simulations that show how the system works. If appropriate, you can add an element of gamification, which adds incentives to the learning module.

You can also have short, microlearning modules on the organization's portal. These short modules will focus on a single, targeted learning objective. Microlearning modules are ideal when the client simply needs a refresher on how to interact with the system.

Regardless of what type of format is used, after training, you'll want to give everyone a chance to process the information they've received. In addition, you might want to have a short follow-up so that you can answer questions and review concepts.

Along with choosing an appropriate format for training, you may need to select an individual to either conduct or manage the training process. It's important to find the right fit so that training is successful. Let's see what's involved in selecting a trainer.

Selecting a trainer

Training is a critical aspect of any new deployment. The users need to be able to understand how to correctly use the system and embrace the new technology. If you decide to use the vendor supplied instructor, that individual will have all the skills required to effectively educate your users on the new system.

However, when an organization opts to use live, in-house training, or uses the "train the trainer" option, you'll want to select a trainer with the right mixture of skills and patience.

If possible, have a dedicated individual that coordinates and conducts the training process. That way, the format can be standardized so that everyone is receiving the same message. In addition, all materials will be kept updated, and if there are any system changes, the coordinator can disseminate the information in a consistent manner. Furthermore, the trainer can be a liaison between the clients and the technical support staff, in order to answer questions and troubleshoot common issues.

While it may sound reasonable to put an **Information Technology** (**IT**) person in charge of the training process, it might be a better fit to select a non-IT person. When training non-IT individuals, you'll want someone who has excellent communication skills and can engage an audience.

It's key to know your audience so that you select the right format for training. In the next section, we'll review ways we can tailor training for each group.

Customizing the training process

In a large, diverse organization with thousands of employees, you'll most likely need to include customized training for the individuals that will work directly with the system. Users can include end users, system administrators, and the technical support staff.

The training process should be customized for each group, as follows:

- **End users**: This includes anyone that will use the system and represents the largest group that the team will need to train. The training process for the end users should focus on the functional areas of how the user will interact with the system.

- **Technical support staff**: These are people that help with system-related issues once the system is operational. The training process for this group will include everything the end users receive, along with system training in performance monitoring and troubleshooting.

- **System administrators**: These are people who work with the system on a day-to-day basis. This group will encompass all of what is required for the technical support staff, along with additional education in the technical aspects of the system. Training will include learning how to manage upgrades, run reports, monitor transactions, debug the system, tune the thresholds, and enable and disable users.

Both the technical support group and the system administrators will be more involved in the day-to-day operation of the system. As a result, they'll be able to participate in discussions on future improvements and enhancements.

When deploying a new system, education, training, and awareness should be part of the transition. Because of the differences in each system, during training, the user should be given guidelines on the best way to interact with the system. For example, if using palm vein technology, you'll want to stress to the client that they do not have to touch the device. After the training process, do a brief survey to give clients the ability to rate their experience.

The team should continue to offer support, even after the initial training. In addition, the training process should be a part of on-boarding new employees.

Once training is underway, it's time to enroll the users in the system. Let's take a look.

Enrolling users

Throughout the training process, the clients are made aware of the benefits of the biometric system and are told that enrollment will be necessary. As a result, once the system is up and operational, the next step is to enroll the users in the system.

In this section, we'll take a look at the process of enrolling the users. We'll outline some of the considerations when adding a new user to the system, as well as the importance of providing feedback. Finally, we'll see how, if there are issues with the biometric system, we can use some troubleshooting techniques that can improve the process.

Next, we'll step through the process of enrolling a new user.

Stepping through the enrollment process

During the enrollment process, the user presents their biometric identifier for the first time. The identifier is then stored in the system database for later comparison. After the subject is enrolled, they can present a biometric sample, and the system will determine whether there is a match.

In most cases, the system should be designed with intuitive instructions and self-guided prompts. However, it's always best to have someone monitor the enrollment process so that they have an idea of how to properly use the system.

We'll explore how to add a new user next.

Adding a new user

Once fully deployed, you may have to enroll a large number of people into the system. Take your time when completing the enrollment process. You'll want most of the clients to successfully enroll into the system and have a positive feeling about the process.

A secure enrollment process maintains the integrity of the system, particularly for access control. Therefore, the first phase will be to manually verify the identity of the individual before the enrollment process, by using an employee badge or documentation. After this verification, the user will be cleared to move through the enrollment phase.

If the team is enrolling a large group, try to have enough members present, and keep the pace steady. In most cases, the biometric system will have an interface where you'll see a series of prompts. This process may go as follows:

1. Select the user, then select the **Enroll Biometric** menu choice.

2. Depending on the biometric, the system will prompt with a message regarding how to present the biometric. For example, if you're using palm vein technology, you might see a prompt that states **Place your hand over the device. Once you see the green light, remove your hand**.

3. Once the system has successfully obtained the biometric sample, you may see a visual prompt stating **Enrollment Complete**.

4. As a follow-up step, it's best practice to verify the client's enrollment in some way.

Once the client has been enrolled, they are then able to use the system, which we'll discuss next.

Using the system

During informational meetings, or while training on the system, the team should educate the clients on how they will use the system.

For example, the system may work in the following ways:

- As part of a time and attendance system, which enables employees to clock in and clock out of the organization. This helps provide more detailed time recording for payroll.

- To monitor employees' movements in and out of a facility, which provides location awareness for supervisors and co-workers.

- As a way to log into the organization at the employees' desk. Instead of a username and PIN, they will authenticate with their biometric identifier.

It's important to understand the audience and provide appropriate feedback so that the clients can confidently interact with the system. In addition, the team needs to be aware of the fact there can be issues regarding the comfort level with biometrics, which includes ergonomic and privacy issues.

An important element of any biometric system is providing feedback, as discussed next.

Providing feedback

Once the client has enrolled, they will be able to use the biometric system. The client will present the biometric sample, and the system will indicate whether there is a match.

Feedback is information returned to the user regarding the results of the process and can be in one of several forms: audio, visual, or even verbal. When using feedback in a biometric system, this helps the client know the status of the transaction.

As the team prepares the clients for the change, they may even use a combination of visual and verbal feedback. For example, when clients successfully go through the system, the client might see a visual light from the system interface indicating there was a match. In addition, the team member can nod to the client and say, "You're good".

Especially when the system is new, additional feedback helps build the client's confidence that they are correctly interacting with the system. This validation helps keep the process moving.

When using feedback, you'll want to use the appropriate methods, such as the following:

- Visual feedback, using easy to understand symbols
- Audio feedback, in short phrases in the appropriate language

In addition to feedback, the team should be prepared to address concerns over using the biometric system, as we'll discuss next.

Recognizing concerns

Even with careful planning and training, some clients will be hesitant to use the new biometric system. One reason for this hesitancy is simply because of change. An employee who has used the same key card method to gain access to a facility for years might be uncomfortable using a facial recognition system.

A single individual's negative response can lead to widespread groupthink, which can affect the process. As a result, careful planning is important, and we need to quickly address any concerns to ensure that the process will continue to move forward.

More and more individuals and companies that recognize the power of adding biometrics form a layered approach to security. In general, most people will accept the new system; however, there may be a few individuals that will be hesitant to use their biometric system for identification and authentication. This can be for several reasons, as follows:

- Fear that the biometric may identify a medical condition.
- Apprehension of being able to move through the system because of a physical limitation, such as using a walker.

In addition, there may be general concerns over the privacy of the biometric data. Because of this, many corporations take a proactive approach and provide a **Privacy Impact Assessment (PIA)** to all employees. The PIA outlines what data you are collecting, along with how it is used, stored, and protected, and becomes part of the organization's policies.

The team needs to address the client's concerns as soon as possible in order to resolve any issues so that the deployment will continue to be successful.

There are times when the system doesn't respond as expected. In that case, you may need to do some troubleshooting, as outlined next.

Troubleshooting the process

In most cases, the team will do everything to ensure that clients are able to enroll and move through the system. If the system doesn't respond appropriately, the team needs to determine what has happened.

Periodically, enrolled clients may have trouble logging into the biometric system. In that case, the technician should go through proper troubleshooting procedures. For example, they can do the following to resolve an issue:

- Make sure all the cables and the power supply are secure.
- Check the position of the client and/or the device. For example, if, during facial recognition, there is a glare on the client's face, this can interfere with the capture.
- Determine whether the problem is with one client, or multiple clients. If multiple clients are affected, the team needs to contact the system administrator.
- Try to manually authenticate the client with the system. If you are successful, that will mean the user account is valid and that the problem is most likely with the device.

Once the technician has attempted to resolve the issue, have the client attempt to log in again. If they continue to be unsuccessful, you may need to escalate the problem.

Some issues are related to the enrollment process, as some users are unable to enroll for one reason or another. It's possible that the system could not obtain a decent sample or enough features to create a template. Explain to the client that this happens every once in a while, and that it's best to try again.

However, in some cases, the client cannot be recognized for a particular biometric. A scientist named *George Doddington* identified these individuals as goats. He classified individuals according to their ability to be recognized by a biometric system by referring to them as Doddington's zoo. These examples include the following:

- **Sheep** are clients that are easy to recognize.
- **Goats** are clients that are difficult to recognize.
- **Lambs** are clients that are easy to spoof.
- **Wolves** are those that can imitate others.

For the most part, a biometric system will work as expected. However, as outlined previously, issues can occur during enrollment or with identification or authentication. During training, the team should provide instructions to the clients regarding how they report any issues, as well as what action they should take if the biometric system doesn't work.

In the next section, we'll take a look at what modifications we can make so that the biometric system operation is in line with acceptable results.

Fine-tuning the decision process

When thinking about a biometric identifier, we know that it represents some human attribute. Because we are dealing with human attributes, there are times we must make some adjustments to the system so that the system returns an acceptable result.

In this section, we'll see why there may be a need to upgrade the template on file because of significant changes to the client's biometric identifier. We'll also see how human intervention might be required during the matching process, as well as how we can tune the acceptance threshold. In addition, to always get the most accurate results, we'll see why it's important to prevent spoofing.

First, we'll take a look at examining the client's template.

Upgrading the template

A biometric system, like any other system, must be upgraded and maintained. In addition to the system, we must take the users into account. Over time, the system may not be able to make a match because of Template Aging. Template Aging is a result of changes in a user's physiological or behavioral characteristics over time. These biometric characteristics can change due to surgery, illness, or injury. Let's take a look at some of them:

- **Surgery** can include cataract surgery, which can affect iris recognition, or plastic surgery, which could affect facial recognition.

- **Certain illnesses** can influence the effectiveness of biometrics, such as skin diseases, which can affect fingerprint recognition, or throat cancer, which can affect voice recognition.

- **Aging**, such as wear and tear of the fingertips over time, can change an individual's fingerprint, or weakness of the vocal muscle, which can affect voice recognition.

Templates typically don't expire as most biometrics have a permanence to them. However, periodically, the administrator may have to retire a template and have the client re-enroll into the system.

In addition, many systems will capture multiple templates per person to increase accuracy. This is similar to the process where we enroll our fingerprints into a mobile device. We provide multiple captures at different angles and areas of the friction ridge so that the device has additional images to compare.

Although most systems are automated and require minimal human involvement, there may be a need to assist by manually intervening. Let's take a look.

Providing a human touch

If the system fails to provide an appropriate response, you'll need to determine the reason behind the failure. At that point, you may have to fine-tune the decision process. When fine-tuning the system, take a look at the physical premises, and make sure the environment is conducive to the biometric; for example, making sure there is consistent lighting for an iris recognition system.

In some cases, a biometric system may need human intervention. For example, during facial recognition, when a client moves through the system, they will get either a response of match or no-match. However, in some cases, the response might be undetermined. In a solely automated system, an undetermined match will default to no-match. The undetermined results will go to a human for review. In that case, they will use additional methods to provide verification.

A biometric is never 100%; it is a threshold. In some cases, we can tune the decision process to an acceptable level. We'll explore this concept next.

Tuning the threshold

When evaluating the results, the system will provide a level of confidence that there is a match. As shown in the following diagram, if you set the system at a level of .50, you will match a higher number of individuals, and the result will be less accurate. However, if you set the system at a level of .90, you will match a lower number of individuals, but the results will be more accurate:

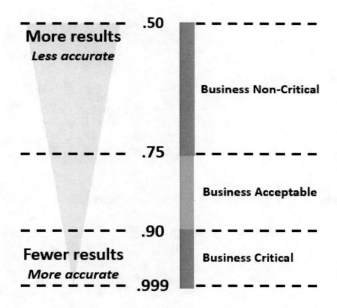

Figure 12.2 – Thresholds and accuracy rates

The default setting will depend on the system; that is, you might see the default setting listed at .65. The system administrator can tune or modify the settings from 0 - 1. However, any adjustments should be in line with the organizational policy.

System settings can be in the following ranges:

- Non-critical activities ranging from .50 - .75 can include activities such as a gym.
- Acceptable activities ranging from .75 - .90 can include activities such as a private club.
- Critical activities ranging from .90 and above can include activities such as financial transactions.

For example, in a low security setting, such as a gym or private club environment, the system may not have to be as rigorous. Depending on the type of business, you can adjust the setting to match the business requirements. For example, if you had a beach or hunting club, you might set the threshold at .85. That would mean anyone that matched with a value of .85 and above would be admitted to the club.

After the system has been in production for a minimum of 30 days, it's important to review the efficacy of the current match threshold. Once you've reviewed the **False Match Rate (FMR)** and **False Non Match Rate (FNMR)**, you may need to adjust the settings.

However, in most cases, a biometric system will return accurate results. With any biometric system, there is the threat that an imposter may gain access to the system. With the sheer amount of faces publicly available, spoofing a system is possible. We'll look at what vendors can do to foil spoofing attempts next.

Preventing spoofing

Companies work hard to prevent presentation attacks. One way to combat spoofing is by testing the system. There are Spoof Bounty programs that reward individuals for successfully spoofing their system. By testing, the vendors can understand their vulnerabilities, and then take proactive steps to prevent others from tricking their system. You can read more on this at `https://www.spoofbounty.com/`.

With more biometrics being used today, vendors continue to improve their systems. Today, there are facial recognition systems that can detect masks, and algorithms are adapting to individuals that have had cosmetic surgery. With these advances in technology and the various enhancements that are available, biometric systems will continue to improve security and privacy in our lives.

Summary

In this chapter, we outlined how testing a system prior to full deployment will help identify bugs and issues with the process early on and avoid problems. We discussed how to prepare for deployment, as well as the various ways we can complete the deployment if we are replacing an existing system. We reviewed the importance of providing documentation for the users and team members. Then, we took a look at what steps to take once the team is ready to move forward to full deployment.

We then moved to the process of enrolling users and outlined some of the considerations when adding a new user to the system. Then, we evaluated some troubleshooting techniques to use if the system is not working as expected. We learned how the template on file may need to be updated because of significant changes to the client's biometric identifier. We then covered examples of using human intervention to improve the matching process. We also learned the we can tune the threshold so that the biometric system is in line with acceptable results, according to the type of business. Finally, we recognized that in order to obtain the most accurate results, we'll want to prevent spoofing.

In the next chapter, we'll take a look at some practical biometric applications in use today. We'll see how law enforcement uses biometrics to identify or verify individuals, along with ways biometrics are used in identifying individuals during a forensic examination. We'll then learn how biometrics can assist in providing recognition for large venues, such as threat management, along with monitoring a prison population. We'll also compare the many different methods biometrics use to restrict access to sensitive computer systems and restricted areas. Finally, we'll see some new uses for biometrics in commercial applications.

Questions

Now, it's time to check your knowledge. Select the best response, then check your answers, which can be found in the *Assessment* section at the end of this book:

1. Vendors regularly test their systems for accuracy, performance, and other variables, in the form of _____ testing.

   a. stub

   b. market

   c. star

   d. beta

2. The team has choices when making the transition to a new system. When running in _____, both systems will be operational. With this transition, the team will determine a start date to phase in the new system, and an end date for the existing system to retire.

   a. parallel

   b. sync

c. cutover mode

d. beta

3. Training can be done in a number of different formats. You might choose an interactive format with a live trainer, or use an online, asynchronous approach with short, interactive_____.

    a. playing cards

    b. videos

    c. geofencing apps

    d. upgrades

4. _____ is information that's returned to the user due to the results of a process and can be in one of several forms: audio, visual, or even verbal.

    a. Gap analysis

    b. Upgrading

    c. Feedback

    d. Geofencing

5. When using the "_____" approach, the vendor trains a single individual in the organization, who then trains the rest of the organization.

    a. beta

    b. geofencing

    c. move to market

    d. train the trainer

6. Template _____ is a result of the changes in a user's physiological or behavioral characteristics over time.

    a. training

    b. aging

    c. moving

    d. feedback

7. One way to combat spoofing is by testing the system. There are Spoof _____ programs that reward individuals for successfully spoofing their system.

    a. Beta

    b. Feedback

    c. Bounty

    d. Mug

Further reading

- To learn the importance of training users on a new system, visit `http://www.saxonslearningsolutions.com.au/blog/tech/the-importance-of-training-staff-when-upgrading-it-systems/`.

- To learn more about beta testing, visit `https://betatesting.com/beta-testers`.

- For an introspective look at George Doddington's Zoo, visit `http://www.cse.msu.edu/~rossarun/BiometricsTextBook/Papers/Introduction/DoddingtonSheep_ICSLP98.pdf`.

- To read more on how cataract surgery can interfere with iris recognition, visit `https://thewire.in/the-sciences/cataract-surgery-aadhaar-iris-biometric-authezit https://tsapps.nist.gov/publication/get_pdf.cfm?pub_id=904876`.

- To read more on liveness detection, visit `https://www.biometricupdate.com/201909/liveness-detection-in-biometrics-is-essential`.

- Learn how systems can detect facial masks by going to `https://gcn.com/articles/2020/06/03/facial-recognition-masks.aspx`.

- For an overview of accuracy thresholds, visit `https://www.kairos.com/blog/the-secret-to-better-face-recognition-accuracy-thresholds`.

- For an overview of the tips for training end users, visit `https://www.princeton.edu/~pshrsys/Implementation%20Plan/Strategies/EndUserTraining.html`.

13

Discovering Practical Biometric Applications

In this chapter, we'll examine the many uses for biometrics in modern-day applications. You'll learn how biometrics are used to enforce the law, and how a large percentage of the countries around the world are adopting some form of biometric recognition. We'll see how biometrics can help deter impersonation attacks and identity fraud, along with the ways the technology can protect children. We'll then briefly discuss the importance of standards, which provide interoperability of biometric data among systems and allow agencies to share biometric data. We'll then take a look at how biometrics are essential in identifying individuals during a forensic examination.

You'll understand how a government-run biometric databases store a large volume of biometric data, which can be used to identify persons of interest during an investigation. We'll take a look at how facial recognition technology is being used for surveillance and monitoring. In addition, we'll see how biometrics can assist in providing recognition for large venues, such as threat management in stadiums and monitoring a prison population. We'll compare the many different ways biometrics restrict access to sensitive computer systems as highly secure areas. Finally, we'll see some new uses for biometrics in commercial applications, such as contactless fingerprint technology and paying your grocery bill with your face or fingerprint.

In this chapter, we're going to cover the following main topics:

- Understanding biometrics and law enforcement
- Identifying individuals during forensics
- Providing recognition for large venues
- Controlling access to assets, buildings, and systems
- Recognizing novel uses for biometrics

Understanding biometrics and law enforcement

Biometrics are the behavioral and physiological characteristics that are unique to an individual. As a result, biometrics can help us in many different ways. One way is by assisting officials in law enforcement.

To enforce the law and provide security, multiple entities, including law enforcement, forensic scientists, and security specialists, provide protection in three separate concepts. These concepts are security, threat management, and forensics, as shown in the following figure:

SECURITY   **THREAT MANAGEMENT**   **FORENSICS**

Proactive   Active   Reactive

Figure 13.1 – Biometrics influence in providing security and upholding and enforcing the law

Although the three concepts are related, they have distinct differences, as follows:

- **Security** includes proactive methods to enforce the law, prevent damage or the theft of physical or logical objects, and ensure the safety of individuals. For example, we secure our systems by providing access controls.

- **Threat management** is actively working to prevent an attack or a system compromise, such as monitoring for threats by using surveillance.

- **Forensics** is reactive, in that these are the things we do after a physical attack, theft, or data breach has taken place. We use forensics to recognize potential criminals or identify the victim of a crime.

In this section, we'll examine how biometrics are used to enforce the law, prevent fraud, and protect children. We'll then take a look at the importance of standards to provide interoperability so that agencies can share the biometric data with one another. Let's start with the ways biometrics can aid in enforcing the law.

Enforcing the law

Officials in law enforcement have recognized the value of using biometrics for many years. Within the last decade, there have been major advances in technology, and a greater interest in developing biometric databases. As a result, we have seen an expansion of the many ways officials use biometric identifiers to enforce the law.

For example, one way to ensure the trustworthiness of an individual is by conducting a background check. This investigates an individual's background, using a variety of sources, such as their driving record, credit score, and criminal record. During this check, anyone in a position of trust, such as teachers, taxi drivers, or individuals working with children, will get fingerprinted. The individual's fingerprints are then checked to see whether they exist in a database of known criminals. After the background check is complete, the individual's prints may be kept in a database for a period of time.

One example is the use of biometric data within agencies in the **United States** (**US**). Let's take a look.

Exchanging data within the US

When law enforcement agencies in the US collect fingerprints while booking a suspected criminal, they share the data with the **Federal Bureau of Investigation** (**FBI**).

In addition to the FBI, there are several other agencies that collect and store fingerprints from individuals, for various reasons. These agencies include the following:

- **U.S. Customs and Border Protection (CBP)**

- **Immigration and Customs Enforcement (ICE)**

- **The Department of Homeland Security (DHS)**

These and other agencies have cooperation and exchange agreements that allow them to share biometric information with one another if they have a suspect in custody.

As the databases grow and evolve, countries are seeing the value in exchanging biometric data with one another, as we'll see next.

Cooperating countries

A large percentage of countries around the world are adopting some form of biometric recognition. Officials are using biometrics to secure our cities and aid in the apprehension of criminals. Some examples of countries that use biometrics include the following:

- The **United Kingdom (UK)** uses a program called IDENT1, which is a biometrics database designed to arm law enforcement with the data they need to track down known criminals.

- The US has several repositories of biometric data, such as the **Homeland Advanced Recognition Technology (HART)** system, which provides data for several agencies in the US. Agencies include those that deal with immigration and border control, law enforcement, and national security.

- Many nations, such as Japan, China, and Canada, are using surveillance in the form of facial recognition.

> **Important note**
>
> The HART system has replaced the legacy **Automated Biometric Identification System (IDENT)** and is the primary biometric repository for the DHS.

Each country uses biometric data in a number of different ways. Uses include border control, securing financial applications, and surveillance.

Several countries recognize the value of sharing their biometric databases with one another. For example, the US and Malaysia have an agreement to share biometric information on terrorist suspects to bolster border control.

In addition to enforcing the law, biometrics help provide an important role in preventing fraud, as outlined next.

Preventing fraud

Many countries use biometric identifiers for things such as driver's licenses and cards for social service recipients. The use of biometrics helps prevent impersonation and synthetic identity fraud, which are defined as follows:

- **Impersonation** is where someone pretends to be someone else. Impersonation might be used for a number of different reasons, such as gaining access to a facility or obtaining goods or services.

- **Synthetic identity fraud** is where someone creates a new identity. This type of fraud gathers information from many sources and combines valid information along with credentials that are fabricated. Part of the identity can be a harvested Social Security number from someone, such as an unsuspecting child or a deceased individual.

Impersonation or identity fraud is dangerous and can have devastating effects on an individual, both financially and emotionally. Using biometrics helps to prevent fraud and impersonation, by using one of a few ways:

- **Multi-modal biometrics** or fusion matching will collect and match two biometric identifiers, such as a fingerprint and face. This will provide a higher degree of accuracy and security, and can be used in lieu of **multi-factor authentication (MFA)**.

- **Liveness detection** includes hardware and software techniques that are used to recognize a possible presentation attack – for example, when someone tries to spoof a facial recognition system by using a latex mask. Liveness detection can help provide proof of a real face and not a mask or image. Techniques can include thermal sensing to determine the temperature of the face, in conjunction with detecting facial movements.

In addition to using either fusion matching and/or liveness detection to prevent deception when using a system, companies have been refining methods to detect possible fraudulent records. One method is by using biometric deduplication, which is a technique used to search biometric databases for a duplicate identifier, which may be an indication of fraud.

For example, imagine using a voting process where users are required to present a card with their personal information and their photograph. When using biometric deduplication, when someone registers for the first time, the system will check to see whether there is a duplicate individual or image in the system.

Biometrics can also assist law enforcement in the case of missing or exploited children, as we'll learn next.

Protecting children

Every year, there are hundreds of thousands of children that go missing. A child can be abducted or wander off in a crowded place. This can be terrifying, for the child and the parents or guardians. Immediately after someone notifies law enforcement that a child is missing, efforts begin to locate the child.

One thing a parent can do in case of a sudden disappearance is prepare and update a kit that can help identify the child.

A parent or guardian can craft their own kit, get a kit online, or download a form from sites such as `https://www.ready.gov/sites/default/files/NCMEC_Child_ID_Kit_wc_FEMA_508.pdf`.

The kit can include a form that allows you to add information. Some kits will include a swab for a DNA sample that can be collected. In addition, many kits contain an inkless fingerprint pad or paper, so you can easily obtain the child's fingerprints.

When filling out the form, the parent or guardian should complete the following where applicable:

- Personal information that includes demographics such as name and address, along with physical attributes, such as height and approximate weight.
- Medical information that can be critical during an investigation, such as if the child is diabetic or other issues that require life-saving medication.
- Identifying features, such as scars, tattoos, and birthmarks, should be identified. This should be updated if there is any change over time.
- A photo of the child, which should be updated every 6 months.
- Fingerprints of all 10 fingers should be recorded. This only needs to be done one time, as fingerprints do not change, unless they become scarred in some way.

As you can see, there is sufficient biometric information to provide the ability to identify the child. However, none of the information is maintained by law enforcement. The kit is held by the parents or guardians to present to law enforcement in the case of an emergency.

With the many benefits that biometrics provide for law enforcement, it is of great value for these agencies to be able to exchange information. Standards help provide interoperability between systems, so they can seamlessly exchange biometric data with one another. Let's explore this idea.

Providing standards

Law enforcement agencies obtain biometric data to identify an individual for a variety of reasons. However, the only way the individual will be found is if there is a template in the database in which to compare the sample. Many organizations rely on the cooperation of other agencies to share information. The key element in being able to share biometric data is the standards that define the format for data exchange.

The **National Institute of Science and Technology** (**NIST**) has been involved in this effort for decades. Standards provide inoperability for manufacturers and dissimilar systems. The first standards were for fingerprints in the late 1980s. Since then, other standards have been developed for the exchange of many other types of biometrics, including the following:

- Palm prints, scars, and tattoos
- Iris, voice, and face

Biometrics play an important role in law enforcement and security. However, we also see the value in recognizing the influence in biometrics during a forensic investigation. Let's take a look.

Identifying individuals during forensics

Whenever there is an illegal activity, such as an attack, homicide, burglary, or system compromise, we can use forensics. Forensics can aid in the ability to do the following:

- Recognize potential criminals.
- Identify the victim of a crime.

Part of an effective forensic investigation is collecting evidence, which is necessary in order to solve a crime or identify a victim. Next, let's see what's involved when gathering evidence for an investigation.

Collecting evidence

After an illegal activity or event, investigators will collect evidence in order to solve the case. Once the investigators have solved the crime, the case may have to be presented in court. If that happens, the prosecutors will need to present evidence, which can include the following:

- **Best evidence** is unaltered evidence that is in its original form.

- **Corroborating evidence** is used to support other evidence.

- **Indirect or circumstantial evidence** is combined with other evidence in order to craft a theory or hypothesis.

Biometric identifiers can be an invaluable resource that can provide evidence in a forensics exercise. During an investigation, biometrics can help identify a criminal, bystander, or victim that may have been involved in a crime.

If there is biometric evidence on the scene, investigators will collect the evidence and submit it for analysis. Evidence can include fingerprints, **deoxyribonucleic acid** (**DNA**), facial images, and palm prints.

Certain types of biometric identifiers can be used for evidence in court; however, some can only provide an investigative lead. Let's take a look at the difference.

Providing positive identification

When submitting evidence of a crime, the only two biometric identifiers that are currently accepted in court to provide a positive identification are DNA and fingerprints. All other biometrics require corroborating evidence of identification and culpability.

For example, when gathering evidence, investigators might obtain a facial image from a security camera that has recorded someone committing a crime. The identification can provide a lead to follow up on a person of interest; however, the investigators must provide other evidence in order to make their case. That is because a facial image is not recognized as a foolproof way to identify an individual and cannot be used as the sole basis of an arrest.

The investigators will attempt to identify those that may have been at the scene of the crime. In order to do this, the biometric evidence is run through known biometric databases in order to find a match. Let's explore this concept.

Finding a match

Today, there are many large biometric repositories that are maintained by governments. The databases are used for surveillance and assist in providing national security. Government biometric databases include the following:

- The FBI's **Integrated Automated Fingerprint Identification System (IAFIS)**
- India's **Unique Identification Authority of India (UIDAI)** system

These repositories collect a vast amount of biometric data that includes fingerprints, faces, scars, and tattoos and can help law enforcement to identify a person of interest. In addition to housing a large volume of biometric data, these powerful systems are able to effectively and efficiently search for a potential match.

Another key use of biometrics, typically by a coroner's office, is identifying an unknown person that has died either by natural causes or homicide. This is an important use of biometric identification, as it provides closure for families.

However, there are some limitations on the effectiveness of biometrics identified during an investigation, which can include the following:

- There might not be a sufficient amount of evidence to be able to determine the identity of someone at the crime scene. For example, finding only a partial fingerprint instead of the entire print might not contain enough minutiae points for comparison.
- At times, there are inconsistent standard procedures in collecting and processing evidence among agencies involved in an investigation. This can result in evidence that can't be admissible in court.

During a forensic search, there are different types of searches used to identify an individual. Next, let's take a look at the different types of searches used during an investigation.

Searching for prints

Law enforcement has several basic categories of fingerprint and palmprint searches that are used in an investigation. When doing a search, the fingerprints and palmprints are described as follows:

- Ten print (or tenprint) refers to a collection of a subject's fingerprints obtained and preserved in some manner.
- Palmprints refer to the prints obtained from any area on the palm.

Fingerprints and palmprints may be obtained either by the subject willingly offering their prints – for example, during a background check – or during a forensic investigation.

If obtained during a forensic investigation, the investigators must locate fingerprints that were left on surfaces. Called *latent fingerprints*, these are commonly invisible to the naked eye. The investigators must obtain the prints by using special tools and techniques, such as dusting powder and clear tape, to lift the fingerprints to be used for comparison.

Once either the fingerprints or palmprints are obtained, they can be processed by searching the databases, using any of the following methods:

- Using a ten print or palmprint is a standard search that is used when conducting a background check to see whether the subject's prints are associated with a criminal record.

- Latent fingerprints or palmprints are used to locate an unknown latent print found at a crime scene against a database in order to provide identification.

More advanced techniques use a combination of standard searches along with searching other databases. These advanced searches can help link a subject to a past crime, or even a series of crimes. Let's take a look.

Looking for a missing link

Many states have a criminal justice service that is dedicated to solving crimes. However, some crimes remain unsolved, possibly for years. In some cases, investigators will run additional searches in order to find a missing link to an unsolved crime. Two other searches that use advanced searches include the following:

- Ten-print or palmprint-to-unsolved latent search
- Unsolved latent-to-unsolved latent search

Ten-print or palmprint-to-unsolved latent search is used in conjunction with a standard search. These searches go through an **unsolved latent file** (**ULF**) database that contains fingerprints and palmprints from unsolved crimes. Also called reverse searching, the goal is to match the subject's prints with a print found in the database, and possibly link the subject to an unsolved crime.

This is a powerful search. However, this technique is prohibited by law in some jurisdictions.

The unsolved latent-to-unsolved latent search takes a deep dive into the ULF database. This search compares an unknown latent print against all other unknown latent prints in the database. With this type of search, the goal isn't to provide identification but to link multiple unsolved crimes.

For example, if the investigator obtains a latent print from a crime scene, they can then run the print against the ULF database. The results might show that the print is a match with several other prints. In this case, the investigator might not be able to identify who committed the crime, but they will see that the print was associated with multiple cases. This can then allow the investigators to pool evidence and leads from what appeared to be separate crimes into a single investigation.

As we can see, there are a number of ways that we can use biometrics to identify individuals during a forensic examination. However, biometric databases can also assist in providing active threat management, as well as monitoring for persons of interest, as we'll see next.

Providing recognition for large venues

Along with the massive government biometric databases available today, we are seeing an increase in the use of **Facial Recognition Technology** (**FRT**) for surveillance and monitoring. Some of the examples include the following:

- Employing FRT to observe individuals as they travel through airports and train stations.
- Providing real-time threat management by monitoring traffic in large venues such as shopping malls.
- Using the technology in stores to deter theft. In some cases, a known thief's face is shared among other retailers, which can ban that individual from entering the stores.

Because of the advances in FRT, surveillance and monitoring can be done in large venues to monitor for threats. One example is the use of this technology at *Taylor Swift* concerts. Taylor Swift is a popular American singer-songwriter. Because of the threat of stalkers attending the concerts, security experts built a facial recognition system into a kiosk that showcased Swift's rehearsal sessions. As the onlookers gazed into the kiosk, their faces were scanned and run through databases that held the facial images of known stalkers and subjects who posed security threats.

Another large venue is prisons. Prison officials are constantly seeking ways to more effectively and securely manage their prisoners. Let's see how biometrics can be an effective way to monitor prisoners.

Monitoring a prison population

Keeping tabs on prisoners has been a challenge for many years. That is because, in many locations, the prison population is constantly growing and changing. Using biometrics to track prisoners' movements have been in use since the mid-2000s. While fingerprint technology was widely used, methods have now expanded to include iris recognition to identify inmates. Let's see why this is a more optimal biometric.

Using iris recognition

Many prisons have used fingerprint technology for years to identify their prisoners. However, more and more prisons are moving to iris recognition as a more secure option to identify prisoners.

Iris recognition is a better option than fingerprint technology for a couple of reasons:

- Depending on the inmate's activity, they may have damaged their fingertips, making it hard to get an acceptable sample for comparison.

- Iris recognition is contactless, meaning the inmate does not have to touch a sensor. In addition, there is no sensor to constantly clean. This makes iris recognition a more optimal, sanitary solution.

In some cases, a prisoner may be confined to their home. This is where the prisoner must serve their sentence, generally with restrictions on what they can do while confined. Next, let's see how biometrics can help manage this population.

Confinement to the home

When low-risk prisoners are released to continue their incarceration at home, biometrics technology provides a secure way to check in with prison officials. The prisoners might use one or more techniques to verify their identity. Biometric technology can be used for the following cases:

- To monitor for alcohol use by using an ankle monitor

- To verify identity by using fingerprint or facial recognition during the check-in process

In addition to monitoring for alcohol use and verifying their identity, thermal imaging can be used to assess an inmate's temperature, either while in prison or during house arrest.

Nowadays, we are seeing advances in software and hardware that is readily available and more affordable. That, coupled with expanded internet connectivity, provides the optimal landscape for countries to use FRT to monitor the activity of their citizens. Let's explore this next.

Securing countries

Countries are expanding the use of FRT to locations throughout the nation. Governments are installing a large number of cameras that are used for surveillance, law enforcement, and threat monitoring. Many are in larger cities; however, smaller communities are now installing cameras in various locations too.

Some of the countries that are enhancing their surveillance technology include the following:

- Australia, where FRT is used in airports to help travelers quickly move through security checkpoints.

- Russia is using facial recognition in many locations throughout the country and cities, such as Moscow, to help law enforcement monitor criminal activity.

- Germany is launching FRT in locations such as airports and train stations.

To see a comprehensive list of countries around the world that are using FRT, visit `https://www.visualcapitalist.com/facial-recognition-world-map/`.

To optimize the ability to recognize individuals while using FRT, developers are enhancing our experience by using augmented reality, as we'll see next.

Enhancing our experience

When using threat management, software developers are using techniques that combine the use of augmented reality and information on known identities from the facial recognition database.

> **Important note**
> Augmented reality is a blend of what we see in the real world and an overlay of computer-simulated graphics and text, designed to improve our visual experience.

The technology can be incorporated into a surveillance system. The identifiers can include the following:

- A person of interest, who may be a known criminal or a friendly individual.

- An unidentified person – the individual is either not in the database or the system cannot identify the person.

- A missing person is someone that authorities are trying to find.

- A **Very Important Person** (**VIP**) is someone that may qualify for special access to an event.

Once the system has the necessary parameters, it can then attempt to identify individuals. The settings can be modified for special events. For example, if monitoring only for VIPs and persons of interest, the system can ignore all others. Then, once the system is active, it will provide the best guess on the individuals during recognition, as shown in the following figure:

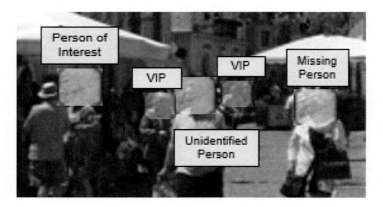

Figure 13.2 – Using augmented reality

Having surveillance coupled with augmented reality will help those in charge of large-scale monitoring. For example, this could be used for border control, **Transportation Security Administration** (**TSA**) precheck screenings, and during a large event, such as the Super Bowl.

Many facial recognition systems are fairly accurate, with accuracy rates averaging around 99.5%. While that might sound reasonable, that rating can potentially misidentify 1 in every 200 individuals that pass through the screening device. As a result, the systems should have a person verifying the identity of a person of interest.

In addition to monitoring a large group of individuals, biometrics can help to control access to computer systems, assets, and highly secure areas, as outlined next.

Controlling access to assets, buildings, and systems

We use access control techniques to prevent an unauthorized individual from gaining access to an asset, computer system, or secure area. Access control can be used in many different ways, in an enterprise network, in buildings, or on our own devices, by using various methods.

Biometrics can provide an efficient method of accurately identifying and authenticating individuals, and can be used to restrict access in the following manner:

- **Physical access control** is limiting access for a physical entity, such as a door or building.
- **Logical access control** limits access to a logical entity, such as a software application or computer system.

Biometrics can simplify the process without having to use a password that can be forgotten or a device that can be lost. We can use biometrics to restrict access in a wide range of industries. Let's see how biometrics can benefit the medical field, government, and business.

Using biometrics in industry and government

Many industries are seeing the benefits of using biometrics, as they are a highly personal, secure way to protect our assets. You are probably seeing a subtle increase in the use of the technology either in your own personal life or at work.

The medical field has seen a lot of benefits in using biometrics. Because medical facilities must ensure patient data is kept confidential, it is very important to limit access to medical records and server rooms. In addition, biometrics can limit access to supplies and medication.

Government agencies have been limiting access to data for decades. For example, the US government and the military classify data according to the sensitivity of the data. This is used because not all data is the same. The level of protection is determined according to the effect on the security of the nation if the data is compromised in some way. The data classifications include the following:

- **Top secret**: If exposed, could severely disrupt national security
- **Secret data**: If exposed, could seriously disrupt national security
- **Confidential data**: If exposed, could disrupt national security

We know that most, if not all, data should be protected in some manner; however, top-secret data is protected at the highest level. Using biometrics to control access can decrease the overall risk of an unwanted theft or a data breach.

In addition to data, governments use biometrics to control access to facilities – for example, using iris recognition to control access to a military base. In this case, iris recognition is an optimal biometric. In some locations around the world, it is necessary for trusted individuals to enter a military base. However, papers such as identification papers can be forged. Instead of a paper document, the officials at the base can use an iris scan to authenticate an individual.

If possible, soldiers in the military have access to a specialized device called a **Biometric Automated Tool Set** (**BATS**). This is a rugged handheld device that can obtain the biometric identifier of an iris, fingerprint, and facial images of an individual. This allows soldiers to provide accurate identification in highly secure areas and checkpoints.

Businesses are expanding the use of biometric technology to gain entry into a building or restricted computer system. For example, businesses can have employees log in to their system using a USB fingerprint reader, or gain entry to a warehouse by using an iris recognition system.

In most cases, when using access control, the system may benefit from a geofencing application on the client's mobile phone.

When the client gets near the biometric system, the system will recognize the client and push a notification out to the mobile device for the client to accept, as shown in the following figure:

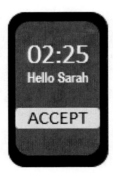

Figure 13.3 – Geofencing app

The client will be presented with the notification. Before interacting with the system, the client will need to select **ACCEPT**. This is similar to a token, and it adds another layer of security.

As technology improves, we will continue to see more biometric access control methods in use in a variety of industries and government. In the next section, let's take a look at some of the expanded uses for biometric technology.

Recognizing novel uses for biometrics

Now is an exciting time, as every day we are seeing more and more advances in biometric technology. In this section, we'll review some newer technologies. We'll look at using contactless fingerprint, the ability of facial recognition to detect facial masks, and the appeal of using a biometric such as our face or fingerprint to make a payment.

Let's start with how we may soon get the ability to obtain a fingerprint without touching a surface.

Obtaining contactless fingerprints

Using fingerprints to identify someone has been used for centuries. In the last decade, we have seen an explosion of fingerprint technology, especially when using smartphones. Although this popular technology has been used for years, it has been a contact biometric, in that the subject must touch a surface to obtain a sample.

The concept of contactless biometrics has a universal appeal, as it provides a more sanitary way to interact with the biometric system. Contactless biometrics include facial, voice, and iris recognition, along with finger and palm vein and gait recognition.

A newer contactless biometric is fingerprints, which has enormous potential. Contactless fingerprint technology uses **three-dimensional** (**3D**) imaging. This advanced imaging has shown greater accuracy and is faster than the classic ink and paper method.

NIST completed a study and found that by using a single fingerprint, a classic scanned image showed superior results than using a contactless method. However, if multiple fingers are scanned, the contactless method shows higher accuracy. You can learn more here: `https://www.nist.gov/news-events/news/2020/05/nist-study-measures-performance-accuracy-contactless-fingerprinting-tech`.

Although the technology is still in development, researchers are excited about the potential this can bring. The device does not need an attendant and can quickly process more users.

With our changing environment, the technology must be able to keep up with the demands and challenges we face, such as using face masks during a pandemic. Let's take a look at how technology is keeping up with these changes next.

Detecting face masks

These days, we are seeing the expanded use of face masks to prevent the spread of disease. As a result, many current facial recognition systems are now turning on the ability to detect whether a person is wearing a protective mask.

With advanced algorithms, developers are training systems to recognize masked faces. This check is incorporated into employee access control systems to ensure employees comply with mask requirements during an epidemic or pandemic.

Face masks can interfere with the ability to verify an individual's face using facial recognition. As a result, developers are creating devices that recognize the use of a face mask, and then obtain another biometric, such as iris recognition.

Along with providing access control, biometrics can also make our lives easier, such as by enabling you to pay your bill by using a biometric identifier. Let's take a look.

Paying your bill with biometrics

As our digital identity becomes immersed with our biometrics, developers are crafting ways to enhance our buying experience. This technology is called a naked payment, which is using a biometric identifier to make a payment instead of a credit card.

Nowadays, several venues are using this technology, such as baseball stadiums, where you can pay for your hot dogs with your face, fingerprint, or another biometric identifier. The backend is provided by a biometric identity platform that stores your biometric data along with your credit card information. The idea is becoming more popular and is expected to grow within the next few years.

We have only brushed the surface on the true potential of biometric technology applications. Within the next few years, expect to see more possibilities that will help make our world more convenient and secure.

Summary

In this chapter, we saw several exciting uses for biometrics in our world today. We reviewed how biometrics play a significant role in enforcing the law and protecting children. We stressed the importance of providing standards to ensure interoperability. We then reviewed the ways biometrics help scientists identify individuals during a forensic examination.

We also took a look at how massive government-run biometric databases assist officials during surveillance and in monitoring large venues. We also saw the various ways that biometrics help monitor the prison population. We compared how biometrics can control access to assets, buildings, and computer systems. Finally, we saw a glimpse of some newer uses for biometrics, such as detecting face masks and the appeal of paying your dinner bill with your face or fingerprint.

In the last chapter, we'll close our discussion on the many uses, benefits, and expanded uses of biometrics today. We'll take a look at the privacy concerns we all face when using biometrics. We'll cover the different ways the US views privacy compared to Europe. You'll see that although using biometrics can help secure our data, in certain cases, there may be a potential for the government to compel us to provide a biometric sample. Finally, as we move forward to the next generation of identity management, we'll outline some thoughts on whether or not the public will fully accept the use of biometrics.

Questions

Now it's time to check your knowledge. Select the best response, then check your answers with those found in the *Assessment* section at the end of the book:

1. _____ includes proactive methods to enforce the law, prevent damage or theft of physical or logical objects, and ensure the safety of individuals.

   a. Forensics

   b. Security

   c. IAFIS monitoring

   d. Threat management

2. _____ evidence is used to support other evidence.

   a. Best

   b. Corroborating

   c. Indirect

   d. Circumstantial

3. _____ has been involved in efforts to create standards for decades.

   a. HART

   b. ICE

   c. IAFIS

   d. NIST

4. _____ reality is a blend of what we see in the real world, with an overlay of computer-simulated graphics and text, designed to improve our visual experience.

   a. Augmented

   b. Prepared

   c. Missing

   d. Context

5. A(n) _____ is a rugged handheld device that is used by a soldier to obtain a biometric identifier, such as an iris, fingerprint, and/or facial image, of an individual.

   a. ICE

   b. IAFIS

   c. spike

   d. BATS

6. If using _____, when the client gets near the biometric system, the system will recognize the client and push a notification out to the mobile device for the client to accept. This acts as a token and improves security.

   a. spike

   b. BATS

   c. geofencing

   d. IAFIS

7. A(n) _____ payment is using a biometric identifier to make a payment instead of a credit card.

   a. BATS

   b. spike

   c. naked

   d. augmented

Further reading

- Read how using biometrics can help prevent fraud by visiting `https://www.accenture.com/_acnmedia/Accenture/Conversion-Assets/DotCom/Documents/Global/PDF/Dualpub_9/Accenture-Beating-the-Biometrics-Fraudsters.pdf`.

- A history of NIST standards: `https://www.nist.gov/itl/iad/image-group/ansinist-itl-standard-history`.

- NIST shares the results of contactless fingerprint technology in this article: `https://www.nist.gov/news-events/news/2020/05/nist-study-measures-performance-accuracy-contactless-fingerprinting-tech`.

- See how the use of iris recognition is providing a more secure way to manage the release of prisoners in Los Angeles: `https://findbiometrics.com/iris-id-tech-to-identify-l-a-county-prisoners-906231/`.

- Read more on the BAT system by visiting `https://www.army-technology.com/news/modernise-us-biometric-processing/`.

- Learn how Taylor Swift is using facial recognition during concerts by visiting `https://www.theguardian.com/technology/2019/feb/15/how-taylor-swift-showed-us-the-scary-future-of-facial-recognition`.

- To learn more about synthetic identity fraud, visit `https://www.idanalytics.com/solutions-services/fraud-risk-management/synthetic-identity-fraud/`.

14
Addressing Privacy Concerns

Biometric technology is rapidly gaining traction. Massive systems are collecting images of irises, fingerprints, and faces. But who protects our faces, fingerprints and other biometric identifiers? We know that no matter where you live or what you do, it's important to protect your personal information, which includes biometric identifiers. If this information were to fall into the wrong hands, this could affect your security. Because of this, it's time to start thinking about the privacy of our biometric data.

In this chapter, we'll outline the fact that we're seeing how more and more of our personal data can be exposed, and discuss what defines a privacy policy. We'll then examine how Europe and the **United States (US)** view privacy, along with how certain states offer better protection against the misuse of biometric technology. In the US, citizens are protected by the Constitution and the amendments. We'll see how invoking the Fifth Amendment can prevent law enforcement from making someone use a biometric identifier to unlock a device, as it can be self-incriminating.

We'll then take a look at how biometric standards can help ensure interoperability on a global scale. We'll also stress the importance of securing biometric data, along with taking a peek at some biometric organizations. Finally, as we move forward to the next generation of identity management, we'll take a look at the ways we'll use biometric technology to improve and secure our lives.

In this chapter, we're going to cover the following main topics:

- Comparing privacy laws in the US and Europe
- Understanding biometrics and the Fifth Amendment
- Recognizing the push for standards
- Accepting biometrics and the future of biometrics

Comparing privacy laws in the US and Europe

When you think about privacy, what comes to mind? The term privacy can relate to a couple of concepts, such as the following:

- Not being disturbed or seen
- Keeping private information private

Because of today's always-connected world, there is already quite a bit of information that may have been considered private in the past that is now in public view.

Many of us willingly share our private information on social media. Perhaps you have shared your birthdate or allowed geotagging on your cellphone so that your movements can be tracked and posted.

When using social media, many sites provide ways for us to lock down our information to only allow certain individuals to view our content. Periodically, social media sites will remind us to do a privacy check to make sure the settings are in line with how we want to protect our information.

When thinking about biometric data, it is a real possibility that more and more of our data will be collected within the next decade. Who will ultimately be the owner of these biometric identifiers, and will you have control over how the organization will use the data? You might have control of the biometric data, if it is on your own personal device. But what happens if you are using a company-owned cell phone?

Similar to social media, companies might include disclaimers for employees in the future. The statement might include information on who controls the data, where it is stored, and how the company will handle the biometric identifier.

Today there are massive government biometric databases available, along with industry-driven implementations. Next, let's take a look at an example of a government database.

Collecting biographical and biological data

In India, the Aadhaar Act began in 2009 to collect data on all citizens over the age of 18. The process is required for every resident of India and is collected and stored in the **Unique Identification Authority of India (UIDAI)**. The UIDAI collects the following information:

- Biographical data, such as name, gender, and birthdate
- Biometric identifiers, such as facial, finger, and iris prints

An individual's profile is created using this information, and the subject is then assigned an Aadhaar number. This process adds biometric identifiers that provide more than just a number (such as a Social Security number) to uniquely identify someone.

The project has been under scrutiny for years over privacy issues. India's Supreme Court has ruled that privacy is a basic right under India's law. Therefore, the system has some limitations and oversight on what information can be accessed and where it can be used. Read more on the Aadhaar Act here: `https://uidai.gov.in/what-is-aadhaar/the-aadhaar-act.html`.

Many countries have their own way of viewing privacy. In this section, we'll discuss what defines a privacy policy. We will then examine how Europe and the US view privacy. Let's start with a discussion on the importance of a privacy policy.

Creating a privacy policy

For many years, if a company collected consumer and employee information, it was implied that the company would protect the data. Many, but not all, companies adhered to a set of guidelines that outlined how to treat customer data. However, that was not always the case. As time passed, it became evident that not all companies treated consumer data with respect. One reason is that there is a distinct difference between a law and a guideline:

- A *guideline* is a set of best practice principles that outlines a course of action.
- A *law* is a legal requirement issued by some governing body.

While guidelines encourage a company to use best practice techniques if desired, laws require the organization to treat consumer data with respect.

Because so many companies have mishandled consumer information over the years, several laws now define how companies treat consumer data. In most cases, companies must collect and treat sensitive consumer information in a responsible manner.

Many businesses and organizations have privacy policies. The policies outline the following:

- What data the company collects
- The manner in which the company uses and shares the data
- How the company stores, secures, and disposes of the data

Many organizations post their privacy policy so that consumers are aware of how their personal data is managed.

In addition to a privacy policy, there may be the need to develop a **Privacy Impact Assessment** (**PIA**). Let's explore this concept.

Assessing risks to privacy

If either a commercial or government entity develops an information system, they should develop a **Privacy Impact Assessment** (**PIA**), which evaluates risks to the privacy of **personally identifiable information** (**PII**). A PIA is an assessment that steps through the data flow to identify where there may be a risk to privacy.

The process identifies who has access to the data and how the data is collected, maintained, shared, and protected. The assessment makes an organization drill down and examine what organizations or processes might pose a risk to the privacy of the information. Some of the questions might include the following:

- How does the system collect, maintain, or distribute PII?
- Is there a major change in the management of the system?
- Will the system interface with a commercial entity?

To see an example of a PIA template, visit `https://www.osec.doc.gov/opog/privacy/PTA_Template.pdf`.

Biometric technology is becoming more popular; however, the lines that define the privacy of biometric data are blurred. There are very few laws that specifically define the protection of biometric data. In many cases, there are vague references to personal privacy and data protection.

As new laws are crafted, we will most likely see the inclusion of protecting the privacy of biometric data. The **General Data Protection Regulation** (**GDPR**) provides a granular framework that outlines data protection and privacy in Europe and internationally. Let's explore this next.

Understanding GDPR

GDPR is a data privacy law that outlines strict guidelines on how companies are to secure consumer data. GDPR affects companies that conduct business in and outside of the **European Union** (**EU**) and Britain, and essentially gives consumers control of their data. The main focus is on data privacy, and if a company violates the rules, they can face a fine of up to 4 percent of total global revenue.

GDPR has several specific provisions, which include the following:

- **International impact**: GDPR has a global reach, meaning anyone who does business with citizens and long-term residents of the EU and Britain must adhere to the regulations.

- **Consent-driven**: A company cannot share personal information with a third party unless specifically granted permission by the consumer.

- **Remove consent**: While consumers have the ability to grant permission for a company to use their data, the consumer can rescind their permission at any time. This is referred to as the *right to be forgotten* rule.

- **Application-driven privacy**: To protect the privacy of consumer data, companies should only collect necessary consumer information, and no more. For example, if the company only needs your email to send updates, it should not collect your home address.

- **Prompt reporting**: If an organization does suffer a data breach, they must inform authorities within 72 hours.

Since its implementation in 2018, there have been many complaints of data protection violations, along with data breaches. In some cases, companies have reported themselves. In addition, several companies have been fined for misusing consumer data. For example, Google received a fine for 50 million euros for conducting targeted advertising.

There are exceptions to the privacy rules outlined by GDPR. Some examples of why there may be an exception include the following:

- A legal request

- Required in the interest of public health

- Necessary for employment options

When thinking about consumer data, we think about biographical data, such as name, address, birthdate, and gender. However, we must now also include biometric identifiers, such as facial, fingerprint, and iris. Let's see how GDPR addresses the issue of biometric data next.

Focusing on biometric data

GDPR has a clear focus on the privacy and security of consumer data. Companies must do their due diligence to ensure their organization is locked down and secure to prevent a data breach. They must also provide for the privacy of consumer data.

With the growing number of biometric implementations in the past few years, GDPR now includes the protection of biometric identifiers. This inclusion illustrates the immense potential of biometrics today, and in the future.

GDPR defines biometric data as a special category, whereby data is obtained by sensors that capture and process an individual's unique physiological, physical, or behavioral features.

By defining and including biometric data in GDPR, many individuals feel that this will help reassure consumers that their biometric identities are more secure. However, this inclusion will require more rigorous accountability and oversight, as consumers will no longer tolerate their personal data being mismanaged.

GDPR has a broad worldwide reach. However, not all companies operate in the EU. In the next section, we'll take a look at how the US protects consumer data.

Protecting biometric data in the US

The US does not have a universal federal law governing the privacy of personal and biometric data. Data privacy is regulated by a variety of state and federal laws.

Several US states, including Texas, Washington, and California, have established biometric privacy regulations. These include the **California Consumer Privacy Act (CCPA)**, New York's **Stop Hacks and Improve Electronic Data Security (SHIELD)** act, and the Illinois **Biometric Protection Act (BIPA)**. Let's start with CCPA.

Understanding CCPA

California is a populous state that has (slightly) more inhabitants than all of Canada and has long been a leader in technology along with data protection and privacy laws.

CCPA went into effect on January 2020 and provides a wide range of provisions designed to protect the privacy of California residents. CCPA is a well-written law that is commonly referenced as a blueprint for a national data privacy law for the US. Much like GDPR, the law protects consumer data.

Companies that do business with Californian residents must adhere to the following provisions:

- The ability for consumers to easily opt-out and be forgotten
- The right of consumers to know what information the company collects and how they use and share the data
- The ability for consumers to see what data is on file and be able to request that their data not be sold or shared
- Fines that provide compensation to consumers in the event of a data breach, in the range of $100 to $750 per consumer

The fines may sound minimal; however, if a company had a data breach of 40,000 client records, they could be facing a fine of 30 million dollars.

Much like GDPR, CCPA protects both biographical data and biometric identifiers. CCPA defines biometric data as an individual's unique physiological, physical, or behavioral features. This includes identifiers such as facial, fingerprint, iris, **deoxyribonucleic acid (DNA)**, and other biometric data that can be used alone or with other data to establish someone's identity.

California is one of several states that protect biometric data. Another state that includes biometrics as personal data is New York, as discussed next.

Protecting data with the SHIELD act

Because of the proliferation of electronic information, the state of New York created a law to protect citizens' data. The law is called the **SHIELD** law and became effective in March 2020.

The SHIELD law requires companies to bolster their cybersecurity defense methods to prevent a data breach and to protect consumer data. The law applies to any company that collects personal information of residents in the state of New York. This includes PII, such as a driver's license, financial account information, Social Security number, and biometric data.

When evaluating privacy laws in the US, one state that specifically includes biometric identification is Illinois. Let's see what **BIPA** is all about next.

Dissecting BIPA

Many individuals feel that it's acceptable to collect biometric data, such as facial images, palm prints, and iris images. However, it's even more important to protect the data. One US state that has enacted a rigorous privacy law that deals specifically with biometric data is Illinois.

BIPA is a robust law that privacy advocates have applauded, as it has several elements that show true respect for an individual's biometric data. These main elements include the following:

- **Consumer opt-in**: The law requires the consumer to opt-in (instead of opt-out) before collecting biometric data.

- **Prohibits the sale of biometrics**: A company cannot sell or profit in any way from a consumer's biometric data.

- **Destroy when done**: The company must destroy the biometric identifier once the data no longer serves a purpose.

- **Seek compensation**: The law allows a consumer to sue for damages in the case of a data breach.

BIPA could be a template for future regulations in other states. In general, any company that does business with a citizen of Illinois must adhere to the guidelines. A company must protect the biometric data, and collect only what is needed. Any violation can result in a hefty fine of up to $5,000 per consumer. To read more about BIPA, visit `https://www.ilga.gov/legislation/ilcs/ilcs3.asp?ActID=3004&ChapterID=57`.

In the US, there are several laws within each state that can be difficult to interpret and can sometimes contradict each other. Because of the complexity of the different laws, many individuals feel the US would benefit from an all-encompassing regulatory body like GDPR. Until then, companies should protect and respect consumer data and biometric identifiers as if there is a governing law.

Laws that govern the use of biometric identifiers are not limited to the US and Europe. Other countries, such as Brazil, Japan, and South Korea, are also seeking ways to protect biometric data. As a result, we'll most likely continue to see an evolution and expansion of privacy laws over the next decade.

Although many are aware of the sensitive nature of biometric data, not all are adhering to privacy guidelines. A fairly comprehensive list of countries and the way they use biometric data can be found here: `https://www.comparitech.com/blog/vpn-privacy/biometric-data-study/`.

In recent years, there has been a proliferation of biometric technology that enables us to use our unique identifiers to control access. Concurrently, there have been several reports of law enforcement requiring an individual to unlock their device by using a biometric. Many individuals question the legality of this coercion. In the next section, we'll examine how the Fifth Amendment of the US constitution can prevent the judicial system from compelling individuals to use their biometrics against their will.

Understanding biometrics and the Fifth Amendment

Nowadays, there is a growing number of applications and uses for biometrics. Many of these are to control access and secure our data in our homes, devices, and computer systems. However, can a governing body or law enforcement compel us to provide authentication by using a biometric identifier such as our face or voice?

Over the last several years, there have been several high-profile cases where someone was requested to provide a biometric to gain access to an electronic device. Whether a defendant or a witness; the question is, "can someone be forced to provide a biometric identifier?"

Let's outline what is included in the Fifth Amendment.

Outlining the Fifth Amendment

The US is governed by the Constitution, which is the highest law of the land. All laws are bound by protecting the rights of the citizens, and any government actions must be in line with the Constitution and the amendments.

The Fifth Amendment protects citizens by providing the following principles:

- Any citizen may not be prosecuted and punished without being fairly processed through the legal system.
- An individual cannot be charged for a crime twice.
- Citizens are protected from "self-incrimination," which is a profession of guilt.
- The government cannot seize personal property without fairly compensating the property owner.

When examining the principles of the Fifth Amendment, the one concept that can relate to using a subject's biometric identifier is the concept of "Citizens are protected from self-incrimination."

For example, in the US, if an individual is accused of a crime, the officer will cite the individual's rights, as they pertain to the Fifth Amendment. Also referred to as the Miranda rights (or warning), this includes verbiage that the individual does not have to speak or answer any questions to avoid self-incrimination.

One of the considerations when dealing with the Fifth Amendment is protecting someone from self-incrimination by forcing the individual to unlock their device. Let's examine this concept.

Unlocking your device

If an individual in the US is accused of a crime, law enforcement agents will attempt to locate the individual and bring them in for questioning. If they are arrested, the officer will recite their Miranda rights. The Miranda warning outlines the rights of a citizen to remain silent and not divulge information that may lead to their prosecution.

If the individual is to testify in a court, they may opt to "take the fifth," which means they choose to remain silent and avoid incrimination. At that point, the individual does not have to be a witness against themselves.

If law enforcement agents were able to obtain a device that is said to contain evidence of a crime, they may try to gain access to the device in some manner. Let's evaluate some of the scenarios that might occur.

Gaining access to evidence

If law enforcement is aware of the fact that reliable and authentic evidence is on a device that is protected in some manner, they will want to gain access to the device. However, if the device belongs to the defendant, the defendant is in control of the evidence.

Here are some of the questions as they relate to forcing someone to give up a password or other private information:

- If agents obtain a safe that is said to contain evidence of a bank heist, could the courts compel the defendant to open the safe or provide the combination?
- If a software application or computer system holds information on a crime, can law enforcement make the defendant give up their password?
- If a mobile device is obtained that contains critical evidence, such as contacts and images, could the defendant be forced to provide a biometric to unlock the device?

When asked, the defendant may choose to NOT give up their password or combination, under the protection of the Fifth Amendment.

In some cases, an individual may decide to waive their Fifth Amendment right and offer their information to unlock their mobile device or other access-controlled software or hardware. However, by doing so, this might provide the evidence required to prosecute them.

Therefore, the question remains: can law enforcement compel a person to unlock a device by giving up information or providing a biometric identifier? Let's evaluate this next.

Using a biometric identifier

While it's legal for law enforcement to seize electronic equipment, forcing someone to unlock the device or software application using a biometric may not be within legal guidelines.

Several, but not all, courts have adhered to this amendment to protect the rights of their citizens. Let's consider both sides of this argument.

Comparing sides

In some cases, the law may assert that requiring someone to use their biometrics to unlock a device is perfectly legal. Many equate this to obliging someone to provide a handwriting sample or offer a blood test. For the defendant, this is a no-win situation, and it may very well force someone to self-incriminate themselves.

Many courts feel that a password or combination is held in someone's mind, which is a constitutionally protected thought. An individual has the right to keep their private thoughts private; however, using a biometric may or may not be considered private.

Some feel that being able to utilize the Fifth Amendment is only applicable if the communication is testimonial or can be spoken. Therefore, if there is damaging evidence on a digital device that is protected by a biometric, some authorities feel the use of the identifier is physical evidence. In that case, the courts may not adhere to the privilege of taking the fifth.

While law enforcement is constantly trying to keep up with technology, and the many ways criminals can conceal information, we must also be cognizant of the rights of citizens. In the future, there needs to be a clear distinction as to where biometric identification falls, as constitutional rights may be affected by changes in technology.

Biometrics are becoming more prevalent and allow access control, as well as help travelers move from country to country and secure physical devices. In the next section, let's take a look at how standards will help simplify and improve our lives.

Recognizing the push for standards

These days, the advances in all types of technology help individuals simplify and secure their lives. Along with this expansion, we see the associated tasks of ensuring privacy and security. Biometric technology is no exception, as we are seeing more and more uses for it. Some of the main uses of biometric applications include the following:

- Law enforcement
- Forensics
- Commercial systems
- Personal devices

It's an exciting time as nowadays, biometric technology can allow us to gain access to different types of electronic devices, applications, and systems, as shown in the following diagram:

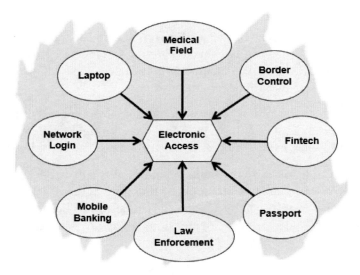

Figure 14.1 – Biometric apps using electronic access

Think about how we can use biometric identifiers to access our laptops, mobile devices, and other applications. Most of the time, each app requires a separate login, using a separate biometric identifier.

Wouldn't it be great to be able to use one biometric – say our fingerprint or palm vein – to unlock multiple applications? Once a biometric infrastructure is built, this could be a possibility. That is if all systems, components, and formats are standardized. Let's explore this possibility next.

Working to create standards

Biometrics systems should be secure and have exceptional performance. While it's not always required for systems to exchange information, being able to exchange data can allow more options and an enhanced system. However, in order for disparate systems to share information with one another, there need to be some standards.

Creating standards will make a system less expensive and improve the workflow. Standards are generally created by a group of individuals in an industry, academia, or in the government so that all aspects are covered during the development of the standards.

Some of the earliest biometric standards began in the 1980s, mainly driven by the need to exchange fingerprint data. Today, several organizations, both national and international, are working together to create standards. These organizations include the following:

- The **International Organization for Standardization** (**ISO**): A recognized entity for creating and disseminating international standards.

- The **International Electrotechnical Commission** (**IEC**) has over 100 technical committees and subcommittees in a wide range of industries, such as lighting, cabling, and electricity.

- The ISO/IEC joint technical committee develops standards for biometrics that include technical interfaces and data interchange formats, along with other topics, such as interoperability, cloud computing, and security.

- The **International Civil Aviation Organization** (**ICAO**) ensures the interoperability of **machine-readable travel documents** (**MRTD**), such as electronic passports that store biometric data.

- The **International Telecommunication Standardization Sector** (**ITU-T**) guides and oversees standards for telecommunications and **Information Communication Technology** (**ICT**) around the world.

Over the years, these and other groups have developed many international standards for a variety of applications. In this section, we'll talk about standard image formats, along with proper formats for exchanging and securing biometric data.

Next, let's talk about the group that focuses on ways to retain image quality.

Storing digital images

When storing biometric images, it's important to provide standards that define methods to extract the components, features, and resolutions, while preserving image quality.

The **Joint Photographic Experts Group (JPEG)** is a working group comprised of ISO/IEC, along with the **International Telecommunication Union (ITU)**. The JPEG standards are significant and include work on some of the following: compliance testing, extensions, and the File Interchange Format.

JPEG continuously examines image processing and defines the proper format and compression techniques for storing digital images. Read more on this working group by visiting `https://jpeg.org/about.html`.

Important Note

When working with images, you may see the following formats: JPEG, JPG, or JPEG-2000. The JPEG working group oversees the JPEG image standards, which differ in performance. JPEG (or JPG) is a lossy compression method; therefore, when an image is saved using JPEG (or JPG), some of the quality is lost. JPEG-2000 has both lossy and lossless compression; however, when saved, the image maintains much of the original quality.

In addition to defining standards when dealing with biometric images, there also needs to be a standardized format to exchange and transmit data between systems. Let's take a look at the **Common Biometric Exchange Formats Framework (CBEFF)**.

Exchanging biometric data

CBEFF is an ISO/IEC framework that outlines a data structure that properly formats or readies biometric data for exchange between two systems. The data structure, as shown in the following diagram, outlines the method to create what is called a **Biometric Information Record (BIR)**:

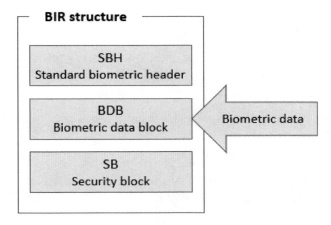

Figure 14.2 – CBEFF

A BIR consists of the following:

- A **standard biometric header** (**SBH**): This defines the metadata describing the biometric characteristics.

- A **biometric data block** (**BDB**): This is flexible, in that it is not defined by CBEFF, and can be in a proprietary or standardized format.

- A **security block** (**SB**): This is an optional component. If used, this block will list encryption and integrity protocols used to protect the BIR.

Along with providing standards for data formats, we'll also want to use standards to secure biometric data. Let's take a look.

Securing biometric data

Along with providing interoperability between systems, we must also protect the data, either at rest on a server or in motion while traveling over the network. The goal is to ensure the following:

- **Confidentiality**: Which protects data against unauthorized disclosure. For example, if someone is able to see the contents of a payroll file, this would be a violation of confidentiality.

- **Integrity**: Ensures data remains in its original form and has not been modified in an unauthorized or accidental manner. For example, if someone were to go into their own personnel file at work and change their salary from $30,000 to $80,000, this would be a violation of integrity.

- **Authentication**: Assures the identity of a system entity. For example, when sending data from the client to the server, authentication protocols provide assurance that parties communicating with one another are authentic and not imposters.

By using cryptographic practices and procedures, we can securely transport and store biometric data. To achieve this, we use encryption standards that include the following:

- **Block cipher standards**: Such as the **Advanced Encryption Standard** (**AES**).

- **Hash algorithms**: This includes the **Secure Hash Algorithm** (**SHA**), which includes SHA-1, SHA-2, and SHA-3.

- **Digital signature algorithms**: This includes the **Digital Signature Algorithm** (**DSA**), **Rivest–Shamir–Adleman** (**RSA**), and **Elliptic Curve Digital Signature Algorithm** (**ECDSA**).

Keep in mind that this is only a partial list of the many protocols and methods used to secure data. To see a list of cryptographic standards and guidelines as defined by the **National Institute of Science and Technology (NIST)**, visit `https://csrc.nist.gov/projects/cryptographic-standards-and-guidelines`.

Standards for storing digital images, along with exchanging or securing biometric data, are key to providing consistency and interoperability while protecting the privacy of biometric data.

While it's important to develop standards, it's also essential for professionals to gather and exchange information on the latest trends and technology. Let's take a look at some of the organizations actively involved in biometric technology next.

Identifying biometric organizations

Keeping updated on current trends in biometrics is important for organizations to be competitive in today's changing market. Some of these organizations include the following:

- The Biometrics Institute is an organization comprised of government and industry leaders that share information on the latest techniques and advances in biometric technology. The organization provides a positive platform for promoting responsible and ethical best practices.

- **International Biometric and Identity Association (IBIA)** is a leader in providing guidance and education on biometric trends, policies, and privacy. Established in 1998, IBIA has several working groups, which include Privacy and Public Policy Advocacy, Financial Services, and Advances in Biometric Technologies.

- **European Association for Biometrics (EAB)** provides guidance and support for biometric initiatives throughout Europe. By working with industries, academia, and citizens, the EAB seeks to improve and support digital identity systems to improve the overall quality of life.

Take a minute and visit each organization's website, found in the *Further reading* section, at the end of this chapter. Once at each site, you'll find out more information, news, and trends on current biometric technologies today, along with the next generation of identity management. Next, let's get a glimpse of the future of biometrics.

Accepting biometrics and the future of biometrics

Growth in biometric systems in commercial and government applications continues to expand. In addition to providing biometric identity management, businesses and organizations are seeking other ways to use biometrics to improve our lives.

Industry is evaluating how to best use biometric technology to improve everyday experiences, by investigating innovative solutions in a number of different areas.

Next, let's take a look at an example of how using biometric technology can improve the travel experience.

Traveling with ease

The process of navigating through the airport, checking in with the airline, boarding the plane, flying, and then landing and gathering your baggage can be tiring.

Many governments are actively working on ways to improve the traveler's journey. In regions throughout the world, such as Asia, the Caribbean, and the European Union, there are efforts being made to implement biometric systems within airports.

Much of the proposed efforts can optimize the use of existing systems, such as the US **Customs and Border Protection** (**CBP**) programs. The CBP manages **Automated Passport Control** (**APC**), which allows travelers to complete a self-check-in process, using an automated system.

The goal is to facilitate end-to-end effortless travel. Some of the efforts include using biometrics to achieve the following:

- Manage border control by using an **APC** system.
- Expedite the boarding process by integrating with the cloud-based facial recognition **CBP** program.
- Permit access to proprietary lounges by using methods such as facial, fingerprint, or palm vein biometric technology.
- Simplify security checks by using facial recognition.

Because of the complexities of international travel and the varying laws regarding biometric data, true collaboration will take time. Once this type of travel is in place, travelers may see its value and embrace the technology.

The use of facial recognition is expanding, for identification, border control, social media, and surveillance. However, despite all of the benefits, facial recognition technology can still be met with resistance. Let's take a look.

Identifying without consent

Facial recognition is a two-edged sword. Many individuals tout its ability to easily provide identification and access control. In addition, facial recognition can help law enforcement provide threat management and monitor the roadways for traffic violators.

Concurrently, there are growing concerns about the overuse of facial recognition and, more specifically, for surveillance. Many are concerned with the overuse of facial recognition, and whether or not this can threaten our freedom.

Several countries around the world, such as India and Sweden, are resisting the overuse of facial recognition. In addition, many cities and states in the US are beginning to ban its use, such as the following:

- San Francisco, California
- Boston, Massachusetts
- San Diego, California

The **Electronic Privacy Information Center** (**EPIC**) has a website that lists concerns over facial recognition. You can find out more here: `https://epic.org/banfacesurveillance/`.

US legislators are encouraging technology giants to self-monitor to avoid overuse of the technology. However, it might come down to government laws that restrict governments and private industry from abusing the technology.

Biometric technology holds a great deal of promise to improve, simplify, and secure our lives. However, along with this comes responsibility, and the need to respect the rights and freedoms of the citizens that use the technology.

We'll most likely see a great deal more play out in the coming years.

Summary

In this chapter, we took a closer look at how biometric technology is generating more and more of our personal data, which, if not monitored, can result in a violation of our privacy. We reviewed the concept of a privacy policy and then compared how Europe and the US view privacy, along with some of the laws that influence the way we protect consumer data.

Along with examining the many ways that we can use biometrics, we debated whether or not an individual can be forced to use their biometric data to unlock a device or computer system. We reviewed the Fifth Amendment of the US constitution and saw how this may be a way to protect ourselves from self-incrimination during a legal investigation.

In addition, we saw the need to provide interoperability among systems and the importance of providing standards. We reviewed standards in image processing, along with exchanging and securing biometric data. Finally, we took a look at the potential that biometric technologies can bring, along with the need for responsible governance and the protection of biometric data.

Questions

Now it's time to check your knowledge. Select the best response, then check your answers, found in the *Assessment* section at the end of the book:

1. A _____ is a set of best practice principles that outlines a course of action.

    a. law

    b. forecast

    c. CCPA directive

    d. guideline

2. _____ affects companies located in and outside the EU and essentially gives consumers control of their data.

    a. CCPA

    b. GDPR

    c. SHIELD

    d. BIPA

3. _____ is a well-written California law that is commonly referenced as a blueprint for a national data privacy law for the US.

    a. CCPA

    b. GDPR

    c. SHIELD

    d. BIPA

4. If an individual in the US is arrested and must testify in court, they may opt to "take the _____," which means they choose to remain silent and avoid incrimination.

    a. CCPA act

    b. fifth

    c. BIPA rule

    d. fourth

5. In the US, if an individual is accused of a crime, the officer will cite the _____ rights, which includes verbiage that the individual does not have to speak or answer any questions to avoid self-incrimination.

    a. BIPA

    b. SHIELD

    c. CCPA

    d. Miranda

6. The _____ is an ISO/IEC framework that outlines a data structure that properly formats or readies biometric data for exchange between two systems.

    a. CBEFF

    b. BIPA tool

    c. CCPA

    d. RSA

7. We can securely transport and store biometric data by using encryption standards, which include block cipher standards, such as _____.

    a. SHA-1

    b. RSA

    c. AES

    d. DSA

Further reading

Please refer to the following links for more information:

- To find out more about IBIA, go to `https://www.ibia.org/`.

- More information about EAB can be found at `https://eab.org/`.

- The ISO/IEC joint technical committee provides a multitude of standards. Read more at `https://www.iso.org/committee/313770.html`.

- Learn more about the Biometrics Institute by visiting `https://www.biometricsinstitute.org/`.

- For a comparison on GDPR and CCPA, visit `https://www.bakerlaw.com/webfiles/Privacy/2018/Articles/CCPA-GDPR-Chart.pdf`.

- Read more about the Fifth Amendment by visiting `https://www.ducksters.com/history/us_government/fifth_amendment.php`.

- To compare the differences between a law and a guideline, go to `https://www.tempe.gov/home/showdocument?id=41925`.

- See how biometrics are used in the prison system by visiting `https://www.correctionsone.com/products/police-technology/investigation/biometrics-identification/`.

- To learn more about the US constitution, visit `https://www.whitehouse.gov/about-the-white-house/the-constitution/`.

- Here are some thoughts on privacy in the age of emotional AI: `https://www.ohchr.org/Documents/Issues/DigitalAge/ReportPrivacyinDigitalAge/AndrewMcStayProfessor%20of%20Digital%20Life,%20BangorUniversityWalesUK.pdf`.

Assessments

In the following pages, we will review all practice questions from each of the chapters in this book, and provide the correct answers.

Chapter 1– Exploring Biometric Technology

1. b. Password or PIN
2. a. Smart card
3. d. Authentication
4. c. Physiological
5. b. Behavioral
6. a. 1924
7. b. Behavioral

Chapter 2 – Biometrics and Mobile Devices

1. b. Logical access controls
2. a. Integrity
3. a. Token
4. d. MFA
5. a. PCI DSS
6. b. Haptics
7. c. Photoelectric

Chapter 3 – Recognizing Biometric Characteristics

1. b. Universality
2. c. Collectability
3. c. Acceptable
4. d. Enrollment
5. b. Authentication
6. c. Filtering
7. c. Three-dimensional

Chapter 4 – Comparing Advantages and Modalities

1. c. Facial
2. a. standalone
3. d. middleware
4. b. FNMR
5. d. multimodal
6. b. FRVT
7. a. MINEX

Chapter 5 – Implementing Fingerprint Technology

1. a. Henry
2. d. deltas
3. c. capacitive
4. d. loops
5. a. noise
6. c. spur

7. c. third

8. b. physical

Chapter 6 – Using Facial Recognition

1. c. prosopagnosia

2. a. eigenface

3. b. infrared

4. a. LIDAR

5. d. triangle

6. b. knowledge

7. c. spoof

Chapter 7 – Learning Iris Recognition

1. c. Collectability

2. a. Uvea

3. c. Dyscoria

4. d. Hamming

5. b. Infrared

6. b. Retinal

7. a. Daugman's

Chapter 8 – Using Voice Recognition

1. c. physiological

2. a. analog

3. d. Markov

4. b. 7

5. c. text-independent

6. a. NIST

7. a. signature

Chapter 9 – Considering Alternate Biometrics

1. c. 1980s
2. c. palm vein
3. d. midstance
4. a. STR
5. b. online
6. a. helix
7. d. retinal

Chapter 10 – Selecting the Right Biometric

1. c. Requirements
2. a. Anthropometrics
3. c. **False Non-Match Rate (FNMR)**
4. b. capture
5. d. Spoofing
6. d. BaaS
7. a. smart card

Chapter 11 – Integrating the Biometric System

1. d. star
2. a. bandwidth
3. d. baseline
4. c. Confidentiality
5. b. permissions
6. a. incident
7. c. disaster

Chapter 12 – Testing and System Deployment

1. d. beta
2. a. parallel
3. b. videos
4. c. Feedback
5. d. train the trainer
6. b. Aging
7. c. Bounty

Chapter 13 – Discovering Practical Biometric Applications

1. b. Security
2. b. Corroborating
3. d. NIST
4. a. Augmented
5. d. BATS
6. c. geofencing
7. c. naked

Chapter 14 – Addressing Privacy Concerns

1. d. guideline
2. b. GDPR
3. a. CCPA
4. b. fifth
5. d. Miranda
6. a. CBEFF
7. c. AES

Other Books You May Enjoy

If you enjoyed this book, you may be interested in these other books by Packt:

Mastering Identity and Access Management with Microsoft Azure

Jochen Nickel

ISBN: 978-1-78913-230-4

- Apply technical descriptions to your business needs and deployments
- Manage cloud-only, simple, and complex hybrid environments
- Apply correct and efficient monitoring and identity protection strategies
- Design and deploy custom Identity and access management solutions
- Build a complete identity and access management life cycle
- Understand authentication and application publishing mechanisms
- Use and understand the most crucial identity synchronization scenarios
- Implement a suitable information protection strategy

Learn Kali Linux 2019

Glen D. Singh

ISBN: 978-1-78961-180-9

- Explore the fundamentals of ethical hacking
- Learn how to install and configure Kali Linux
- Get up to speed with performing wireless network pentesting
- Gain insights into passive and active information gathering
- Understand web application pentesting
- Decode WEP, WPA, and WPA2 encryptions using a variety of methods, such as the fake authentication attack, the ARP request replay attack, and the dictionary attack

Leave a review - let other readers know what you think

Please share your thoughts on this book with others by leaving a review on the site that you bought it from. If you purchased the book from Amazon, please leave us an honest review on this book's Amazon page. This is vital so that other potential readers can see and use your unbiased opinion to make purchasing decisions, we can understand what our customers think about our products, and our authors can see your feedback on the title that they have worked with Packt to create. It will only take a few minutes of your time, but is valuable to other potential customers, our authors, and Packt. Thank you!

Index

V

W

Manufactured by Amazon.ca
Acheson, AB